THE MOST FASHIONABLE VARIETY HOUSE in the WORLD

The Edwardians

J. B. Priestley

Heinemann
London

William Heinemann Limited
LONDON MELBOURNE TORONTO
JOHANNESBURG AUCKLAND

Designed and produced by
George Rainbird Limited
Marble Arch House
44 Edgware Road
London W2

Picture Research: Mary Anne Norbury
Design: Pauline Harrison

First published 1970

The text was set in
Monophoto Imprint 11/13 by
Jolly and Barber Limited,
Rugby, Warwickshire
The text was printed by
Butler & Tanner Limited,
Frome, Somerset and bound by
Webb Son & Co. Limited,
Southgate, London
The colour plates and jacket were
originated and printed by
Westerham Press Limited,
Westerham, Kent

S.B.N. 434 60332 5

Colour Plates:
(reverse of frontispiece)
A poster advertising the Palace Theatre, 1904

(frontispiece)
The Mantelpiece, *c.* 1907, by Walter Richard Sickert

Contents

Part Three 1911–14

List of Colour Plates

Preface

Readers will soon notice – not unfavourably, I hope – that as a junior Edwardian I keep popping up in this chronicle. I did not have to persuade the publishers to allow me to do this; they insisted that I should. Now and again it may irritate my contemporaries (at our age this is easily done), but I agree with the publishers in believing that for younger readers the fact that I keep popping up in it will make this era seem less remote. And, after all, this is far from being a formal piece of social history.

Checking facts and going in search of opinions I have gone through many Edwardian volumes, most of them now out of print. But the authors and books I am particularly indebted to I have mentioned in the text, and I have included them in the short bibliography, which should be useful to readers who wish to follow up a subject. My thanks are due to the authors and publishers concerned for their permission to use various quotations.

As this is very much an illustrated book and space for the text is limited, as in its companion volume, *The Prince of Pleasure and his Regency*, I have left some subjects – notably architecture, decoration, fashion and sport – entirely to the illustrations and their captions, allowing the eye to do its work here. This would not have been possible without the expert and enthusiastic co-operation of Mary Anne Norbury, who has been responsible for the illustrations. My warmest thanks go to her and to John Hadfield, one of the most patient and sympathetic editors I have known during a long writing life. I also want to thank Geoffrey Green for his help with the illustrations of sport.

J.B.P.

Acknowledgments

Quotations in the text have been taken from the following copyright works, and acknowledgment is made to: Crown Publishers Inc. for the quotation from *Lloyd George* by Richard Lloyd George; Harcourt, Brace and World Inc. for the quotation from *From Sarajevo to Potsdam* by A. J. P. Taylor; Rupert Hart-Davis Ltd for the quotation from *The Rainbow Comes and Goes* by Diana Cooper; The Hogarth Press Ltd for the quotation from *The Edwardians* by V. Sackville West; MacGibbon and Kee Ltd for the quotation from *Memories* by Desmond MacCarthy; Macmillan & Co. Ltd for the quotation from *Mutiny at the Curragh by* A. P. Ryan; Methuen & Co. Ltd for the quotation from *The Common People 1746–1946* by G. D. H. Cole and R. Postgate; Frederick Muller Ltd for the quotation from *Lloyd George* by Richard Lloyd George; John Murray (Publishers) Ltd for the quotation from *Scott's Last Expedition* by Robert Falcon Scott; Mr Nigel Nicolson and Mr Benedict Nicolson for the quotation from *The Edwardians* by V. Sackville West; Martin Secker & Warburg Ltd for the quotation from *A Modern History of the English People 1880–1922* by R. H. Gretton; Thames and Hudson Ltd for the quotation from *From Sarajevo to Potsdam* by A. J. P. Taylor; Mr M. B. Yeats for the quotation from *From the Green Helmet and Other Poems* by W. B. Yeats; the Executors of the Estate of H. G. Wells for the quotation from *The New Machiavelli* by H. G. Wells.

1. Young Bertie

It would be cheating to accept the word *Edwardian* while attempting to keep out or even to diminish the king who gave his name to the age. It is true, as we shall see, that many things typically Edwardian were far removed from King Edward VII. Yet, even so, he changed the whole look and appeal of the monarchy. I was only a child when he succeeded Victoria in 1901, but I can testify to his extraordinary popularity. He was in fact the most popular king England had known since the earlier 1660's, the first years of Charles II's Restoration.

He was born on November 9, 1841, the second child but the eldest son of Queen Victoria and Albert, her adored Prince Consort. His arrival received an uproarious welcome from the nation. He was christened Albert Edward, and he used both names until his accession, when he wisely dropped the Albert. In the family he was always called 'Bertie'. Here, having the future king always in mind, I shall call him Edward. When he was born, Victoria was still an enraptured girl bride, delighted by the thought that her son might 'resemble his father in *every, every* respect both in body and mind.' Later, when this son grew up to be completely unlike his father, Victoria's disappointment largely explains her severe and unwise treatment of him. But severity and a lack of wisdom were evident from the first. Guided by his German adviser, Baron Stockmar – generally considered, outside Windsor Castle, a pedantic busybody – the Prince Consort laid down a set of rules for his son's upbringing and education that almost guaranteed Victoria's later disappointment. We can see how much of Edward's behaviour and character as a man came out of a rebellion against his boyhood.

The christening of Albert Edward, Prince of Wales, in St George's Chapel, Windsor, January 25, 1842 (detail), *c.* 1842–45, by Sir George Hayter

The boy was to be controlled, closely watched, reported upon, almost hour by hour, and he was to be kept away from other boys of his age. So, as soon as he grew up and was free of Windsor Castle, he became excessively gregarious, never happy in his own company. Governesses and tutors imposed courses of hard dreary reading on him. So as a man he read as little as possible. The whole atmosphere of his childhood and early youth was thick with Teutonic pedantry and priggishness, together with a stiff consciousness of rank and royal prestige. Almost the only escape the boy had was an occasional visit to the theatre, usually to some enchanting pantomime. Later, Edward was able to combine a feeling for rank and precedence with a love of playgoing and even more frivolous pursuits.

He had been admired and petted as a very small child, when he had some claim to rather delicate good looks. But then his parents, with several more promising children by this time, began to find him vaguely unsatisfactory and no longer gave him such loving attention. After that he seemed a rather wistful, rather melancholy lad, and perhaps even then he was dreaming of all the attentive pretty women he would come to know as a man. However, he was fondly attached to his eldest sister, Vicky (another Victoria), who was to marry Prince Frederick William of Prussia and bitterly regret the match, both before and after she became the mother of the future Kaiser Wilhelm II. Vicky soon detested Germany and the Germans, and it is worth remembering that from their earliest years she and her brother shared many likes and dislikes.

The one brief but glorious break in the grim routine came from a visit to France. It was the first time the thirteen-year-old boy had gone abroad. After all, however backward and unsatisfactory he might seem to be, young Edward was Prince of Wales, so Victoria and Albert took him and Vicky with them on their state visit to Napoleon III at the Tuileries. It was the summer of 1855: the Second Empire was at its most brilliant if rather flashy height. After sober old Windsor Castle and

(right) The Royal Family at Balmoral, September 29, 1855. This was the day the Princess Royal, aged 14, became engaged to Prince Frederick William of Prussia. *(Left to right)*: Prince Alfred, Prince Frederick William, Princess Alice, the Prince of Wales, Queen Victoria, Prince Albert and the Princess Royal

(centre right) The Prince of Wales at Frewen Hall during his studies at Oxford, 1859–60. *(Left to right)*: Colonel Bruce (Governor), F. W. Gibbs (Tutor) and the Revd Charles Turner (Director of Studies and Chaplain)

(below) The Prince of Wales during his visit to the United States in 1860

gloomy London, the Tuileries and Paris, bright in the sunshine, were an enchantment to the boy, a pantomime come true and grown gigantic – all flags and cheers, cavalry escorts out of a storybook, martial music in the daytime, waltzes at night. And nothing, nobody, formal and stiff and severe, from the smiling Emperor and his beautiful Empress Eugénie downwards, all friendly, almost free-and-easy. The small fair Prince of Wales, wearing Highland costume (a clever stroke this), was the darling of the Paris people, who never stopped cheering him. It was all so wonderful that on his last day the boy, suddenly brave, implored the Empress Eugénie to let him stay longer. When she replied with a smile, that his mother would not be able to spare him, he said solemnly, 'Don't you believe it. There are six more of us at home, and Mama won't miss me at all.' But, if he could not linger, I think the enchantment itself lingered and never entirely faded from his memory. For ever afterwards, up to the last few weeks of his life, he was always happy to return to Paris; he never fell out of love with France.

During his later 'teens Edward was allowed some travel, but never to do as he pleased. He always went with a full and unenticing programme and under the strictest supervision. A Colonel Bruce, a dour martinet, had now been appointed his governor, just as if everywhere he went was an extension of some prison. He spent some time at three universities, Edinburgh, Oxford and Cambridge, but being somewhat removed from collegiate life, knowing only a few visiting professors, he was carefully protected from any advantage a university might have offered him. However, the summer of 1860 brought him a break, and one he immensely enjoyed. Queen Victoria had found it impossible to accept repeated invitations to pay an official visit to Canada and a private one to the United States. So she offered them her eldest son, the Prince of Wales; and off Edward went, surrounded by an official suite and still under the stern eye of Bruce. Both visits, packed with engagements, demanding a great deal from a youth of nineteen, were triumphantly successful. The young Prince might be inexperienced, but now, away from books and professors, on show as a smiling royal personage, he was at last moving in his natural element. His parents might have learnt something from this; as it was, backward and unsatisfactory 'Bertie' was clamped again into the grim routine of books and Bruce. If Victoria and Albert had been determined to turn him into a rip as soon as he was free of them they could not have worked harder at it.

Towards the end of November, 1861, Albert went to Cambridge to give his son more good advice. He caught a cold, returned to Windsor only to go down with typhoid fever, and died on December 14. Queen Victoria, wild with grief, fled to Osborne, her house on the Isle of Wight, and refused to leave it, so the Prince of Wales was the chief mourner at the funeral. He was a genuine mourner too, for a reverent deep affection for his father, which never left him, had always mastered any resentment he might have felt. Doting on her husband, Victoria had always

(opposite) Nanny in Kensington Gardens, *c.* 1910, by Brake Baldwin

(overleaf) The Imperial Hunt in the Forest of St Germain, August 25, 1855. Standing in front of the hunting lodge are *(left to right)* the Prince of Wales, Prince Albert, Queen Victoria, the Princess Royal and Napoleon III

TEMPLE
PIE HOUSE
220
PATENT
COMB & BRUSH
PROUT

happily agreed with every plan he made – and Albert was a great planner. Now, in her rigid widowhood, Victoria began to develop her own formidable resources of will and domination. Every plan of Albert's must be carried out.

Not long before his death Albert had been giving much earnest consideration to the question of young Edward's marriage. Naturally he had turned first to Germany, his own country and one that had enjoyed almost a monopoly of royal-marriage-business for the past hundred years. A string of German princesses was examined and reported upon, but for one reason or another none was thought to be suitable. Finally and surprisingly, the Prince Consort abandoned Germany for Denmark, fixing his choice on young Princess Alexandra, known familiarly as Alix.

With Alix we are in a fairytale atmosphere. (But then, among her family friends was Hans Andersen.) Not only was this Princess beautiful, charming, kind – she was also quite poor. Although her father, Prince Christian, had been accepted as the heir to the Danish Crown, he had to live on a pittance. He and his family scraped along as best they could in a mouldy ruin of a palace miles from anywhere. Alix and her sister Dagmar shared the same draughty attic bedroom, made their own clothes, and, on the rare occasions when their parents felt they could entertain anybody, they waited at table. But now, in spite of protests from Berlin, Victoria insisted upon carrying through her Albert's plan. She sent for Alix and gave her several lectures on conjugal and domestic themes. She arranged for Edward to meet her – they examined the battlefield of Waterloo together – and then learnt that the young people had taken to each other at once. So in March, 1863, Alix left her attic, dressmaking and tureen-holding for ever, and found herself Princess of Wales. The other girl in the attic, Dagmar, became Empress of Russia and mother of the unfortunate Nicholas who was swept away by the revolution of 1917.

Even if we heavily discount the flattery of royal personages, I think we ought to agree that Alexandra was a remarkable woman, a shining piece of luck for Edward and for Britain. She really earned her enormous popularity. She may never have been quite the great beauty she was declared to be, but she certainly kept her splendid good looks throughout her long public life. ('But then they have their faces *enamelled*' I overheard, as a boy, some women telling one another, and then found myself haunted by the idea of this strange practice). She was the perfect wife for Edward, who was far from being a perfect husband. On show with him she looked dignified, magnificent, yet was always charming and easy in manner. At home with her five children, relatives and intimate friends she was simple and affectionate, undemanding and often high-spirited, greeting mishaps – and they were fairly frequent – with a peal of laughter. (Perhaps more young princesses should have shared attic bedrooms, made their own clothes, and served the soup.) Though Edward's attentions to pretty women were notorious, somehow she seemed to float serenely above any idea of herself as a neglected wife. And when Edward

The Arrival of Princess Alexandra for her marriage to the Prince of Wales: driving through the City at Temple Bar, March 7, 1863 (detail)

The Prince of Wales descending a timber slide near Ottawa in 1860

was dying, it was she who sent for Mrs Keppel, who had been his favourite for some years. She was indeed a remarkable woman, and the people, sensing her quality and her genuine warmth of heart, loved her. To raise money for one of her favourite charities she instituted an annual 'Rose Day', when roses were bought in every main street, perhaps chiefly to please Queen Alexandra, a kind of rose herself.

Now, in 1863, very much the Prince of Wales and a married man, Edward was given £100,000 a year and as his London residence Marlborough House. To these were added the mansion and the fine country estate of Sandringham in Norfolk, excellent for training race-horses and for rearing pheasants and partridges that would come thudding down every shooting season. Victoria had settled into her implacable widowhood, avoiding London and all public appearances, living in black seclusion at Windsor, Osborne or her favourite Balmoral in the Highlands. (Her chief ministers, compelled to go up there, cursed the place.) Somebody had to represent the Crown, both at home and abroad; so it had to be the Prince of Wales. Fortunately he enjoyed such official occasions and, soon losing his shyness, became adept at making impressive appearances. He was even able to improvise effective little speeches in idiomatic French and German. Acquiring complete command of French had probably been a labour of love. German he had heard all round him since childhood. Victoria and Albert in their domestic life had probably spoken more German than English. Ed-

(below) Sandringham, Norfolk

(bottom) Marlborough House, London

ward's own English never quite lost the deep guttural tone, the rrrolled r's, the separated syllables, associated with a German style of speech. It must have influenced the whole family. I remember that in the 1930's, when I had a house in the Isle of Wight, Edward's sister, old Princess Beatrice, was then Governor of the Island, living in some discomfort in Carisbrooke Castle. One summer afternoon she descended upon us, and I was astonished to discover what a thick German accent she had. I also remember, with more pleasure, my small son Tom bowing in an odd jerky fashion, and telling myself how queer it was that he was looking at a woman who had been nursed by Queen Victoria. As I have said before – we are all in history.

(top) The Prince and Princess of Wales at Sandringham, autumn 1863

(above) Queen Alexandra, founder of the Rose Day, in 1912, receiving a rose from a small child

2. Prince of Wales

Though Victoria allowed Edward to represent the monarchy on so many occasions she still mistrusted his character and capacity. She inflexibly refused him any part in the government of the country. He was not to be told anything important. Indeed, it was not until the middle 1890's that, at Gladstone's request, the Prince of Wales, now well past his fiftieth birthday, was permitted to see Cabinet papers and other official documents that would now be labelled 'Top Secret'. Edward naturally resented being banished from all the more serious affairs of state, even while performing as its figurehead. But he lived in such awe of his mother, an awe rising to sheer terror as she became more rigidly intolerant and formidable, that he shrank from pressing his claims. It could be argued that this long exile, lasting thirty years, from state affairs and domestic political life did him more good than harm – that is, as a future king. I am not thinking now of the way in which it concentrated his attention on foreign affairs. This was not altogether a good thing. But because he was outside domestic politics, he was not associated in the public mind with one political party. What is perhaps even more important is that while Edward was always ready to meet his responsibilities, they left him with sufficient time and energy to enjoy himself. Some of his experiences may have been far from edifying, but the sum total of them soon turned him into a tolerant and affable man of the world, a sharp contrast to his stiff and priggish father. It has been said that he owed his popularity to the fact that his subjects regarded him as a typical Englishman. But this is too simple. What his livelier subjects – and there were plenty of them – saw in him was a typical Englishman *with the lid off*.

He overdid it at first, of course, like a colt let out of a dark stable. With £100,000 a year and his own establishment, he went, we might say, 'on the town'. And the town was the London of the 1860's, much of it very

Caricature by Max Beerbohm entitled: 'The Rare, the rather awful visits of Albert Edward, Prince of Wales, to Windsor Castle'

disreputable indeed, far worse than the London we know now. It might house Dickens's Mr Podsnap and his friends, worrying about anything that might 'bring a blush into the cheek of the young person'. But its customary late-night scenes were enough to embarrass the bosun of a whaling ship. It offered wild young bloods, 'heavy swells' on the loose, a wide choice of dubious midnight company. It ranged from notorious cocottes like 'Skittles' and her kind in their St John's Wood villas to the anonymous pretty girls to be found at Cremorne. Its scene moved from the private supper rooms of fashionable restaurants to the cockfights, rat-killing contests, sailors' booze haunts and opium dens further East. Edward's late-night companions were the wilder young members of that aristocracy which had long regarded Victoria's Court as stuffy, too German, almost bourgeois. They were soon known, with much head-shaking, as the 'Marlborough House Set'.

Catherine Walters, 'Skittles'

Then for Edward, setting out not as the Prince of Wales but as Baron Renfrew or the Earl of Chester (two of his actual titles) there was always Paris, the almost hysterically gay Paris of the last years of the Second Empire, set to music by Offenbach. We have no clear picture of Edward's larks and sprees in the 1860's, but we do know there was more and more gossip, fed by scandal-sheets like *The Tomahawk*. The London popular press of the 1860's and '70's was far bolder and more scurrilous than any newspapers we have now, and was often quite ready to offend the Royal Family. So, in one way or another, disturbing rumours reached the Queen herself, even though she might be in remote Balmoral. Her Bertie, it was obvious, was not behaving himself.

Then early in 1870 gossip and rumours were confirmed: a scandal like a giant rocket burst over London. Harriet, the wife of Sir Charles Mordaunt, a member both of Parliament and of a well-known family, had just given birth to her first child – she was only twenty-one – and was in great distress because the baby was in danger of losing its sight. Blaming herself, she then told her husband he was not the father of the child, and blurted through her tears that she had been very wicked, having had many lovers. She named two of the Prince's closest friends, Lord Cole and Sir Frederick Johnstone, and then the Prince himself – together, she added, with 'others, often, and in open day'. This last addition suggested she had received her lovers during the afternoon, when her husband was at Westminster. And unfortunately this was the very time when Edward liked to pay her a call. Was she a young nymphomaniac, with whom the Prince and his friends liked to amuse themselves when there was no racing in the afternoon? Or was she the victim of some puerperal disorder (still common then) that turned her confession into so much lunatic raving? This is what her family believed: they were ready to produce medical evidence to prove she was – or at least had been – insane. But her husband never doubted the truth of her confession and so insisted upon a divorce. It was an extremely complicated case, and, being fully reported, was unsavoury meat and drink for millions.

In his evidence Sir Charles Mordaunt said that the Prince of Wales had never gone to the house at his invitation, that in fact he had warned his wife against His Royal Highness because, he added vaguely but not without a damaging effect, he had heard 'in various quarters certain circumstances connected with the Prince's character . . . . .' Some letters written to Harriet by the Prince were produced and actually found their way into the press. At no time did Edward allow himself to be eloquent on paper. These brief letters seemed quite harmless: *Tomorrow and Saturday I shall be hunting in Nottinghamshire; but if you are still in town, may I come and see you about 5 on Sunday afternoon?* – all that kind of thing. But cynical persons felt that something might be read between the lines, and wondered aloud why the Prince of Wales should want to write at all to this particular young woman.

Edward actually appeared in the witness box, but there were no

Cremorne Gardens (closed 1877): 'The Chinese Platform', 1857

startling revelations. He was examined by his own counsel and not cross-examined by Mordaunt's. As part of a divorce case, his appearance was a fraud. A few polite questions established – at least for the benefit of the court and the reporters – that the Prince had met both the Mordaunts on various occasions, and that he might be regarded, no matter what Mordaunt himself had said, as a family friend. The final question asked if there had ever been any improper familiarity between himself and Lady Mordaunt, and his Royal Highness replied firmly there had not. There was then some applause, echoed throughout the country by loyal citizens and the more responsible press. But in some low radical papers suspicious queries could be discovered. Why had the Prince been allowed to go without any cross-examination from the other side? Why these visits anyhow when the husband was always out? There was a sudden drop in the Prince's popularity, and even some hisses and booings in his favourite public places, the theatres and racecourses.

Popular sympathy went his way again when he was seriously ill during the winter of 1871–72. After a rather protracted convalescence, spent yachting in the Mediterranean, he returned in summer and proceeded to give enormous garden parties, astonishing in 'the number and range of invited guests'. It may have been the dubious variety rather than the number of these guests that compelled Gladstone to speak to the Queen. Braving her displeasure, though he was innocently unaware of the fact that she detested him, Gladstone solemnly declared it was time the Prince of Wales was offered some official regular employment – in India perhaps or Ireland. But the Queen, though agreeing in principle, offered objections to every definite proposal. So nothing came of it. Yet it would have been a wise move. There was now increasingly sharp criticism of the monarchy. There were even suggestions, in the

(above) Sarah Bernhardt as *Théodora*, 1902

(right) The Prince of Wales, photographed by Bassano, *c.* 1875

radical press and in speeches by public men, that Britain might do well to follow the recent example of France and become a republic. People asked what the Queen, whom they rarely saw, did with all the money the nation gave her. By remaining in mourning, and not holding any splendid courts, she was bad for trade. And while the Londoners seldom set eyes on her, a promoted Balmoral gillie, John Brown, a rough Highlander who was allowed too much whisky, saw her every day. He was now her personal attendant, quite brusque with her and extremely rude to everybody else. Some foolish people believed they were secretly married. Her unpopularity must have lasted some time, long enough for her son Edward to become very friendly with Sarah Bernhardt, because once when she had been angrily complaining to him about attacks on her in the press, he replied, '*Ma chère amie,* you are not as badly spoken of as is my mother.'

Neither was he, but he did not escape criticism. Indeed, it was one of the arguments against continuing the monarchy that this heir to it was far from being a solidly responsible character. If his mother was blamed for not being seen and spending too little money, he was blamed for being seen everywhere and spending too much. All this racing and gambling, fast company, trips to Paris, women here and women there! As late as 1891, when Edward had to make a second appearance in the witness box, the people who had been shaking their heads over him for years were offered a fine chance to enjoy some righteous indignation. He had been one of a party staying at a house called Tranby Croft. There had been some high play every night at baccarat – an idiot game that has long had a rakehell air about it – and one of the party, a distinguished army officer, had been accused of cheating. It was not the cheating but the fact that the Prince of Wales should have been there, gambling away night after night, that created the scandal. He was forced to complain about 'the most bitter and unjust attacks' coming not only from the press but also from 'the low church and especially the nonconformists'. So from then on he avoided baccarat, at least when in England. But as he enjoyed card games, he took to bridge, which he played regularly for only moderate stakes and apparently with only moderate skill.

The head-shakers, whether shocked nonconformists or aggressive republicans, did not in fact treat Edward fairly. He had a tremendous zest for pleasure but he also had a real sense of duty. As Prince of Wales he did whatever was demanded of him, and almost always, both at home and abroad, bettered expectation. It was not his fault that he was not offered greater responsibilities. And it had not taken him long to create an impressive *persona.* He grew a beard that lengthened and strengthened his face; he broadened out and began to look massive; his voice was stronger and deeper; and, indulging a lasting passion for dressing up, he took care that his innumerable uniforms and suits improved his appearance. Just as the other Edward, Prince of Wales, his grandson, set the fashions in the 1920's, so throughout the 1870's and 1880's our Edward's style of dress and various mannerisms were eagerly copied in high society, not only in London but also in the European capitals he had visited. At the same time he caught the fancy of people at the other end of the social scale. The fact that he was a sportsman, yachtsman, inveterate playgoer, and when off duty a man about town who enjoyed a good dinner, a large cigar, and lively pretty women, did not alienate the working class. It gradually brought him the admiration and affection of the more cheerful, often feckless, members of that class. Typical of these were the Cockneys, who wanted to live vicariously through somebody and to give that somebody, themselves enlarged and with the lid off, a cheer: 'Good old Teddie!' they began to shout.

Victoria, now a stout little old lady, recovered some of her early

(above) Four generations: Queen Victoria, George V, Edward VII and Prince Edward of York (the present Duke of Windsor), 1899

(opposite) Queen Victoria's funeral procession at Windsor, February 2, 1901. Behind the gun-carriage drawn by sailors walk Kaiser Wilhelm II, King Edward VII and his brother the Duke of Connaught

popularity when the Jubilee of her reign was celebrated with much pomp in 1887. The English love to acclaim sheer survival, so there was even more cheering, in 1897, when her Diamond Jubilee blazed and thundered with all its Imperial pageantry. But Edward was not lagging behind. The cheers for him were louder too because his racehorse Persimmon had won both the Derby and the St Ledger in 1896. (This may seem absurd until we remember Chesterton's remark that the English people in general were not interested in the equality of men but in the inequality of horses.) So while Victoria's death, in January 1901, was genuinely mourned by the nation, there were also feelings of relief and expectation. A change at last! Fashionable society was eager to welcome its own man. The people had their 'Good old Teddie!' His coronation was delayed until the summer of 1902, when the heirs (not the rulers themselves) to all the empires and kingdoms in the world arrived in London. But almost at the very last moment there had to be a further delay. Edward had to have an urgent operation for what was soon to be called appendicitis. (It became fashionable too.) I can still remember when I first heard this news. I had been spending a day in the country with my parents, and a farmer drove us in his trap, through the gathering dusk, to the nearest railway station: on the way there, a man shouted the news at us. The postponed coronation was something of an anticlimax, if only because all the royal visitors who had arrived in June had departed before August. But the ceremony and its processions were sufficiently splendid. This was the first coronation for sixty-five years. The people had been eagerly looking forward to it, and for many weeks, perhaps months, I had heard the singing in the streets:

We'll be merry,
Drinking whisky, wine and sherry.
Let's all be merry
On Co-ro-nation Day.

The Prince of Wales leading in Persimmon after winning the Derby in 1896

LONDON
COUNTY BANK

3. The Crown

It is worth returning to the day after Victoria's death. Edward had had to go to London, to meet the Privy Council and take the various oaths of sovereignty as King Edward VII. He then made a speech, beginning, 'I am fully determined to be a constitutional sovereign in the strictest sense of the word.' It was an impressive speech, surprising too, for not only had he used no notes, he had spoken without asking his chief ministers what he ought to say, so breaking a tradition. There is a great deal of Edward to be discovered here, in his first appearance as King. He was genuinely determined to be 'a constitutional sovereign in the strictest sense of the word', and this he proved to be. At the same time, within the allotted limits, he was going to be his own man, to be Edwardian and not Victorian. For example, he took the monarchy back into London, using a richly re-decorated Buckingham Palace as his base. Instead of being almost invisible, as Victoria had been, he showed himself all over the place, leading the parade, so to speak, as a good constitutional monarch should do. The small and dreary court circle was now immensely enlarged. Little tea parties were out; glittering evening receptions, with champagne and a band, were in. (Did he still remember the Tuileries in 1855?) He wasted no time and energy, as Victoria had done, trying to extend the political power of the Crown. He never wrote long and querulous letters to his ministers. But he did give an astonishing amount of time and energy to doing all that could be expected of a constitutional monarch – and doing it very well. This was astonishing not because he had now entered his sixties, but because he never abandoned his old role of the pleasure-loving wealthy man of the world. Somehow he still contrived to visit Biarritz in the early spring and Marienbad in late summer, to go racing and yachting, to pay royal calls abroad, to join house parties for bridge, good food and wine, and amusing pretty women. Incidentally, he was not alone in these tastes; many of his chief ministers shared them too: hence Hilaire Belloc's sardonic epigram: 'On A Great Election':

> The accursed power which stands on Privilege
> (And goes with Women, and Champagne, and Bridge)
> Broke – and Democracy resumed her reign:
> (Which goes with Bridge, and Women and Champagne)

Edward VII was brilliantly successful because, first of all, *he enjoyed being a king*. Here I think he was very different from his son and grandson, George V and George VI. Edward was an experienced relisher of life. If, after waiting so long, it brought him a Crown, he would enjoy that too. He had lost, years and years ago, any trace of shyness and diffidence. The one person he was frightened of, his mother Victoria, had vanished from the scene. He was a cunning old hand at tact, affability, charm. But he was not going to be too easy a king, allowing

(opposite) King Edward VII, 1907, by Sir Arthur Stockdale Cope

His Majesty King Edward VII.

Her Majesty Queen Alexandra

H.R.H. the Prince of Wales.

H.R.H. the Princess of Wales.

bridge partners, racing companions, the women he favoured, to take liberties when he appeared before them as their monarch. He had a sharp eye for any faults in dress and manner on Court occasions, when all were on parade. A misplaced decoration or a wrong ribbon was noticed at once and brought an immediate reprimand. Unpunctuality, never a fault of his, was severely condemned. Even when he was off duty and at ease it was dangerous to take advantage of his smiling good humour, to forget that the stout elderly gentleman with his glass and his cigar was also His Majesty King Edward the Seventh: the purring cat suddenly growled like a tiger. This may have been deliberate policy, part of his cleverness in handling people. In point of fact, Edward as a man was tolerant and good-natured, never out of temper long, never vindictive. So I cannot help feeling that keeping this danger alive, making friends and courtiers realise that if they went one step too far they would be immediately in trouble, was a deliberate policy. It gave an edge and excitement to his company. It brought into high relief those times when he really did seem to be all affability, charm, companionable ease, when if some of the mob from Newmarket, Epsom or the Mile End Road could have looked through the window, they would have cried 'Good old Teddie!'

Kings who retreat into their inner worlds, searching for jewels of experience in the darkest recesses, have always invited failure. Hamlet would have been a disaster as King of Denmark. Edward succeeded because he was the complete extrovert. Not for him the poet Dyer's famous boast: 'My mind to me a kingdom is'. He lacked entirely the inner resources that come from wide reading and much reflection. Throughout his reign he probably never entertained one abstract idea; but this left him with more opportunity to entertain and be entertained in the outer visible world. However, it also meant that he was always being threatened by boredom. Edwardian high society knew only too well the danger signals – his heavy eyelids falling, the voice deepening and slowing up, a drumming on the arm of his chair – and then some lively attractive woman would have to be rushed to his side. He was reasonably conscientious in attending to all the tedious formalities of royal business, but he took care to reduce them to a minimum, always dreading boredom and knowing he had something more amusing he could do. But our inner worlds resent being completely neglected; they can begin to throw shadows over the jolliest scenes. I may be prejudiced here but I do seem to detect in Edwardian high society and even in Edward himself, especially in his last years, a certain strain of melancholy, common enough among over-extroverted lovers of pleasure. Oh yes, it's a wonderful party – but the band sounds tired, the women and champagne are losing their sparkle, the latest cigar smokes badly, boredom and satiety come creeping in, and the night is waiting outside to put its dark old questions.

Coronation postcards of 1902

However, if King Edward could not read books, he could read people.

Princess Alexandra on the occasion of Queen Victoria's Golden Jubilee, photographed by Bassano, 1887

He was an acute judge of character, unlike most monarchs. Having long been 'no better than one of the wicked', he had acquired in all manner of places much valuable experience. He shared with very successful financiers and business men the knack of rapidly absorbing all the information he needed simply from talk. He welcomed the company of wealthy international financiers, mainly Jewish; and at least one of them, Ernest Cassel, became an intimate friend. The old-fashioned gentry – as distinct from the smarter aristocracy, always fascinated by money – grumbled about the King's association with these Jewish plutocrats from nowhere. But then, as Proust observed: 'Princes know themselves to be princes, and are not snobs; besides, they believe themselves to be so far above everything that is not of their blood royal that great nobles and "business men" appear, in the depths beneath them, to be practically on a level.' It was widely assumed that Edward, trying to cope with his extravagant style of living, accepted large loans from these millionaires, especially Cassel; but this was not true: what he did get from them were stock-market tips he was able to turn to advantage. Not another

The Coronation of Edward VII, August 9, 1902, painted in 1904 by Laurits Tuxen

George IV, always hopelessly in debt, Edward was level-headed about money, spending freely but always able to meet his obligations. I think what really attracted him, market tips or no tips, to these international financiers was their shrewd sophisticated talk over the brandy and cigars, their knowledge of the world. They represented boldly one side of his own character. Being international they paid close attention to foreign affairs, and here King Edward was just as much concerned as they were.

Partly because he had been kept out of government and politics at home, partly too because he had made so many journeys abroad, Edward as Prince of Wales had acquired a deep and lasting interest in foreign affairs. As King he felt he could do more than he had been able to do as Prince. He was *in* foreign affairs anyhow, being related in one way or another to so many emperors, kings, princes. (The French said he was the Uncle of Europe.) Now a tremendously impressive figure, he enjoyed having confidential talks with important ministers when he was abroad. Like most people who thoroughly enjoy themselves and have no quarrel

(top) President Kruger

(below) Rudyard Kipling

with destiny, the last thing he wanted was war. He saw himself helping to maintain a nice balance of the major European powers that would preserve peace. But his diplomatic moves were entirely his own affair, so many rides on his hobby-horse. He was never acting on behalf of his Foreign Office, which did not want the King to represent it – and indeed was all too often reluctant even to represent itself.

Edwardian Foreign Secretaries would have felt much relief if the King had spent all of his late hours abroad in a frivolous fashion. The trouble was, some heads of state and their foreign ministers could not understand that King Edward was not acting on behalf of official British policy. They saw him as a super-important, glamorous and artful ambassador-cum-agent. In Berlin, which had a rather neurotic foreign department inclined to believe anything except the truth, he was regarded as a Machiavelli-de-luxe. The Kaiser, who was even more neurotic than his expert officials, half-despised and half-feared this majestic uncle of his, so much at home among the decadent French, so cynically unappreciative of Teutonic aspirations and vast Wagnerian fantasies. To all this we may have to return later: here I merely add one query. Did Edward, coming so late to the Throne, fully realise, for all his knowledge of the world, how the rapidly increasing facilities and enterprise of journalism could bring every move he made into the fierce light of publicity? The simplest friendly chat might now be misinterpreted. For example, on one occasion he was caught talking to Sir Henry Campbell-Bannerman (his first Liberal Prime Minister) who, like the King, was taking his annual 'cure' at Marienbad. Under the photograph of them earnestly conversing was printed *Is It Peace Or War?* Campbell-Bannerman said afterwards, 'Would you like to know what the King was saying to me? He wanted to have my opinion whether halibut is better baked or boiled.'

We read that Henry James very privately denounced Edward as 'an arch-vulgarian' and declared that his reign would be ugly, all 'vulgarity and frivolity'. This seems to me quite wrong, but then I have never been able to accept Henry James as a novelist who understands English life and character. And Edward was altogether too full-blooded for him. No doubt, in the Jamesian sense, there was a vulgar streak in Edward – all that wining and dining with pretty women and rich financiers, all those racecourse appearances! But as King Edward VII, somehow he contrived to surprise a great many of his more intelligent subjects. There was more in him than met the eye. For instance, the nineteenth-century monarchy had been traditionally Tory in its sympathies. But Edward, while avoiding any obvious bias, tended to be Liberal, even though he always refused to recognise the fiercely radical Lloyd George. He was on the whole, as he once described himself, 'a liberal-minded man'. Indulgent to himself, he was inclined, except in the formalities of court dress and etiquette, to be indulgent to others. When he could use the royal prerogative he was lenient, never severe. He was not the kind of man to spend weeks visiting factories, stifling yawns as all the mechanical processes were laboriously explained to him; but a list of the public engagements he did accept, very often to lay foundation stones, does suggest he had a genuine interest in hospitals, universities, schools. He was not a social reformer, but even so he was something more than the patron of semi-official charities. Somehow or other he created an atmosphere in which philanthropy could make way for social reform.

Lord Roberts

It was the same with the arts and sciences. Nobody could pretend that Edward was a felicitous lover and patron of the arts; yet again, perhaps out of a genial tolerance, a refusal to impose his own private standards, he helped to create an atmosphere in which the arts could flourish. (So, for instance, we know that he delighted Elgar, who for all his pomp-and-circumstance *persona* was in fact a wincingly sensitive man.) And it was this 'arch-vulgarian' who early in his reign created an Order of Merit that really was – and still is – an order of merit, not just another title and ribbon to reward contributors to party funds or to compensate politicians kicked out of the Cabinet. It was the very order, initialled as O.M., into which Henry James himself was admitted, early in the World War when he took British citizenship; and perhaps looking back, remembering the founder of the order, he may have decided that this man had not been so utterly vulgar after all. No indeed, there really was more in Edward than met the eye, even though as 'Good old Teddie!' he always seemed willing and happy to meet the eye.

(right) Lord Kitchener

(far right) Christian de Wet

4. Beating the Boers

King Edward's short reign, only nine years, was soon to be splendid and glorious, but it began at a bad time. In 1901 Britain was so unpopular abroad that even if official court mourning had allowed the King to resume his rounds of visits he could never have risked the hostile demonstrations in one foreign capital after another. At home his subjects were so bitterly divided that old friends shouted one another down (I know, because I overheard some of them) and political meetings often ended in uproar and brawls. The trouble was that the Boer War had not yet been brought to an end. It was now in its last but ugliest phase. From the first it had been denounced abroad, where some serving army officers had been allowed to join the Boers, who were seen as brave farmers prepared to defend their South African homeland against greedy and aggressive British Imperialism. Liberal opinion in Britain might agree that old President Kruger was too obstinate and reactionary, but it was felt that there had been something fishy about the case built up against him and his fellow Boers, basically by financial men who cared nothing about votes and farms but cared a great deal about South African gold and diamonds. There were, however, numbers of influential people – their laureate was Kipling – who were not cynical and self-seeking but were swept forward towards the war on the great glittering tide of Imperialism. They believed, like the government and its military, that this would not be a real war but only another brief colonial adventure. Boer farmers could not be expected to face for more than a few weeks the highly-trained regular troops of the British Army.

They were wrong, and towards the end of 1899 the British Army suffered several astonishing and humiliating defeats. The men, brave enough, were no longer fighting Kipling's *Fuzzy-Wuzzy* and his kind. The Boers were surprisingly well-armed and even had heavy artillery. They were campaigning in difficult country that they knew very well. They were mostly mounted, so that if they were repulsed they could vanish in a cloud of dust while the wretched British infantry, cursing their thick uniforms and heavy gear, were wiping the sweat out of their eyes. The Boer leaders were masters of guerilla tactics, while many of the senior British officers were slow to learn and made bad mistakes. But this could not last, of course. More and more troops – some from the other colonies – and better equipment were sent out. Lord Roberts and the formidable Kitchener, the victor of Omdurman who utterly defeated the Mahdi in the Sudan, went to take supreme command. This meant that earlier generals like Buller, White and Methuen had to take orders as well as give them – or retire. We kids, I remember, had been wearing – and constantly swapping – their portraits on celluloid brooches, a publicity device not repeated in the two World Wars; and I do not think we threw these things away after Roberts and Kitchener assumed command. Indeed for many years after the Boer War, whenever anybody on

(opposite) This typical example of the popular-patriotic art of the period, by W. H. Y. Titcomb, 1913, was originally entitled 'Cheering the Chief Scout', but later was used as recruiting propaganda with the title 'Send Us!'

the variety stage mentioned Buller, who was immensely popular among his Tommies because he took great care of them, there was always immediate applause.

The unified command and the presence in the field of the beloved Lord Roberts and the grimly determined Kitchener soon changed the course of the war. By the end of summer, 1900, the larger Boer forces had been defeated and scattered, British prisoners had been released, the way was open from Cape Town to Johannesburg, and President Kruger had fled to Europe to ask for help. The real war was over, and Roberts returned home in November, 1900, leaving Kitchener as Commander-in-Chief. To his disgust, Kitchener had to soldier on, after a fashion, because a number of the best Boer leaders, including the elusive and brilliant de Wet, a guerilla fighter of genius, refused to surrender. Not only did they and their 'commandos' avoid capture but they scored, by daring raids or artful ambushes, various unexpected victories, not important in themselves except that they made the great British Empire look foolish. Moreover, this irritating guerilla phase of the war proved to be very expensive. Kitchener had an enormous territory to cover, and what with guard duties everywhere and the various 'commando-hunting' expeditions, he had to keep a large army active in the field. The Boer leaders knew this, of course, and their tactics were to keep Britain frittering away time, patience and money, against increasing protests at home, until the European powers sympathetic to the Boers insisted upon a compromise peace settlement. But they reckoned without Kitchener. He detested this expensive and frustrating tip-and-run warfare, in which remote farmers suddenly turned themselves into guerilla raiders and then in a few days were farmers again. Moreover, he was very anxious to be free of South Africa so that he could accept an invitation to become Commander-in-Chief in India. But he had taken on the duty of putting an end to this wretched war; his whole great reputation had been based on his inflexible determination and slow-but-sure method; so he would stick it out but would now attempt far more drastic measures.

Kitchener by all accounts was not an endearing character. He was big, overbearing, inclined to be brutal in manner. He was a tremendous methodical worker, unwilling or unable to surround himself with men to whom he could delegate power, and this weakness brought about his failure as Secretary of War from 1914 to 1916, when he was drowned on his way by sea to Russia. But he was a most impressive and formidable figure. (Oddly enough – or is it odd? – one of his few recreations was planning the decoration and furnishing of his residences, and he had a taste, almost a passion, for delicate china.) I saw him only once but had a close view of him. This was early in the Great War when I was a private soldier in the first New Army he had raised, often known as the 'First Hundred Thousand'. We were stationed in Aldershot and one day the whole division was drawn up on parade, outside the town, to be inspected by Kitchener. We waited for hours, and it rained all the time,

The Doctor, by James Pryde, exhibited 1909

dont Forget Majuba
NO FEA
BOER NO FEAR

(opposite above) A blockhouse in South Africa

(opposite below) An evacuated Boer dwelling

so long and so hard that the blue dye began to run out of our absurd forage caps. And then at last there he was, glaring at us rank by rank – a huge figure with an outsize purple-swollen face – no, not the result of drink, because he was then strictly teetotal – and through this unmoving mask the strange eyes moved, stared, glared. I must confess that to me, just turned twenty, standing there rigid, with blue rain running down my face, feeling, as I was often to do in the army, idiotic, he seemed a monster. But he was not a monster. Grimly devoted to duty, ready to work day and night, he could be rough and tough, but there was no deliberate cruelty working in him: he was no sadist. The point has to be made because of what follows, when we return to South Africa at the beginning of 1901, just when Edward succeeded Victoria.

Kitchener decided to adopt drastic measures to compel the Boers to sue for peace. He began to build blockhouses for his man-hunting troops, and divided his enormous territory into fenced-off divisions. Within these areas, which became smaller as more blockhouses were built, a scorched-earth policy in reverse was carried out. Livestock and supplies were removed from the Boer farms, and then the farms themselves were burnt. (But after the peace settlement their owners were given compensation.) Before the war was over Kitchener had built about 8000 blockhouses covering between 3500 and 4000 miles. And he had about 150,000 troops, mostly mounted now, either on guard or out hunting the guerillas. But what became of the Boer women and children whose homes had gone up in flames? To answer this question is also to explain the tremendous outcry that rose not only in Europe and America but also in Britain itself. These women and children were removed – and it was the first appearance of this sinister term – to 'concentration camps'. (Later we had to answer the taunts of Goebbels on this subject.) Though he had come to detest the whole Boer population, Kitchener intended no deliberate cruelty. But a lot of good people could have flung at him, like a dart, Clough's stinging couplet:

> Thou shalt not kill; but need'st not strive
> Officiously to keep alive.

His policy was rough-and-ready, but too rough and not sufficiently ready for one that involved the lives of women and children. Many of the camps were overcrowded; supplies were often late or inadequate; the spread of disease was hard to check; and out of 117,000 persons in the camps, about 20,000 died. (The sunlit *veldts* of South Africa were curiously unhealthy, and far more British troops were killed by disease, chiefly enteric, than by shells and bullets.) It is said that Kitchener himself never inspected a camp – he attributed the insanitary conditions to the filthy habits of the Boer women – and he was so busy trying to capture the last guerilla forces, and spending hundreds of thousands of pounds a day doing it, that he was glad to transfer responsibility for the camps to civilian authorities, under the Colonial Office. Its minister, the Colonial Secretary, was Joseph Chamberlain, an aggressive Imperialist with a gigantic popular following. This was in March, 1901. Not long afterwards some of the camps were inspected and reported upon by Emily Hobhouse, who had been sent out by an influential group of women. But when she returned to Cape Town in October, 1901, Kitchener, who said she had not asked for his permission, immediately had her arrested, to be deported. She was seen violently resisting her guards, and all this was widely reported, to swell the chorus of protests throughout Britain.

The people were more sharply and emotionally divided than they have ever been since. The division on the whole followed political opinion, most Tories supporting the Tory government and the war, most Liberals and all radicals and socialists denouncing everything that was happening and the men in authority who were allowing it to happen. Feeling against Kitchener was so strong that a group of prominent Liberals decided to bring an action against him, but counsel's opinion, probably based on the fact that he was after all a serving soldier, dissuaded them. There were some Tory members of Parliament, deeply shocked, who sided with the protesters. On the other hand, some important members of the Liberal Party, while deploring Kitchener's drastic methods, felt that he should now be allowed to bring the war to an end as soon as he could. But popular opinion and feeling, mostly feeling, ran to extremes. From the first, the Tory government and its press, a large majority of the newspapers, had played a gambit now all too familiar: you rush out troops, and then any reasonable protest against the war and its aims is heatedly denounced as treachery, an insult to 'our boys out there'. But in this last phase of the war the snarling cry of 'Pro-Boer' was heard more often. There were large meetings at which any mention of 'Pro-Boers' was greeted with howls of rage. There were also other large meetings, sometimes ending in riot, at which any reference to the intrepid and agile Boer guerilla, de Wet, was enthusiastically applauded.

To give one example of this division and heat of popular feeling we can turn to December, 1901. The fiercest of the Liberal anti-war orators was young David Lloyd George. (I never heard him then, of course, but many years later I did, and considered him the best political orator I ever did hear, far better than Winston Churchill.) Lloyd George very courageously agreed to address a big meeting in Birmingham Town Hall. Joseph Chamberlain had long been associated in the public mind with events in South Africa, before and during the Boer War, and Chamberlain was a native son of Birmingham and its darling. The idea of 'Pro-Boer' Lloyd George daring to denounce Chamberlain in their Town Hall infuriated the Birmingham crowd. A huge angry mob defied and fought with the police, smashed the Town Hall windows, broke down a door and stormed in, even firing shots. One man was killed, and ninety-seven police were injured. Lloyd George escaped, disguised as a policeman, through a back door, a heavy fall of snow coming to his aid.

My late friend Kingsley Martin, for thirty years the editor of the *New Statesman*, described in his reminiscences of early childhood how, at this time, his family had its windows broken. His father was a Unitarian minister in a quiet cathedral city, but his windows had to be smashed because he had spoken out against the war and was another 'Pro-Boer'. Nothing so dramatic happened to us in Bradford, though my father was certainly a 'Pro-Boer' and, unlike his only son, was argumentative and rather hot-tempered; and I can remember that there seemed to be trouble in the air, loud with arguments that led to furious quarrels. England at the beginning of Edward's reign did not resemble at all the long golden Edwardian afternoon described in so many memoirs.

The Boer War actually came to an end in May, 1902. Though Edward delighted in continental travel, he had had to stay at home because Britain was so unpopular abroad. It was not until March, 1903, that he risked a cruise in the royal yacht, calling at Lisbon, and then, by way of Naples, going to Rome, to see the Pope and King Victor Emmanuel. All this was easy enough, for he was still outside the range of anti-British feeling. But a three-day visit to Paris, which he had planned, was a very different matter. Though official France was ready, even eager, to receive him, it was felt in Whitehall that the Paris crowd might be very hostile and create some unpleasant scenes. However, the King, who loved Paris and had not seen it for several years, must have felt that he knew the French better than his Foreign Office did. It was all very difficult at first. As he rode with President Loubet in an open carriage from the railway station, there were angry shouts, jeers and boos from the crowd all along the way. It was not much better at the Comédie

Souvenir election postcard of 1906

(opposite) Edward VII after his arrival at Bois de Boulogne station, Paris, May 1, 1903, driving away with President Loubet

Française that first night. There was no applause, even some hisses, for King Edward. Yet before the three days were gone, all the jeers had turned to cheers. He achieved an immense personal success. He captured Paris and with it all France. He did it by preserving his dignity and smilingly ignoring all demonstrations against him, by his tact and easy charm in private, and by the warmth of his various impromptu speeches in praise of France. This complete reversal of public feeling, begun and completed within seventy-two hours, seems to me worth a volume of admiring tributes to his quality as King. It is clear evidence of his self-confidence and capability: he knew what he had to do and how to do it. For three years his ministers and generals had been busy alienating the French, and in three days he put it all right again. There was a lot to be said, in 1903, for a King who was also a pleasure-loving man of the world, who had known for a long time, being no better than one of the wicked, how life could be enjoyed in Paris.

Edward VII in Paris, a caricature by the German, Bruno Paul, 1905

5. The Imperial Mystique

The Boer War and its division of the British into supporters of the war and 'Pro-Boers' were part of a larger issue and a deeper and more lasting division. This was between the enthusiastic Imperialists, whose poet and prophet was Rudyard Kipling, and the more radical Liberals and

Cecil Rhodes, 1896

the socialists who were contemptuously dismissed as 'Little-Englanders'. The debate between those two opposed types of mind continued long after the war in South Africa had ended, went on throughout these Edwardian years, and indeed, in one form or another, even survived the First World War, partly brought about by rival imperialisms. It has been said that it was in 1897, the year of the old queen's Diamond Jubilee, that British Imperialism reached the peak from which, willy-nilly, sooner or later, it would have to descend. Its new acquisitions both in Africa and Asia came fastest during the 1880's, but its pride and propaganda were more evident in the 1890's, especially after 1895 when Joseph Chamberlain, very forceful, very popular, became Colonial Secretary. A successful business man himself, Chamberlain appealed to other business men to remember that, through the empire, new markets could be created and old markets 'effectually developed', that 'the empire is commerce'. Such statements might be compared to loud tunes for the brass section. But other prominent speakers brought in all the quivering strings. So Cecil Rhodes, who had made a great fortune in South Africa, said, 'If there be a God I think that what he would like me to do is to paint as much of Africa British-red as possible'. And in 1899, Lord Rosebery, who had been a Liberal prime minister but was also strongly imperialist, took off another lid by declaring, 'It is the mission of England to take care that the world as far as it can be moulded shall receive the Anglo-Saxon and not another character'. Meanwhile, Rudyard Kipling, in his 'Recessional', one of the few notable poems first printed in a daily paper *(The Times)* that had an immediate sensational effect, had warned his fellow countrymen that they must be worthy of their great destiny:

If, drunk with sight of power, we loose
  Wild tongues that have not Thee in awe,
Such boastings as the Gentiles use,
  Or lesser breeds without the Law.

To some of us much of what Kipling wrote then and later does not suggest a dependable sobriety. On the contrary, those 'lesser breeds' suggest an Imperialism at least slightly intoxicated.

As an idea, a policy, a course of action, Imperialism was as infectious as the various fevers that killed so many of the young men it sent far abroad. Even the United States could not entirely resist it. There the last frontier had gone; the whole continent was now wide open and yet closed in; the idea of planting the flag in distant places, as the European powers were so busy doing, was tempting; and the U.S.A. had a navy fit and ready to go anywhere – to Hawaii and far down in the Pacific to the Samoan Islands or to help the Cubans rebelling against Spain. There were newspaper publishers like Hearst crying out for war, glory and larger circulations. On the other side were wise men like President

(right) William Randolph Hearst depicted in caricature by Oliver Herford as a contender for political power, who would like to conquer the Governorship of Albany and the Capitol. By his ear is a bug, the leader-writer of the Hearst Press, Arthur Brisbane

(below) Theodore Roosevelt, the 26th President of the United States of America

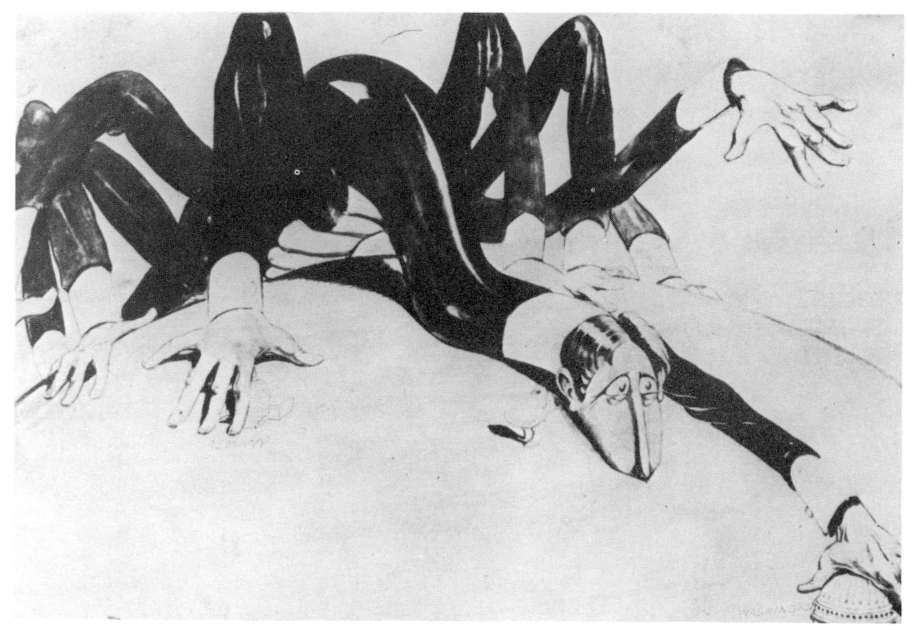

Cleveland, who could declare that 'the mission of our nation is to make a greater country out of what we have, instead of annexing islands'. A man who could easily have encouraged a fiery jingoism and imperialistic designs in America was Theodore Roosevelt, who was in favour of the Spanish War and fought in it himself with notable courage. He was one of those men who, having deliberately overcome various physical weaknesses in childhood and youth, are in their maturity unusually energetic, bold, sharply aggressive. There is a kind of imperialist flavour in Teddie Roosevelt's style as a man. But in fact during his two terms as president, though he built up the army and the navy, finally sending a formidable fleet of battleships round the world, he made use of his energy and aggressive qualities in a war with the big corporations and the financial interests, and with all the local opponents of his plan for national conservation. There may have been a touch of imperialism, for example, in his dealings with Panama, but there were no more far-flown adventures. He kept his country busy with and excited about itself. After all, at that time American capitalism had a whole continent in which to expand and develop.

After the British, the French were the most successful imperialists. During the 1880's and '90's, they acquired a great deal of valuable territory in Africa and the Far East, and they did it with rather less cant than the British had done. Even so, the average French citizen was persuaded to accept colonial expansion as an ideal, for which certain sacrifices might have to be made, not without an air of romance. But the French businessman, not on the whole a romantic type, was soon able to see that money spent on developing North and West Africa and Tongking might be returned tenfold. French products entered the colonies

Edward VII and the Kaiser during the State visit to Berlin in February 1909

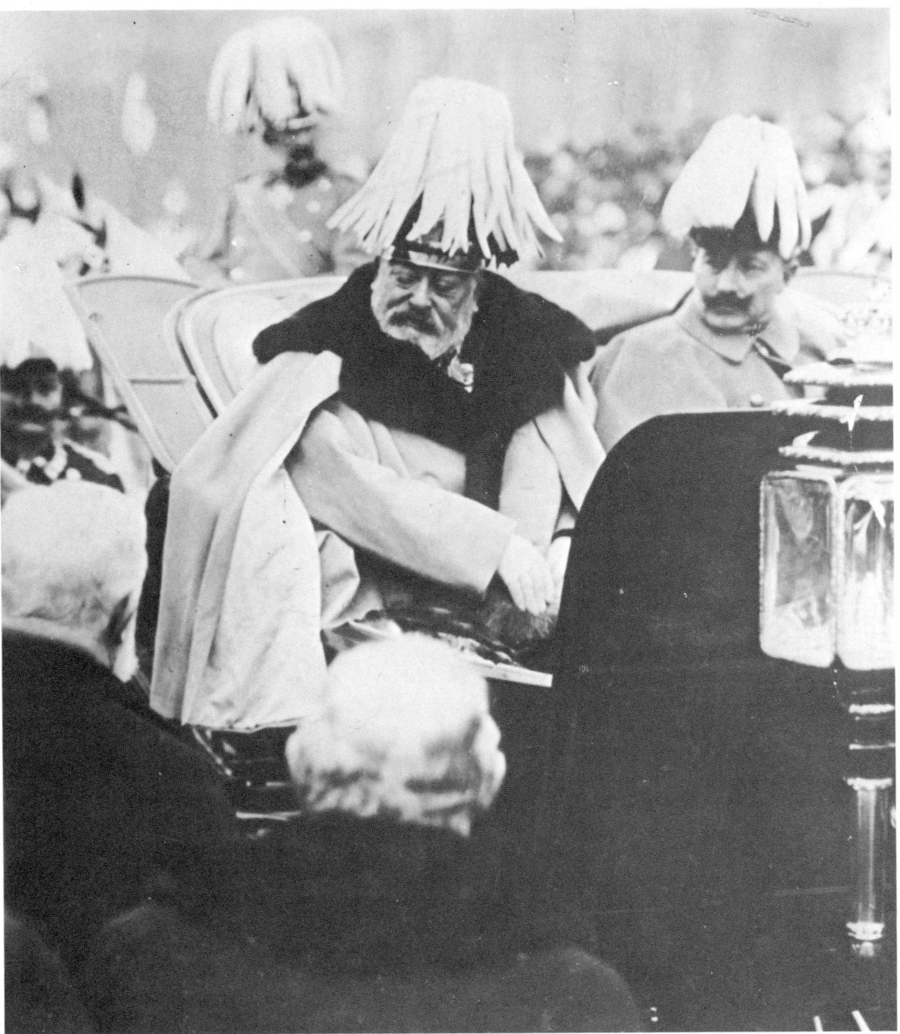

free of tax whereas, to protect French industries and agriculture, a tariff was imposed on most colonial products entering France. So French Imperialism was no more altruistic than any other, but it did some of its colonising with a certain ease and grace, largely uncomplicated by any colour prejudice. If France had cut herself a huge slice of Equatorial Africa, so had King Leopold II of Belgium, who, until 1908 when the Belgian state took it over, had personally owned the vast mysterious region of the Congo. There the natives were flogged, tortured, mutilated, to make sure they collected sufficient rubber and ivory and so enjoyed the benefits of European rule. Dreadful rumours and then detailed reports came out of this *Heart of Darkness* (as Conrad called it), and the final outcry, together with the execration of King Leopold, not only put an end to the worst horrors of the Congo but made the other imperialist powers increasingly anxious about what might be happening in their colonies.

We are told that Leopold's agents could sell for about £52 an amount of rubber that had cost them under £3. Imperialism did not always do as well as that, of course, but there, writ large, is the dominant economic motive. Its aggressive capitalism had to expand. 'The empire is commerce'. One favourite British device was to allow a trading company to take over an undeveloped lump of Africa, and then, when the company ran into trouble, to let the Colonial Office, plus a few Gatling guns, take charge of the territory, after which larger companies moved in. Even so, I think it is possible to be too Marxist-minded about Imperialism. I am not thinking now about defence, which explains some of Britain's acquisitions, really uneconomic but important as coaling stations for the navy or as army bases. Almost all the Asiatic moves were connected with the defence of India. But what lies outside the usual Marxist approach is national prestige, the kind of imperialist mystique that explains a Kipling, who was never worrying about commerce. (It also explains the very popular music-hall songs I well remember, songs created, delivered, received, in an almost fevered flush of patriotism.) Imperialism was not all hard-headed calculation. There was working in it, heating it up, an irrational element, more dangerous in the long run than anything coolly worked out at a board-room meeting.

(below left) A South African comment on the Tory government's decision to allow the importation of Chinese labourers into Transvaal

(below right) A popular poster used by the Liberals in 1906

(opposite) Britta the Danish ballerina as the 'Spirit of the Flag' in *Our Flag*, a ballet at the Alhambra Theatre in 1910, painted by Spencer Gore

I cannot help feeling that it was prestige and a new nationalistic fervour that dominated German Imperialism. Germany was late entering the race for colonial possessions. It stayed hungry when Britain and France were glutted. Shrewd old Bismarck, having created his German Empire at home, wanted no adventures overseas. However, he and his successors, during the 1880's and '90's, got their hands into the grab-bag, picking up a bit of this, a bit of that: Togoland and the Cameroons, various islands or parts of islands in the South Seas, and a couple of treaty ports in China. In the end, this other German Empire contained about twelve million persons, with whom the Germans, good solid immigrants rather than colonists, were rarely on rewarding terms. The total territory, mostly land hard to develop, covered over a million square miles, which may look impressive but was a mere backyard compared with the huge British and French Empires. So the Germany of Kaiser Wilhelm II – a prestige man if there ever was one – was left colony-hungry, dissatisfied, envious. It was not a healthy situation.

Too often the imperialist powers went half-blindly blundering around, like big arrogant men who had forgotten their spectacles. So, back in the 1890's, Britain and France had nearly gone to war over a single incident that was largely a question of prestige. An exploring French officer, Marchand, had crossed equatorial Africa to reach Fashoda on the White Nile. There, in true imperialist fashion, he had promptly hoisted the French flag, only to be confronted soon by Kitchener and a considerable force. In the crisis that followed there was even a partial mobilisation of the British fleet, in the middle of an angry dispute between officials in London and Paris still ignorant of Nile geography. It was touch-and-go before Marchand went, taking his tricolour with him. Then, in 1903, there was a fairly typical imperialist blunder in South Africa, based on arrogance, a contempt for popular feeling. Balfour, as prime minister, accepted a recommendation from a Transvaal Commission that indentured Chinese coolie labour should be brought in to work the valuable mines on the Rand. This blew up a storm of protest in Britain, and I can remember staring, as a small boy, at the cartoons and posters with their Chinese faces and caricatures of bloated capitalists using slave labour. It was this popular indignation that largely helped to sweep Balfour and his colleagues out of office and to bring in the Liberals. Imperialism was not wearing well.

As everybody knows, the British Empire finally dissolved itself, though not without some pressure from its possessions. There is irony here. The new nationalist politicians, who so frequently and fiercely denounced colonialism, even after they were free of it, were the very men who had gained most from colonialism, which had given them opportunities to be educated and trained. A sterner empire would have kept them sitting about in their tribal villages. A further and grimmer irony can be found in the fact that when the brutal British finally departed, many of the people in their former possessions began

slaughtering one another on a horrifying scale which the Empire had never known. Not that I am defending Imperialism; I remain a 'Little-Englander', believing that no people are good enough to rule other people thousands of miles away. Again ironically, it was the later developments of Imperialism that did most harm. When the Colonial Office sent out young bachelors to act as district commissioners, it was not too bad. Most of these young men, as I know from personal experience, were more than conscientious, were eager to know and understand the people they were sent to govern. They learnt the languages, appreciated the value of local customs. But later, when white women went out, together in some instances with unimaginative army officers, then came the exclusive clubs and compounds and the colour bar was down. All manner of proud people were insulted. So, for example, in the Chinese treaty ports, the 'old China hands' would clap and shout 'Boy!' to be served perhaps by an elderly man who felt that he represented a civilisation far older and wider than anything these arrogant barbarians knew. (This rankles yet with the Chinese, even though they may be idiotically busy destroying what is left of that civilisation.) Then, to my mind if not perhaps to most people's, even while it was being increasingly denounced and opposed, Imperialism was most dangerous because it was rapidly destroying traditional ways of life. The power it wielded encouraged a belief in, an imitation of, the industrial civilisation it represented: the freed colonial peoples also wanted factories, industrial processes, machine guns, cars and airplanes, newspapers and radio and contemptuously dismissed the traditional life of their forefathers. Yet now it is clear we urgently need not fewer but more experiments in living. The human race should not be compelled to sink or swim with only one kind of civilisation. It is beginning to look as if we are all being packed into one leaky boat.

British Imperialism, far stronger at the beginning of these Edwardian years than it was at the end of them, existed in a bad atmosphere. It was too arrogant, too boastful, and when it was not too boastful it talked too much cant and humbug. Always it gazed outward, not inward. Cleveland's 'The mission of our nation is to make a greater country out of what we have' may have been applied to a continent and not to a modest island; but it remains wise counsel. *And what should they know of England,* cried Kipling, *who only England know?* To which the 'Little-Englanders' could reply that they knew a great deal that Imperialism chose to ignore. While it was so busy painting so much of the world map a bright red, hundreds of thousands of houses down England's mean streets could have done with a lick of paint. In the centre and heart of the Empire on which the sun never set there were too many people on whom the sun hardly ever rose. A mile or two east of London's Mayfair, into which the wealth of Empire was poured, there were some of the foulest slums in Europe. Between the rich and the poor there was still an appallingly wide gap.

A leaded glass panel for Miss Cranston's Willow Tea Rooms, 1903, by Margaret Macdonald who was a leading member of the Glasgow School

(above) Fashions seen at Ascot, 1905

(opposite above) Waiting for parcels of food in Cheapside, London, 1901

(opposite below) Waiting for Lights Out in the Salvation Army Shelter, Medland Hall, 1901

6. High Society

Edwardian high society added a little chapter – and surely the most recent, unless we are going to be silly about the 1920's – to the myth of the Lost Golden Age. During the years between the turn of the century and the First World War the glitter of rank, wealth and fashion was not of course confined to England. Paris had its Faubourg Saint-Germain, haunted nightly by Marcel Proust, whose huge dark eyes missed nothing. These were the last years of the legendary Vienna, still capital of the Austro-Hungarian Empire, the city of the endless waltzes, the cavalry officers in magnificent uniforms, the late-night suppers in the discreet little rooms upstairs. Among the Americans, Newport, Rhode Island, still flowered every summer, New York still heard and read about the Four Hundred, the crazily extravagant parties of the millionaires, the export of 'dollar princesses' to London, Paris and Rome. All this, together with much more of it elsewhere, may be said to have existed in the same atmosphere, with a considerable amount of cross-fertilisation, assisted by a world press that employed more and more gossip-writers and photographers. But it was the English Edwardians who occupied and decorated the central position and did most to bring the myth of the Lost Golden Age into the twentieth century.

Ah! – those wonderful parties in town, Season after Season, when we danced until dawn – those long summer afternoons, when we sauntered through the gardens of the great houses that entertained us in those days, those afternoons that somehow shrivelled, faded, then vanished from the world! What days, what nights! What nostalgia, what regrets! But nobody must be deceived; I am merely being rhetorical. I never enjoyed such days, such nights, except in print, and it did not take me long to stop enjoying them even there. The truth is: not only was I far removed from Edwardian high society but *I never set eyes on a single member of it* – not, that is, until I became a soldier, when I had to take orders, often ridiculous, and reprimands from various specimens of the English ruling class, and listened to accents so extraordinary that they might as well have been foreigners.

Why did this Edwardian high society create so soon a legend, smiling at hundreds of thousands of wistful or envious readers? The Victorian Age, so long and rich in events and famous personages, created no such legend. Following the social myth, we have to jump straight from the Regency into the Edwardian years. How then, in legendary terms, did this brief and comparatively recent era and its society work the trick?

I think there is no simple answer. Many different things combined to create the legend. We must take into account first the influence of King Edward himself, who restored the monarchy to London, who lit up and flung open Buckingham Palace, who shared the tastes of this society as his mother had never done. It was an era when the new wealth of the

Laundry Girls, 1906, by Albert Rutherston

Maid darning socks, *c.* 1910, by Brake Baldwin

financiers was added to the old wealth of the great families of landowners. Direct taxation was still so low it could almost be ignored. The cost of living had not yet risen. Masses of domestic servants, on whom this society depended, were willing to be hired for absurdly small wages and, what is more important, considered it a privilege to serve such grand people, the nobility and gentry. (Edwardian novels testify to this.) So the rich scene is set. But it is transformed into (I quote a publisher) 'the now fabulous Edwardian age' by the autobiographers who look back not only at their own youth but also at a scene all the more radiant because it is on the other side of the huge black pit of war. They are remembering the time before the real wars came, before the fatal telegrams arrived at every great house. The Edwardian was never a golden age, but seen across the dark years afterwards it could easily be mistaken for one. When it dined and wined, laughed and made love, it had not yet caught a glimpse of the terrible stone face this world can wear.

The term 'idle rich' was often seen and heard in those days. But in fact the rich were not idle at all. No matter how much money they may have, very few people can face empty days, months, years. If they have no useful work, then they invent useless work. If they have no ordinary duties and responsibilities, then collectively and very solemnly they make up duties and responsibilities. The void must be filled somehow, so fashion and the social round are called in to act as ferocious task-masters. To keep in, to keep going, members of Edwardian high society toiled harder than overworked clerks or warehousemen. It was a dreadful nuisance, of course, but a fellow would have to go down to Cowes for the first week in August, then go up North to shoot the grouse or stalk the deer. A woman invited for a weekend at one of the great houses would have to take several large trunks, and then would have to be changing clothes – and always looking her best – half-a-dozen times a day. A free-and-easy life in theory, in practice it was more highly disciplined and more wearing than the life of a recruit in the Life Guards. A regular decent job would have seemed a rest to most of these people, so sternly pursuing pleasure all day and half the night, the men longing to smoke a quiet pipe somewhere, the women wanting to take their shoes off, dab on some eau-de-Cologne, and then lie down. And if this weekend visiting was hard on the guests, it was even harder on their hostesses, though they might be assisted by a social secretary, housekeeper, butler, and platoons of chefs, footmen and maids. That would be punishment indeed for some of us – suddenly to find ourselves transformed into very rich, very smart, very ambitious Edwardian hostesses.

Though a great deal 'went on in town' or in Homburg or Marienbad, Cannes or Biarritz, the Golden Age memorialists and the novelists of Edwardian high life, frequently satirical, make it plain that what shone brightest, there in the centre of it all, were the famous weekend house-parties. The houses themselves were not only very large, for they might have to accommodate thirty guests, but were often very old, renowned in history, quite beautiful, with lawns and rose-gardens out of a dream, with melting vistas of pastures and woods. (Nowadays, they admit crowds of visitors at so much a head, run tearooms, even miniature zoos and swings and roundabouts.) Most of the guests belonged to the same rich smart set. However, some senior politicians like Balfour or Asquith would be welcomed, even a writer or two if they were sufficiently amusing and knew what cutlery to use at the dining table; and there might be, if only to make other hostesses envious, one of those 'catch-of-the-season' types, the young man who had been very brave on the North-West Frontier or had just returned from remote reaches of the Amazon. Even apart from these odd visitants, this society was not entirely without cultivated men and women. But they were the exceptions. Taken as a whole, it was not a society that accepted social or cultural responsibilities, unlike earlier aristocratic societies that had set admirable standards and produced notable patrons of the arts.

Following King Edward himself, who off-duty was a member of it, this society did insist upon social discipline, upon a certain level of behaviour, upon appearances being kept up, no matter what went on behind locked doors. Thus one of its men, discovering that his wife had a lover, might refuse for years to speak to her in private, while still playing the devoted husband in public. Old titled families insisted upon a *noblesse oblige* attitude at least as far as outward appearances were concerned. These people were expected to be 'loyal to their class', which

(opposite) In Sickert's House, 1907, by Harold Gilman

Maid cleaning silver (detail), *c.* 1910, by Brake Baldwin

meant that they had not to be sufficiently foolish to be found out so that all manner of dreadful envious people might jeer at them. Hypocrisy wore the cloak of social, even political, responsibility, political because so many of these men sat, when they felt like it, in the House of Lords. ('The House of Lords,' said Augustine Birrell, a Liberal wit, 'represent nobody but themselves, and they enjoy the full confidence of their constituents.')

Taken as a whole, and now that its Golden Age glow is fading, this Edwardian high society can justly be regarded as shallow, self-indulgent, stupid, not worth to the community a thousandth part of the money it spent trying to amuse itself. And those readers who will not accept this judgment of a North Country radical – of lower-middle-class origin too – should look at *The Edwardians*, a semi-documentary novel by the Hon.Victoria Sackville-West, born at Knole Park, Kent. She grew up in this society and she is far more damning in her judgment than I propose to be.

It might be found that any society nearing the end of its high time, making hay while the sun still shines, overdoes everything. Exaggerating all its features, it pulls itself out of reasonable proportion. It does not tamely follow fashion, it is now fashion-mad. Where £100 might have been spent earlier, it spends £1,000. Champagne is served at moments when a glass of barley-water might have been acceptable. It is lavish when no lavishness is required. Its men change their clothes too many times; its women wear too many jewels. There is such a multitude of servants that elaborate hierarchies have to be created below stairs. Housekeepers, butlers, valets and personal maids are even more relentlessly snobbish than their masters and mistresses. Weekend parties – and I am now firmly back with the Edwardians – have to be organised like small expeditionary forces. Remote Oriental capitals have been taken and annexed by the Empire with less fuss. Self-indulgence is no longer idle and easy but almost ruthless, as if it represented some rigid and wearing duty. Toiling away at pleasure, these drones and butterflies might as well be worker ants. We are told that these people in Edwardian high society believed in its permanence, had no suspicion that anything would ever be changed, and therefore existed in a complete smiling self-confidence. This is not my opinion. I think that obscurely, just below the conscious level, there was a vague feeling that the end was almost in sight, that their class was now banging away in the last act. So they overdid everything.

Let us take, as an example, the food that was provided at these weekend house-parties. No doubt rich English landowners had always wanted to make sure their guests did not go hungry. There may have been equally large single meals at earlier times in history, but people then ate little before or after them. In these Edwardian great houses, however, there were processions of food and drink from eight in the morning until late at night. Not since Imperial Rome can there have been so many

(opposite) Cowes Regatta with the Royal yacht (centre), July 1909

(right) Edward VII shooting at Sandringham, *c.* 1907

(below) The visit of King Carlos I and Queen Amelia of Portugal to Windsor Castle on November 15 and 16, 1904. *(Left to right, back row)*: Princess Victoria, the Prince of Wales, Queen Alexandra, the Marques de Soveral, Prince Christian of Schleswig-Holstein, the Hon. H. G. Legge and two others; *(front row)*: the Duke of Connaught, the Queen of Portugal, King Edward VII, the King of Portugal and Senor A. E. Villaca

(opposite) The Butler, 1910, by George Percy Jacomb-Hood

(below) A spring morning in London, 1911

signposts to gluttony. No wonder these Edwardians went to Homburg or Marienbad to 'take the cure'. The Edwardian breakfast alone would make one of our Christmas dinners look meagre. First-comers arrived about eight o'clock, late-comers finished eating about 10.30. There was porridge and cream. There were pots of coffee and of China and Indian tea, and various cold drinks. One large sideboard would offer a row of silver dishes, kept hot by spirit lamps, and here there would be poached or scrambled eggs, bacon, ham, sausages, devilled kidneys, haddock and other fish. On an even larger sideboard there would be a choice of cold meats – pressed beef, ham, tongue, galantines – and cold roast pheasant, grouse, partridge, ptarmigan. (Harold Nicolson wrote: 'No Edwardian meal was complete without ptarmigan. Hot or cold.') A side table would be heaped with fruit – melons, peaches and nectarines, raspberries. And if anybody was hungry, there were always scones and toast and marmalade and honey and specially imported jams.

This kept people going until lunch, usually taken at 1.30, and it might consist of anything between eight and twelve courses, some of them very rich indeed. (Though perhaps not quite as ambitious as one mentioned

by a Rothschild, who said that quite a good dish could be confected by first taking the roes of nine hen lobsters.) Then, after a walk in the park perhaps, it was time for tea, just to keep body and soul together until dinner. And there was no cup-and-a-biscuit nonsense about this tea; toast and brioches and hot scones and all the jams again; a fine choice of sandwiches; several kinds of rich sticky cake. And if King Edward – a real glutton, I am afraid – happened to be there at teatime he would probably insist upon having his usual lobster salad. Dinner at 8.30: a dozen courses perhaps, with appropriate wines, and even richer food, probably including, if the chef were up to it, one of those quasi-Roman idiocies, in which birds of varying sizes were cooked one inside the other like nests of Oriental boxes. And surely that is enough? But no, a fellow can feel peckish after a few rubbers of bridge; so round about midnight, in a neighbouring room, he would help himself to sandwiches, devilled chicken or bones, the brandy and whisky and soda; and then he could get through the night and be ready to welcome his early-morning tea and biscuits.

However, he may not have spent the whole night in sleep. It is fairly common knowledge now that the Edwardian house-party, while severely determined to keep up appearances, discreetly provided opportunities for lovers, not necessarily young, to enjoy themselves, the males having been fortified by a final drink or two, a last ham sandwich or a bit of devilled chicken. So long as some care had been taken in advance, many of these huge rambling mansions might have been designed for late-night sexual enterprise. But a conscientious hostess was needed. We are offered an account of one in the Sackville-West novel, *The Edwardians:*

> . . . The name of each guest would be neatly written on a card slipped into a tiny brass frame on the bedroom door. This question of the disposition of bedrooms always gave the duchess and her fellow-hostesses cause for anxious thought. It was so necessary to be tactful, and at the same time discreet. The professional Lothario would be furious if he found himself in a room surrounded by ladies who were all accompanied by their husbands. Tommy Brand, on one such occasion, had been known to leave the house on the Sunday morning – thank goodness, thought the duchess, that wasn't at Chevron! Romola Cheyne, who always neatly sized up everybody in a phrase – very illuminating and convenient – said that Tommy's motto was 'Chacun a sa Chacune'. Then there were the recognised lovers to be considered; the duchess herself would have been greatly annoyed had she gone to stay at the same party as Harry Tremaine, only to find that he had been put at the other end of the house. (But she was getting tired of Harry Tremaine.) It was part of a good hostess' duty to see to such things; they must be made easy, though not too obvious. So she always planned the rooms carefully with Miss Wace, occasionally wondering whether that upright and virtuous virgin was ever struck by the recurrence of certain adjustments and coincidences . . .

Tranby Croft, September 11, 1890

I think most of us take for granted the reference to 'recognised lovers'. After all, this was a society in which many marriages had been arranged by parents and their lawyers, wanting either to join two great estates or to provide one of them, already in debt, with funds from the other. Divorce being out of the question, the victims of young loveless marriages could be forgiven if they carried on long secret affairs with the people they ought to have married. (But there were always a few scandalous 'bolters', women so deeply infatuated that they left everything and 'bolted' with their lovers, usually abroad. Somerset Maugham's sardonic comedy, *The Circle*, perhaps his best play, is based on this situation.) No, it is not the reference to 'recognised lovers' that opens our eyes, it is the passage dealing with that notorious Lothario, Tommy Brand, who could not enjoy a weekend unless wives unaccompanied by husbands were available along the same landing. It looks to us as if Tommy and his good-humoured ladies were cheerfully promiscuous.

Beauty without make-up, 1902

Well, what if they were, now they are all dead and gone? Who cares? The answer is that I do, for one, not because of what these people did inside their bedrooms: it is what they did outside them that is important. This high society, with its complaisant duchesses, its Harry Tremaines and Tommy Brands, was an extremely influential section of the general Edwardian establishment, which utterly condemned and immediately silenced any attempt in public to discuss sex seriously. What had been accepted in other countries was not allowed here. (Havelock Ellis – to take one example – was published in America long before he was in Britain.) The Tommy Brands were discreetly accommodated at week-ends by the very people who publicly declared that writers like Shaw and Wells were a disgrace to the country. Sex was fun along the landing at 1.30 a.m., but not an essential human activity, a drive, to be seriously examined and sensibly reported upon. So countless numbers of the ordinary English remained bewildered and unhappy, trying to come to terms with sex.

Some of these country-house and London-Season sexual intrigues may have come out of sheer boredom. The comparatively few intelligent persons who were allowed to enter these exclusive circles, the gossip writers' paradise, have told us how boring they could be. The talk throughout most of those long luncheons and dinners was vapid, the women prattling, the men uttering pompous nothings. Any subject worth discussing was generally barred. How tempting then to start an illicit affair, to let eyes meet across the dining table for a dangerous second or two, to feel for a fleeting but meaningful moment the pressure of a hand, to play, late on Saturday, the only exciting game the day had offered on tiptoe from bedroom to bedroom! The very keeping-up of appearances made it all the more enticing.

There was, however, something else that could account for all these liaisons and this bedroom-visiting. I think that Edwardian life on this high social level – though not on the level I knew best – was strongly charged with sexuality, which behaves oddly, at least from the masculine point of view. It is not when it bursts out, loudly proclaiming itself, all over the place, as in the 1920's, for example, or at the present time, that it is most fascinating and disturbing, flowing like a deep current below appearances and changing also the very atmosphere in which they exist. These Edwardian garden-party ladies, with their elaborate and ridiculous hats and padded coiffures, with their tight-lacing and tiny waists and well-covered prominences in front and behind (so they always seem as if they are about to bow), with all their hidden petticoats and long trailing skirts, with nothing of them clearly seen except eyes and mouths and helpless-looking dimpled hands – may appear to be anything but temptresses. But the older I get, the more deeply am I convinced that that is exactly what they were. And their lusty males, crammed with all that Edwardian food and inflamed by all its drink, were constantly tempted, were avidly longing to discover what the women were really like once the frippery and finery and social disguise were removed. So the illicit affair, however dangerous, the little tap on the bedroom door behind which the delicious creature, with heroic bared bosom and those great marmoreal thighs, was waiting – oh it was all irresistible! Such longings, such imaginings, such thoughts, charged the very air with sexuality. Or so – not without evidence, though none of it direct and personal – I suspect.

It was certainly an age that prided itself, under royal patronage, on its beautiful women. They were always being photographed, usually looking pensive and very, very feminine. Society beauties, a familiar type then, in need of a little pin money, could collect fees from fashionable photographers. There was a gigantic trade in picture postcards of musical-comedy actresses – Marie Studholme, Gabrielle Ray, Gertie Millar, Lily Elsie, Zena and Phyllis Dare. To my mind, these famous Edwardian 'beauties', whether in high society or on the stage, were not

(below left) The Corset of 1903

(below right) 'Gibson girl', Miss Camille Clifford, 1906

(opposite, above left) Zena and Phyllis Dare

(opposite, above right) Gabrielle Ray

(opposite, below left) Marie Studholme

(opposite, below right) Gertie Millar as 'Mitzi' in *The Girls of Gothenburg*, Gaiety Theatre, 1907. The diablo became fashionable during Edwardian times

really beautiful at all. A Garbo at her best would have made them look like pink marshmallows. They were altogether too feminine, almost swooning with it, and were so many very pretty sexual objects, not persons. I do not mean that in themselves they were not persons – of course they were – but that they were not photographed and presented to the public as persons, but just as so much generalised femininity, like the women who arrive in young men's erotic dreams. I shall come to the suffragettes later, but it is worth remarking here that some of these brave women, always appearing in cartoons as hideous viragoes, were in fact far more beautiful than the fashionable 'beauties'. They received no help from the rich. The house-party hostesses were still leading their laborious and anxious lives of pleasure, still overloading their tables with luscious food, still making sure that Tommy Brand's bedroom was not too far from some serviceable women.

7. The Lower Orders

So now we go from the rich to the poor, from London's West End to its East End, from the splendid dining tables of the great country houses to the cottages of the men who supplied those tables with beef, mutton, ham. After wandering among statistics, and brooding over this section, I have found myself anything but eager to begin writing it. I am reluctant because I keep feeling I am being pushed back to the 1850's not the early 1900's, well within my own lifetime. I know of course there were many changes, many reforms, during that half-century, yet somehow the material I must use, the figures I must produce to clinch an argument, seem so Victorian, not at all Edwardian, that I would rather be writing about something else, something that takes its particular shape and colour from Edward's reign. On the other hand, there is no dodging the fact that these millions, still engaged in sweated industries, living in slums condemned in theory but not in practice, in mean streets just behind the mills or close to the coal pits, in sweet little cottages that were menacingly insanitary, were King Edward's subjects like the duchess, Harry Tremaine and Tommy Brand. They probably turned out to give him a cheer. I was alive when they were alive, even though I was learning how to play football or to draw battleships (a favourite subject then) while they were putting in twelve hours a day or, being out of work, hoping to earn a shilling or two somewhere to give the family some idea of a square meal.

Compared with what we have to pay now, the Edwardian cost of living seems absurdly, almost unbelievably low. But in fact, during most of these years working people in the mass were rather worse off than they had been during the later years of the last century. Prices were at

Waiting for work, London

least a little higher whereas most wages were much the same. People in general – though not, of course, industrialists, landowners, farmers – were fiercely opposed to the protective tariffs so many Tories wanted: the prices of bread and meat, for example, would have gone up at once. These people ate a great deal of bread, often with cheese or covered with butter or margarine and jam, with lard or beef dripping; and they filled up with dumplings or heavy suet puddings. Meat, usually imported, they bought when they could, usually having a joint of some kind for the midday meal on Sundays. They had to make a little money go a long way. Ordinary farm labourers, perhaps casually employed, might take home 14 or 15 shillings for a week's hard work. (This would be well under 2 dollars, at the current rate of exchange then. I suggest that American readers take the £1 as the equivalent of $2.40, the shilling (s.) as 12 cents, and the pence worth 1 cent each.) Men permanently attached to a farm, all with some agricultural skills, were considerably better off than the labourers, having, in addition to wages, at about £1 2s. a week, free cottages and gardens, and possibly fairly generous allowances of potatoes and wheat. With garden produce, poultry and a pig or two, fresh milk and cream, these men probably ate better than any other members of the working class. And certainly the small farmer had plenty to eat. As a small boy, staying in the country, I often shared one of his meals, almost hearing the table groan.

But during these years too many of the people could only be described as poverty-stricken. A third of the population, living at the centre of this huge Empire, were below any humane level of subsistence. They were overworked, underpaid, and crowded into slum property that ought to have been pulled down years before. Conditions were so bad that it was believed they were producing degenerate physical types, anaemic mothers of rickety children, young men incapable of defending the Motherland and the Empire. There were persons, quite a lot of them, well-fed and comfortably housed themselves, who declared, perhaps to get rid of the awkward subject, that all this poverty and misery could be attributed to idleness, fecklessness, drink. But intelligent Edwardians realised that such talk was merely trying to escape the problem. Many Tories suggested tariff reform, but the Liberals of this period, who already had the problem on their consciences, pointed out that anything short of free trade, admitting cheap food, would make the poor still poorer. Meanwhile, in London, the West End was already establishing 'missions' in the East End, just as the Victorians had sent their missionaries to India, China, Darkest Africa.

What the East End, a giant city in itself, really needed was not more library books, soup, talks on temperance, but more regular work with decent hours and conditions and more money. Its huge docks were a chaos, shockingly organised, with no proper relations between employers, foremen and the dockers themselves. Regular men earned between £1 and £1 5s. a week. Then there were thousands of casual dock labourers who, after standing about in the rain, might be lucky enough to earn about three shillings and sixpence, under a dollar, a day, and if they were married might be living in one room. The bitterness of the dockers seeped down through generation after generation, and has not gone, even today. The men who were treated like outcasts began to look

Ploughing on the Downs, 1907, by Robert Bevan

(opposite above) Dancing to a street organ in the slums of the East End of London during the early part of the century

(opposite below) Taking the air in Whitechapel, London, 1901

and behave like outcasts. Some years later, but before the Great War, I went abroad for the first time, going by sea to Copenhagen. When we were tied up there, I looked down and saw a number of clean and comfortable middle-aged men, standing around and smoking cigars. Wondering who or what they were, I was astounded to learn they were the Danish version of our wretched dockers, and I felt ashamed of my country.

One section of the East End belonged to the tailoring trade. Much of the work was done at home, which meant that for some men and women, doing piece work on the 'sweating system' perhaps for fourteen hours a day, 'home' was a combined workshop, bedroom, living room. The rates of pay varied according to the class of trade: lucky women in 'the better-class trouser and vest trade' might earn up to sixpence (say, twelve cents) an hour. Among these workers, and often among the best of them, were Jewish immigrants from Eastern Europe, and some very useful and indeed distinguished British citizens, notable in the arts and sciences, came from these tailoring families. The bootmakers, mostly in Hackney, could go up to 35 shillings (nearly $4) a week if they were top skilled men, but on a lower level, with the work very irregular too, they rarely made more than 25 shillings a week, working a twelve-hour day, snatching meals without leaving their seats. The skilled cabinet-makers, Bethnal Green way, might even reach to £2 and over, but their assistants and labourers, doing 52 to 60 hours a week, often came out with under £1.

A Primrose seller of 1905

The West End and the East End were two different worlds, though linked by commerce. The society ladies at one end and the factory girls at the other probably never exchanged a single look, but still the link might be there. I have before me a list of weekly wages for women and girls in East End factories, and from it I choose some items that would not have been without interest to the ladies in the West End: *Artificial flowers* – 8s. to 12s. per week; *Bookbinding* – 9s. to 11s.; *Brushes* – 8s. to 15s.; *Corsets* – 8s. to 16s.; *Fur-sewing* – 7s. to 14s.; *Umbrellas* – 10s. to 18s. Whatever the cost of living might be, clearly this is shockingly bad pay, which would still be bad if the hours were short and the conditions pleasant – and they certainly were not.

I was never anywhere near the East End during these years; I was growing up two hundred miles to the north, in a highly industrialised textile city, sprouting tall mill chimneys all over the place. There the wages would be rather higher, if only because most mill workers, women as well as men, had certain skills. But the point I want to make is this – that while protesting against these wages, hours, conditions, I would be dishonest if I left in readers' minds a picture of gloom and misery. Our own mill girls in their clogs and shawls were often high-spirited, poor but gay. I doubt if many of the workers in the East End, if they were not too unhealthy and had regular jobs, were very different. I am not defending the system, which was rotten; but it would be wrong to create the

(opposite above) An artist's impression of a tailor's sweat shop in the East End of London, 1904

(opposite below) Women at work in a cycle factory, *c.* 1901

impression that the working class of these years was altogether downtrodden, dispirited, wretched. Somehow a large number of them rose above it, no doubt with some help from ale and porter at twopence a pint; they were certainly ready to roar out their favourite music hall songs, the very songs our radio and T.V. revive when they want to suggest a jolly evening. Working people were gloomier after the First World War than they were before it, perhaps because their world had lost its innocence and too many faces were missing.

Coal miners, often called 'colliers' round about 1900, were generally cut off from the rest of the community. They lived in their own small towns or villages, nearly always very ugly. Their hard and dangerous work underground demanded much mutual dependence, and this was found too among their wives and families. Miners had their own habits, customs, a whole style of life different from that of other workmen. One of the very best accounts – truthful, vivid, very much alive – of a miner and his family can be discovered in the early chapters of *Sons and Lovers* by D. H. Lawrence, who was born and brought up in a mining village in the Nottinghamshire coalfield. Lawrence's childhood memories are pre-Edwardian; he was born in 1885 and his recollections, I imagine, chiefly belong to the period 1890–95 or a little later; but I doubt if there were many important changes during our years, 1901–05. The father's earnings fluctuate considerably; sometimes the family is very poor indeed; at other times it seems to have a fair amount of money to spend; but this is what happened when a man was working at the coal face and was being paid strictly on results. Lawrence's descriptions of the family's simple joys are at once true and touching. The later chapters show us a young Edwardian, exceptionally intelligent, sensitive, and more ambitious than he imagines, pulling himself out of the working class during our years. But the childhood memories are best.

I have just realised that a once-familiar, almost archetypal figure of my Edwardian youth no longer makes an appearance in the contemporary scene. The Tramp – 'bum' or 'hobo' across the Atlantic – has vanished. I know, of course, that rootless, homeless, wandering men have not entirely ceased to exist. Even so, not one of them restores to me the Tramp of my youth. There was then a kind of quintessential Tramp, who was neither clean-shaven nor fully bearded, wore the ruin of a hat, no collar or tie, not always a shirt; a ragged coat usually too big for him, baggy patched trousers, and enormous gaping boots. He came into novels and short stories, plays and music hall sketches, and in hundreds of comic drawings in *Punch* and the magazines. His appearance varied little but he did not always play the same character. There was the Comic Tramp; there was the Sentimental Wistful Tramp; there was the Menacing Sinister Tramp. And now there is only the vanished Tramp. It cannot have been by accident that he was portrayed so often in the early years of this century. A lot of men in those days must have decided they could no longer work so hard for so little, thus creating a whole school of wanderers and beggars, able to read the chalked signs on gates, telling them that in one house they might expect a bit of cheese and some bread, that in another, best left alone, there would be nothing but a shake of the head and perhaps an angry dog. One of the characters in an old melodrama used to cry to the gallery, 'It's the poor that helps the poor'. And, after all, the Tramp was poorer still.

Certainly the poor were everywhere in Edwardian England. Many well-meaning persons were troubled and tried to do something about it, but during these earlier years neither of the two great political parties, neither Tories nor Liberals, could offer any real remedy. I am not an economist, but looking back I ask myself why one party had not already suggested fixing minimum wages well above the current rates of pay. There may have been apparently sound economic arguments against this, but of one thing I am certain – there was one argument against it that was not economic at all. The English class system, still almost a caste system when Edward reigned, strongly favoured both long hours of work and very low wages. Unless they happened to turn themselves into good gardeners, footmen or maids, these common working people must be kept in their place and out of mischief. Give them more leisure and more money – and God knows what they might get up to! And this prejudice was as strong among all but the best of the middle class as it was among the nobility and gentry. There was a vicious circle here. Many workers were brutalised by long hours, unhealthy conditions, low wages, bad housing. Their social superiors had only to assume they were all like that, not the victims but somehow the creators of their environment, to declare then with a clear conscience that anything better would be wasted on such people. Though it survived as a joke, it was said quite seriously at first that if baths were installed in their houses these people would only keep coal in them. I remember when, a little later than this, there arrived a rumour that some miners were actually *acquiring pianos*. Miners with pianos! Oh – the solemn protests, the sarcastic comments! It was as if some huge law of nature, welded into the very structure of the universe, had been impiously defied. Edwardian England, and indeed the England that survived him, had many severe economic problems, but there is no doubt in my mind that they were complicated and bedevilled by a class system, a class feeling.

8. Portents

In Britain in 1902 Lord Salisbury had produced a private memorandum in favour of continued isolation and so ended any further talk of an Anglo-German alliance; his office as prime minister was taken over by his nephew, A. J. Balfour, a delightful man with a brilliant mind who was not a success as head of a government; Chamberlain's campaign for Imperial Preference was a failure; the Tory government itself was generally regarded as a failure, and by 1905 the Liberals eagerly awaited a return to power. In America, President Theodore Roosevelt ('Speak softly and carry a big stick') was busy at home with his anti-trust and conservation programmes, but was really more successful abroad, where he compelled recognition of the U.S.A. as a great power, proving his case in 1905 by acting as peacemaker between Russia and Japan. France was still sharply divided by the Dreyfus affair; there was a strong anti-clerical movement; much-needed social reform was ignored and this would lead to trouble after 1905; and the *Entente Cordiale* began to make itself felt in Anglo-French affairs. In Germany, Chancellor von Bülow tried to steer a steady anti-democratic course while his embarrassing Kaiser kept saying the right thing at the wrong moment or the wrong thing at the right moment. In Russia, the Emperor had no will of his own and the Empress had too much; the bureaucracy was still inefficient; industry had been rapidly developed and with it a Marxist proletariat; and in 1905, following the disasters in the Japanese War, there were protests, demonstrations, strikes, riots, assassinations, and wholesale murder by the troops and police in St Petersburg. To all these we could add topics from the Austro-Hungarian and Turkish Empires, from Italy and India, from the Near East to the Far East. But they can be left to the real historians of these years, 1901–05. I prefer to turn aside.

Does this mean we must leave the main road to wander along various byways? I doubt it, and for this reason – that what looks like a byway to one type of mind may seem a main road to another. What I propose to do now is to pick out from these years 1901–05 what we might call, with only a touch of exaggeration in some instances, 'portents'. Many of these things seemed of little importance at the time, but now we know better. Thus, in 1901 H. E. Booth invented something that came to be known as 'a vacuum cleaner'. If we ask who cares about that then we are defeated by a chorus of 500 million housewives. No byway there.

It was in 1901 that Max Planck gave the world his *Laws of Radiation*, that Marconi sent messages from Cornwall, England, to Newfoundland by wireless telegraphy, and that we had the first – and I wish it had been the last – motor cycle. Dr Normann, a German, discovered how to harden liquid fats by a process of hydronisation, while another German, surprisingly young, Thomas Mann, in his *Buddenbrooks*, might be said to have liquidified and then liquidated another lot of fats, all belonging to one Baltic family. In Vienna, Freud gave us his most entertaining and most widely-read book – on the psychology or psycho-pathology of everyday life, which never looked quite the same again. Verdi (at eighty-eight) left this earth, and Walt Disney arrived on it. As long ago as 1901 Rachmaninov finished his second piano concerto, still the favourite, and 50,000 performances, good, bad, indifferent, began stirring, perhaps even rattling, in the womb of Time.

Guglielmo Marconi at Signal Hall, Newfoundland, with the instruments with which he received the first Trans-Atlantic wireless signals on December 10, 1901

Just to please myself I shall give first place in 1902 to the book that William James made out of his Gifford Lectures, *Varieties of Religious Experience*. Most of our donnish philosophers sneered at James and thought him slapdash and woolly-minded, but out of slapdashery and woolly-mindedness he brought a wise and liberating work, which is more than all but one or two of them contrived to do. Then there was an English physicist who went deaf and retired to Devon, where he kept himself busy discovering or suggesting things. Among these was a layer in the upper atmosphere that would not allow electro-magnetic waves to escape into space. His name being Heaviside, his layer came to be known as the Heaviside Layer, and for many years now we have been bouncing radio programmes against it. Also in 1902 Bayliss and Starling discovered 'secretin', the hormone that splendidly comes to the aid of our digestive processes. In Bamberg the first Bosch sparking plugs were being made, after Honold of Bosch's had invented the first high-tension magneto. I can only hope that these clever fellows in Bamberg never had a horrible vision of every pleasant square in Europe being ruined by the mass of motor cars parked in it. I gather that osteopathy was then brought from America into Britain, but whether this was good or bad I do not know, not having needed, *so far,* its particular manipulative system. Important books were being published, pictures painted, music composed, but we can attend to them later.

Just before 1903 slipped away into history Orville and Wilbur Wright got up into the air with a gasoline engine, which meant that soon men would be flying and would then be hard at work devising and perfecting new methods of killing other men – and indeed women and children. Taking us further into civilization, this year the Krupp Works, at Essen, were founded. A Gyro Compass was patented, also in Germany. The

(above left) Wilbur Wright

(above right) Samuel Franklin Cody, the first man to make an officially recorded aeroplane flight in Great Britain in 1908

(below) Poster for England's first aviation races at Doncaster, 1909

first motor taxicabs arrived in London and possibly were not well received, leaving a mistrust of passengers not entirely forgotten after sixty-seven years. It was in 1903 that G. E. Moore, of Cambridge, published his *Principia Ethica*, at the early age of thirty. But who, outside philosophy, cares about Moore and his attacks upon metaphysical idealism, his neo-realistic theory of epistemological monism? Well, I do, for one; and I do because Moore's heightened commonsense, scepticism, and the supreme value he attached to aesthetic enjoyments and personal relationships powerfully influenced a whole remarkable group, based on Cambridge, that included among others Maynard Keynes, E. M. Forster, Lytton Strachey, and Leonard and Virginia Woolf. This group in turn strongly influenced thousands of other intellectuals, who may never have been near Trinity College, Cambridge, nor even read anything by Moore himself. I believe the intellectual climate of Britain and America between the two World Wars would have been quite different if G. E. Moore had not published *Principia Ethica* back in 1903.

High among 'portents' of 1904 was Rutherford's book, *Radio-activity*, announcing his conclusions after a series of experiments in Montreal with Frederick Soddy. It challenged the very idea of the indestructibility of matter, to the horror of most established scientists, and it took physics and chemistry into a new age, bright with promise yet edged with darkness and menace. (Rutherford of course went from radio-activity into the atom, driven by the *daimon* of scientific genius. I met him only once, when we were fellow guests at a small dinner party. He was a large and loose kind of man who talked freely, entirely without conceit and grandeur, in an uncommonly loud voice. He could have led an army; but then, on second thoughts, that is what he did.) 1904 also gave us the photo-electric cell, the ultra-violet lamp, the first safety razor blades, and the initial section of the New York Subway, a mode of transport I for one try hard to do without, even if I have to walk in the rain. Two other inventions of this year were Alexander Fleming's thermionic valve, and Cellanese (acetate rayon) by P. Schutzenberger – needless to add, a German contribution.

Notice how these 'portents', many of them hardly noticed at the time, are creeping up on us, already secretly shaping and colouring our own age, apparently far removed from King Edward's golden days. So, in this last year of our brief period, 1905, an obscure examiner of patents in Berne, Switzerland, ventured to publish his first *Theory of Relativity*, and a few people wondered what this Albert Einstein thought he was doing. Neon lights were tried out. Two Swedes, Platen and Munters, invented a new and more efficient type of refrigerator. Wood's laminated safety glass arrived, and it was thought that such a thing might be of some use to manufacturers of automobiles, together with the new anti-dazzle car lamp. Throw in Freud's *Three Treatises on the Theory of Sex*, published this year, and we are almost home in 1970, so much of the foundation of our own age having been quietly laid between 1901 and 1905. When we boast of our science and technology, sometimes we forget what our Edwardian grandfathers did for us. They could not put men on the moon, but, even so, H. G. Wells's *First Men on the Moon* came out in 1901. No doubt modern technology was in its infancy up to 1905, but then some things are better during their infancy. We had more room then, more quiet, far less pollution – and we had our jovial King Edward, enjoying pretty faces and lobster salad for tea.

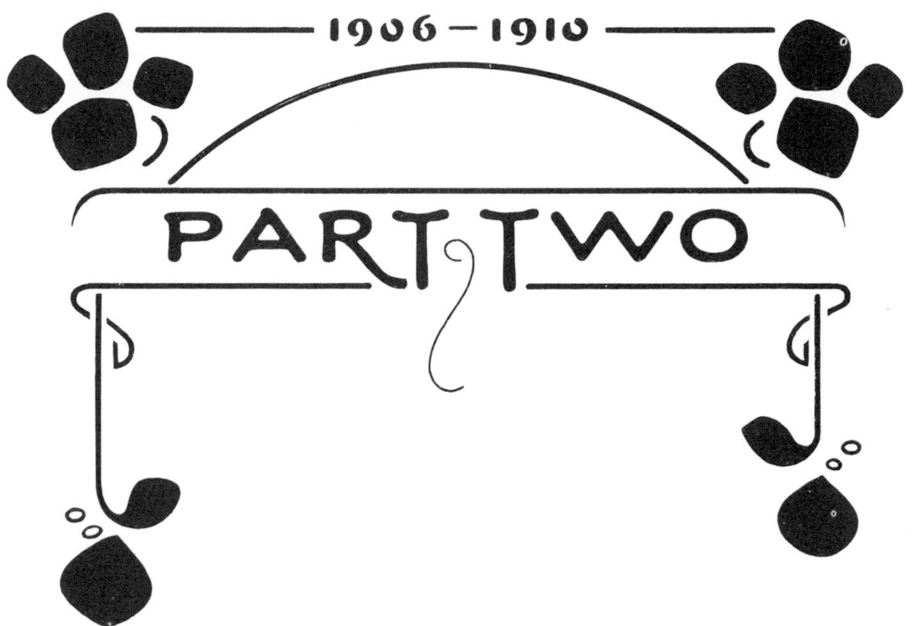

1. A Time of Tension

The idea of Edwardian life as a Golden Age has already been dismissed. Another idea, applied at least to the years up to 1911, and so including the whole of Edward's reign, must now be considered. It found expression in progressive quarters at the time, just after Edward's death, and has since been repeated now and again, with even less excuse. It asks us to believe that the Edwardian Age was simply a prolongation of the Victorian. This I cannot accept. To begin with, it ignores the fact that the Victorian Age, which we really associate with the period 1840–80, was already losing much of its former character, especially its complacency, during the 1880's and 1890's. It ignores the arrival of a *new century*, which had an effect perhaps all the stronger because it was irrational, as if our lives were governed by calendars. This effect probably explains the fashion, during the later 1890's and early 1900's, of calling so many things *New*. It ignores – what we have already noticed – the change in style and appeal of the monarchy. It makes too little of the spread of education, the growth of the popular press, the inventiveness of the new era. Finally, it is strangely insensitive to the atmosphere, the *feel*, of the Edwardian Age.

Many fairly typical Victorians, some of them very influential, were still to be found in Edwardian England. A large proportion of the upper and lower middle classes was Victorian in its outlook, values, judgments. But this is where some writers on the Edwardian years go wrong. They take away all the clever people, then tell us how stupid this age was. They point, let us say, at the banning of *Ann Veronica* by the circulating libraries, and declare that this was all very Edwardian, forgetting that

H. G. Wells and his protesting colleagues and all his admirers were Edwardians too. They tell us that the Royal Academy was typically Edwardian, when in fact it was still rigidly Victorian, and the challenge to its values and authority by unacademic painters and art critics was typically Edwardian. Indeed, if we are to have this division, then I am ready to say that it is the clever and not the stupid people who share and colour the age. What is peculiarly Edwardian, making it a new age, is not the solid lump of conformity it carried over from Victorian England but the various challenges, denunciations, rebellions, all the attempts to break away from it, to push forward into a freer atmosphere. It is the new ferment and not the stiff old complacency that gives the age its character. Even King Edward himself, for all his limitations, was a new kind of king.

If these Edwardian years had been a mere prolongation of Victoria's I would not be writing about them. This age is fascinating, just as the Regency is fascinating, because while it is brief it is also charged with character, and while it has a flavour of its own it is very hard to define – rather like a good mixture for the pipe. It is a kind of short interlude between two long acts, just as the Regency is: a col between two plateaux, the Victorian Age and our own, which began in 1914; a bridge passage, brief but complicated, in the great symphony of two centuries; a time when a lot of people are trying to cling to the past while many others are trying to hurry themselves and everybody else into a future of their own devising. Most of the adjectives tacked on to this age – *spacious*, *leisurely*, and the rest – seem to me quite wrong. It was an era of tensions between extremes.

Clearly, as we have already seen, some Edwardians were far too rich and many others were far too poor. This made thoughtful people think all the harder: I shall consider them later. But the tension I have in mind now, the sharpest and most important, was not produced by the extremes of wealth and poverty, by the contrast between the extravagant lives of the rich and smart and the narrow hard existence of the working class. The gap between them was too wide, only bridged uncertainly by the gossip and photographs of the popular press. Short of violent revolution, there was no area in which the people at each extreme could clash. The rich and smart, bent on entertaining themselves and hoping to entertain the King, were mostly shallow and silly, addicted to the exchange of scandalous anecdotes, senseless games, a daft slang of their own (as they might have called it 'a deveen privato slangino'), and – what, for me, puts any society back into the schoolroom – the constant use of nick-names. They were too busy rushing about and spending money – and it is said that one of their weekends cost an American $150,000 – to complete an iron fortress of privilege, to anticipate the Fascism of the 1920's. And, with exceptions among the nonconformists in the industrial North, the Edwardian working class tended to be equally shallow and silly, the women particularly, perhaps having relatives among the

(opposite) Lytton Strachey, 1914, by Henry Lamb

UNDERGROUND

FLYING AT HENDON

hordes of country-house servants, and enjoying vicariously the remote lives of the rich and smart.

So we must look elsewhere for the kind of tension that will bring the Edwardian Age alive. We shall discover it flickering and then often flashing among the people neither very rich nor very poor, belonging of course to the middle classes. I have declared earlier that a large proportion of the upper and lower middle classes was Victorian in its outlook, values, judgments. But these people had lost something the Victorians had had. They no longer felt secure. The old confidence had gone. Behind their imposing mask of moral indignation, all the fiercer because they were not sure of themselves, was fear. The members of the upper middle class felt that property and position were being threatened. In the lower middle class respectability itself, often newly-won, had to be guarded. There was a feeling that religion, the family, decency, social and political stability, the country itself, were all in danger. And where were these constant threats coming from? Certainly not from King Edward and his set, even though their frivolity and extravagance were regarded with suspicion and disapproval. But they were not 'clever', a pejorative term; and they would never come out with 'ideas', also pejorative. On the other hand, only a very few of the working class bothered their heads about this mischievous cleverness, these disturbing ideas. So we are left with the middle classes, to which almost all the clever dangerous fellows belonged, together with their shameless women,far worse as examples than their men. And it is a fact that during these years the English middle classes were at war with themselves. This odd conflict did much to give the Edwardian Age its peculiar character.

Later I shall have to describe some of its cultural antics and irrational animosities. Here it will be enough if I offer a longer look at the large fearful section of the upper middle class. Its denunciation, almost always immediate and loud, of anything new in ideas and the arts was neurotic. That it was hardly ever rational is proved by the fact that it tended to lump everything together into one huge quivering target. A few new ideas, an unusually frank novel, a dubious play, some strange painting or sculpture – and instantly all that was good was in danger. The stream of national life was being poisoned. Religion was mocked. The Family was attacked. Property would soon be threatened. The essential impurity of these clever fellows would contaminate young women, and so weaken and ruin young men that soon they would be unable to stand up and fight for their country, now *in danger of a German invasion.* I know this seems far-fetched, and I will not pretend that every indignant protester ended with the Uhlans galloping down the street. But many of them, leaping like terrified kangaroos, could start from a distaste for *Ann Veronica* or Granville-Barker's play, *The Madras House*, or a painting by Gauguin, then go bounding from one possible disaster after another until they landed in a German invasion. They

Flying at Hendon, 1913, a London Underground poster by Tony Sarg

went so fast and so far because the hell-hounds of fear had come baying and slavering out of the unconscious.

The German invasion scare, which haunted so many upper-middle-class Edwardians, is hard to justify on any rational grounds. Even by 1914, after Germany had been building up its navy for years, Britain still had a larger fleet, and any attempt at invasion demanded an immense naval superiority. At the end of World War Two the bulk of German foreign-office and military archives was captured, sorted out, analysed. From all the documents concerned with the First World War it was proved, for example, that German aggression could not simply be attributed to the Kaiser and his Supreme Command, but that – and here I quote from an *Atlantic Monthly* article by David Kahn – 'world power was a policy of the entire German government, civilians included, supported by almost everyone who counted . . .' But there were no plans for an invasion of Britain even by 1914. Yet there were stories and plays about invasion years before that. (One or two of them, notably the play *An Englishman's Home* by Major Guy du Maurier, brother of the actor and a regular soldier, were propaganda for a stronger policy of National Defence). Military propaganda apart, this invasion stuff confirmed the worst fears of the middle-class protesters against the new ideas and all the clever nasty fellows. But why had it to be *invasion*, not some general European war in which Britain might be defeated? This was certainly not rational. But these middle-class protesters and denouncers could not help feeling, on a deep irrational level, that they and their whole ordered and well-tried way of life were being invaded. And in their own drawing and dining rooms too – by way of a remark dropped by a son, a rebellious look from a daughter: cleverness, ideas,

(opposite, above left) Miss Liebmann's 1906 Darracq car seen outside the Albert Hall, London

(opposite, above right) *La Belle Chauffeuse*, 1904, by Sir William Nicholson

(opposite below) The model for the Rolls-Royce mascot 'The Spirit of Ecstasy', 1911, by Charles Sykes

revolt, were now invading many a detached villa or terrace house. It is a situation, usually based on a clash between generations, that can be found over and over again in the more intelligent Edwardian fiction and drama.

If this middle-class protest, often resulting in swift intolerant action (through official censorship or the commercial banning of books), came from a new feeling of insecurity, spreading fear in the dark of the mind, then what was happening at this time to their enemies, also middle-class, the dangerous clever fellows with all their atheism, sex and socialism? It was hope, not fear, that inspired them. This is equally true of writers not associated with atheism, sex and socialism, men like G. K. Chesterton and his friends. The intellectual Edwardians lived in an atmosphere of hopeful debate. They were ready to argue with one another in private, before an audience, or continually in print. Their disagreements might be wide and deep indeed, but when we look back on them now we see that they shared a common platform – a belief that men might be converted to a cause, that society might be rationally transformed, if they could win the debate.

Later I shall have to consider Edwardian writing in general, but here, to prove my point, I will bring in two writers and men of ideas, Shaw and Wells. To some people they were the leaders, the inspirers, the prophets, and to many others they were the chief mischief-makers. Now Shaw, whose stock was rising rapidly during these years, was nothing if not a confident and witty debater. His greatest achievement as a dramatist, in my view, was his own unique comedy of debate. He

A scene from *An Englishman's Home*, by Major Guy du Maurier, Wyndham's Theatre, 1909

had spent years learning every trick of it. The Edwardian atmosphere of hopeful debate was one in which he flourished. (He also understood, as few other public men did, the value of constant publicity and how to make the best use of disapproval and protest – bouncing himself, so to speak, against it.) Though already middle-aged in these years, the eldest of the brilliant rebels and iconoclasts, he is to my mind very much an Edwardian, really at home in this era. But that is not all. Though he lived on and on, turning himself into a world figure, it seems to me he never stopped being an Edwardian, somehow contriving to continue existing in its particular atmosphere, like a man on the moon in a space suit. That is why after 1914, when a very different world began to reveal itself, he seems curiously out of touch with reality, so that he ends by cheerfully condoning the appalling cruelties of a Stalin, blandly accepting and praising a totalitarian system he could not have endured himself, except as a distinguished visitor, for a couple of weeks.

Unlike Shaw, H. G. Wells never tried to create a *persona*. He was a more honest, if very impatient, thinker. He was never as brilliantly successful in debate as Shaw was, partly because he was emotionally more involved with his ideas. But the hopeful Edwardian atmosphere gave him confidence – and indeed inspired him. These were the years of his best novels, which must be noticed later, and also of his sociological prophecies, *Mankind in the Making, A Modern Utopia,* and *New Worlds for Old*. He might be derided and denounced but he could not help feeling that a scientific and rational Utopia might be glimmering in the future. He was still eager to explain himself and the world later, between the wars, but the old Edwardian confidence, the appeal of hopeful debate, had waned, until the last spark of optimism was extinguished in *Mind at the End of its Tether*. Here we can take a look at a paragraph in the opening chapter of his novel, *The New Machiavelli*, published in 1911 and presumably written in 1910. Wells's narrator, Remington, has retired to Italy and is about to begin his memoirs:

> In a sense it is wonderful how power has vanished, in a sense wonderful how it has increased. I sit here, an unarmed discredited man, at a small writing-table in a little defenceless dwelling among the vines, and no human being can stop my pen except by the deliberate self-immolation of murdering me, or destroy its fruits except by theft and crime. No King, no council, can seize and torture me; no Church, no nation silence me. Such powers of ruthless and complete suppression have vanished. But that is not because power has diminished, but because it has increased and become multitudinous, because it has dispersed itself and specialized. It is no longer a negative power we have, but positive; we cannot prevent, but we can do. This age, far beyond all previous ages, is full of powerful men, men who might, if they had the will for it, achieve stupendous things.

That is how it looked in 1910. Wells might have written some of this, though certainly not all of it, in 1920. By 1930, by 1940, he would not

(opposite) George Bernard Shaw, 1912, by Alick P. F. Ritchie

(right) G. K. Chesterton, *c.* 1907

(far right) H. G. Wells, *c.* 1900

have written any of it. The seizing and torturing, the powers of ruthless and complete suppression, almost unbelievable in 1910, had all come back. It was not these powers that had vanished; it was those hopeful Edwardian years.

So let us try and sum up the tensions of the time. At one extreme in this society there are the King and his friends, the extravagant and all-too-often frivolous rich, outwardly complacent, no doubt, but perhaps inwardly and obscurely aware that this was an Indian Summer they were enjoying, that winter was on its way. At the other extreme was a huge working class, facing long hours, low wages, and a rather desperate insecurity that did not, however, take all the heart out of these people. Such extremes of course create their own tensions that must inevitably bring about political-economic changes, as we shall discover. But the tensions, the sharply opposed attitudes of mind, that do more than anything else to give this age its particular character, are discovered among the people who are neither rich nor desperately poor – the middle class. (I drop the plural simply for convenience.) It is largely this class that produces the ideas, and it is this class that loudly denounces them. It is here that hope dawns and fear grows. It is here we find the wall against which a Shaw bounces himself and where a Wells has to take cover against the batteries of outraged decency. The situation is not unique, not peculiar to England. But I think it reasonable to suggest that it arrived rather earlier in the major countries of Western Europe and rather later in America. In the arts the influences encouraging rebellion came from different directions: they came in music from the Central Europe of Strauss and Mahler; the painters and sculptors looked to Paris; the influences upon new dramatists and the braver producers came mostly from the Scandinavia of Ibsen and Strindberg; and creative writers and a few, all too few, critics took into account the realism and careful construction of French fiction and, what was more important, the liberating genius of the Russian masters, whose work was at last being translated.

These debts must be acknowledged. Having done this, I must insist that what these Edwardian years produced was not a pale reflection of what had already been produced elsewhere. It was on the whole very English, and it was created by a genuine explosion, not world-shaking but a very considerable explosion, of English fine talent, lit here and there by genius. It is always possible that an elderly man is being deceived by the memories of his boyhood and youth, mistaking geese for swans in the haze of recollection; but I have tried to guard against this; and indeed I have long believed that the decade, say, 1904–13 was more richly creative than any decade since then, far more representative of essentially English talent and genius.

Moreover, because I happen to have taken Shaw and Wells as examples, when discussing this age's atmosphere of hopeful debate, this does not mean I see this as a particularly Shavian or Wellsian time, all moving in their direction. It was moving in many different directions.

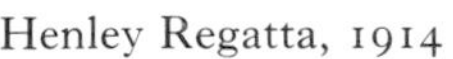

Henley Regatta, 1914

It was opening out, not hurrying one way. What it was opening *from*, so leaving behind, was the decaying bulk of middle-class Victorian belief, thought, feeling, taste, customs, habits. It might be reaching out not to Wells's scientific Utopia but towards India and Theosophy, Irish peasants and leprechauns, Catholicism and the distributive state, Merrie England and the guilds, a quiet life and a new closeness to Nature, Free Love or no Love but plenty of social service. Where it moved at all, the age – as we say now – was wide open.

True, I was very young then, and it is easy to reply that to its young every age is wide open. But I do believe there really were more turnings to take then than in any of our later decades. The roads created by ideas may have been wider afterwards, but there were far fewer of them. We can understand why this should be so if we consider our own age, with its huge wars, iron totalitarian states, savage prejudices and intolerance, world-wide lying propaganda, with every mild prophet silenced, every utopian vista blotted out. Moreover, we were free then from something that has haunted most of us for years, complicating and darkening almost all plans – the thought and the inescapable feeling that now there are too many people. The Edwardian combination of apparent social stability, a low cost of living, and an uprush of new ideas, could not be repeated. As both the ideas and their denouncers came from neither of society's extremes but almost entirely from the people in the middle, it is to them we must now turn our attention.

The Salvation Army Penny Sit-up at Blackfriars, *c.* 1901

(above) In 1908 Mrs Sterry became Wimbledon Ladies Champion for the fifth time since 1895.

Of feminine playing fashions at the time she wrote: 'To my idea nothing looks smarter or more in keeping with the game than a nice hanging white skirt (about two inches off the ground), white blouse, white band, and a pale coloured silk tie and white collar'.

(below) A. F. Wilding, a New Zealander, whose magnificent physique was often copied for statuettes, was Wimbledon Champion from 1910 to 1914. He first competed in 1904 as a Cambridge undergraduate in the days when the All-England Tennis Championships were held at Worple Road.

His death in World War I in 1915, aged 31, was a great loss to sport.

(opposite above) Association football, the sport of the people, in the age of the cloth cap and muffler. 'A game hurtling with conflict, yet passionate and beautiful in its art', it attracted its first 100,000 crowd at the 1901 Crystal Palace Cup Final.

Here the Tottenham Hotspur side of 1912 prepares to face Everton at White Hart Lane, London, framed by a sea of faces, each 'lord of the earth and critic in his own right'. *(Left to right)*: B. Middlemiss, J. Darnell, B. Bliss, W. Tattersall, C. Young, T. Collins, T. Lunn, A. Grimspell, E. Lightfoot, W. Minter, C. Brittan.

(opposite below) The dramatic finish of the Marathon at the White City Stadium, London, in the Olympic Games of 1908. The route ran past Wormwood Scrubbs where prisoners lined the walls and cell windows.

Dorando Pietri, a candy-maker from Capri, was helped over the finishing line first in a state of collapse and later disqualified. Right foreground (in cap) is Sir Arthur Conan Doyle.

YORKSHIRE TEAM 1903.

I. WASHINGTON. D. HUNTER. J. TUNNICLIFFE. L. WHITEHEAD. W. RHODES.

G. H. HIRST. MR. F. S. JACKSON. LORD HAWKE (CAPT.) MR. T. L. TAYLOR. S. HAIGH.

J. T. BROWN. D. DENTON.

(opposite above) The historic touring M.C.C. Cricket party of 1911/12, led by J. W. H. T. Douglas, became the first English side to win 4 Test matches out of 5 in Australia in the fight for The Ashes. While others sported the straw boater of the day, S. F. Barnes, perhaps England's greatest ever bowler, revealed his individualism under a floppy felt hat. (*Left to right top row*): S. P. Kinneir (out of picture), E. J. Smith, F. E. Woolley, S. F. Barnes, J. Iremonger, P. Mead, J. Vine, H. Strudwick; (*left to right middle row*): W. Rhodes, J. W. H. T. Douglas, P. F. Warner, F. R. Foster, T. Pawley, J. B. Hobbs, G. Gunn; (*bottom row*): J. W. Hitch, J. W. Hearne

(opposite below) The Golden Age of Cricket, with Yorkshire the reigning county champions of 1902/3. Lord Hawke and F. S. Jackson (later Sir Stanley, Governor of Bengal) typified the talented, wealthy amateur of the day able to play, as such, on honest and equal terms with the professional.

Lord Hawke once said: 'Pray Heaven, a professional will never captain England'. He died in 1938, nearly twenty years before this came to pass

2. The Middle Classes

Obviously a large number of people neither very rich nor poor, all belonging to a society still intensely class-conscious, could be divided and sub-divided to the point of bewilderment and tedium. So an upper middle class could have an upper-upper, a middle-upper, a lower-upper, and then there could be a middle-middle class, between the upper and the lower, which in turn could have at least three divisions. And now I have given my mind to the subject I believe at a pinch I could describe, with appropriate details, every single one of them, right from upper-upper to lower-lower. I do not know if this might amuse a few readers: what I do know is that it would bore me. Curiously enough, if I did make such an attempt it would be based almost wholly on what I have gathered since that time, from talk, memoirs, fiction and drama. What I personally felt then would hardly come into it at all. Am I suggesting that I was free from class-consciousness in my Edwardian youth? I am indeed. But I claim no personal merit here. Had I been born and brought up in, let us say, a market town in southern England, I would have been as stiffly class-conscious as the next fellow, perhaps worse. As it was, I spent my life up to the age of twenty, all the most formative years, in a Yorkshire industrial city, Bradford. There are various reasons why the usual English class-consciousness did not thrive in Bradford. The upper class was not represented there at all; so without an apex the social pyramid was not a firm structure. Manners were heartily democratic; the gamblers on the wool market who suddenly made fortunes were still called Sam or Joe by characters who wore cloth caps and mufflers; they had to buy a title and acquire a mansion well away from Bradford to find deferential treatment. (The Independent Labour Party was born in Bradford.) Of course there were wide differences in what people could earn and spend, but these existed in an atmosphere of social democracy, familiar enough in America but rather rare in Edwardian England. Finally, in a city like this in the industrial North there was little of the class demarcation by accent.

This division by accent, style of speech, which Shaw used so effectively in *Pygmalion*, deserves a paragraph to itself. It was – perhaps still is – part of English snobbish imbecility. It has nothing to do with speaking the language properly. There are downright bad accents – more in evidence now, I think, than they used to be – that offend the ear because they are careless, slovenly, ugly, almost as if whole sentences were being vomited out. (English Pop singers, when they are not pretending to be American, have a weakness for this slush of speech). Such accents seem to me detestable, but then so do certain varieties of upper-class English speech, often painfully acquired by men wanting to rise to the top. It would be impossible to read poetry properly in these upper-class accents; they have such a wretched poverty of vowel sounds: *Aw waw taw gaw*, they seem to be saying. (There is an ancient recording of Tennyson reading his poetry, and it does my ear and heart good to detect, through the blurring and scratching, his broad and open Lincolnshire vowel sounds.) Much of this *yaw-haw* comes down to us from the drawl of the fashionable Mid-Victorian 'swells', who were suggesting to their listeners that they were doing them a favour by talking to them at all. It is the speech of lazy condescension, and all too often it has been the voice of official Britain. The feminine equivalent, I would say, is a high-pitched staccato, impossible to modulate, rather like a hard stare turned into speech. But the debutante daughters often imitated the drawl of their fathers, only they gave it a stricken-little-girl tone, as if they were about to cry. All the people with these foolish voices regarded with horror anybody with a provincial accent.

Using both my own direct experience and what I have learnt since, I shall now divide the Edwardian middle-class into two – the upper and the lower, as indeed I suggested in the previous section, when I was discussing their Victorian prejudices. The finer shades between them really can be ignored. On the other hand, I must insist that there was a wider range of income and styles of life in the Edwardian upper middle-class than in the lower. This range extended from quite large houses – indeed, 'mansions with extensive grounds', to quote the advertisements – in which six or seven servants might be employed, down to detached villas with small gardens, whose owners would not have more than three servants. (I am thinking now of the provinces, though much of this would apply to the fast-growing London suburbs.) The men concerned might have private incomes or be successful manufacturers, merchants, solicitors, physicians or surgeons with a first-class practice, property owners or speculators. Their wives did no real housework, just a little dusting in the drawing room and some flower arrangements; they were never found in the kitchen except when ordering the meals. Most of the sons went to minor public schools (not to be confused by American readers with *their* 'public schools' – just the opposite, in fact), and then might or might not reach a university. Some of the girls might be sent away to boarding school, perhaps even to the famous one at Cheltenham, but most of them were educated rather sketchily somewhere in the neighbourhood, and then stayed at home, helping Mummy in the garden, taking the dogs out for a walk, and making sure that exciting new young man saw them at the tennis club. In the evening they might play and sing the *Indian Love Lyrics* or something from *The Merry Widow*, or read a ripping new novel by that divine W. J. Locke. The family took its main meal, dinner, in the evening, except on Sunday, but might have to rush through it early if they wanted to go to a theatre or a concert. Four out of five of these families probably belonged to the Church of England and were rigidly Tory in their politics.

Before bringing in a few figures, I must again warn American and other readers who have their own currency that they must forget present rates of exchange, which are very different from those of sixty years

(opposite) Cabyard at Night (detail), 1910, by Robert Bevan

(overleaf) Paulhan flying a Henry Farman machine over the London and North Western Railway during the London to Manchester Air Race, April 1910, by I. E. Delaspre

THE LONDON TO MANCHESTER FLIGHT
PAULHAN OVER THE LONDON & NORTH WESTERN RAILWAY

Delasp

Y394

EL713

R 1909

ago, when the pound sterling, represented not by notes but by actual golden sovereigns, was roughly worth $5.00, 20 German marks, 25 French francs, and so on. So when members of this upper middle class built their own houses – and many of them did, almost always employing an architect – these houses would cost anything between £1500 and £2500, unless of course an imposing mansion was required. They would be extremely well-built too, made to last. The three or four domestic servants might often be better accommodated than they would have been in the great houses of the rich, but there were more of them serving the rich and grand, with a kind of hierarchy below stairs, and with glamorous nobility coming and going domestic service offered more fun and glory. Indeed, later in these years, the upper middle class found it more and more difficult to get good servants; and this difficulty provided the wives in this class with a topic for endless discussion. Wage rates in domestic service varied, but I would say that an efficient cook might ask for £30 a year or more, while the maids, according to their particular duties, ranged between £16 and £22 a year.

It is hard to find an average income for upper-middle-class men, but £750 would be a minimum, with most of them earning (or at least getting) £1000 to £1500, and a comparative few on the top level – Galsworthy's Forsytes, for instance – reaching higher figures. Most of them ate well, probably always having fresh English meat, though their menus would seem dull and stodgy to us today. The men came off better than the women, not only because the meat was good but also because drink and tobacco were astonishingly cheap. Families entertained one another constantly, almost always at home: dining in restaurants was a habit common enough among the rich and smart or the semi-bohemians in London, but which had not yet been adopted by the provincial middle class.

I shall now risk some wild guessing, While it is true I was personally acquainted with a number of Edwardian upper-middle-class families, it is also true that my acquaintance was limited to one small area, to families in or around my native Bradford. (At that time Bradford was an unusually progressive city, therefore not typical.) I could only discover what the upper middle class elsewhere was like from political and sociological articles, novels, plays, and hearsay, because of course I knew young men, some of them on newspapers, who had moved around the country far more than I had. So there has to be guessing, though it need not be too wild. I will do it by tenths. I suggest then that one tenth of this upper middle class, the people with the most money, were madly busy, half-crazy with snobbery, trying to get themselves into the accepted upper class, to mingle at ease with the nobility and 'real gentry', belonging to old landed families, frequently referred to as 'the County'. I did not know any of these anxious persons myself, and they would certainly not have wanted to know me, a youth without any social lustre, invisible to eyes fixed on an altogether higher level.

(above left) 1904 Wolseley; (above right) 1901 Sunbeam Mabley; (centre left) 1912 Lanchester; (centre right) 1909 Rolls-Royce; (below left) 1913 Morris; (below right) 1913 Vauxhall

The Breakfast Table (detail), 1911, by Harold Gilman

With the next group, far larger, indeed representing about eight-tenths of the whole upper middle class, I had some acquaintance. The people in this group might be described as being solidly and complacently middle-class, entirely satisfied with their style of life and deeply suspicious of any other. What they did, thought, felt, seemed to them just right. What they had enjoyed, they were desperately eager to defend. It is these people, I believe, who were responsible for the petty tiresome snobberies so characteristic of English life not only during these years but after the First World War – and even in something like sport, to which they paid great attention. So, in cricket the 'players' (the professionals, generally from the working class) and the 'gentlemen' (the amateurs) used different entrances when they came out to bat or to bowl. Again, they greatly preferred 'rugger' (rugby football) to 'soccer' (association football), partly because the latter game, which has since conquered the world, had been enthusiastically adopted by the working class.

These eight-tenths of the upper-middles, a large group indeed, kept an uneasy eye on the working class, which numbered so many of their employees. But as I suggested earlier, what really frightened and angered them was the revolt against their standards coming from within their own class, often destroying the harmony of that family life so dear to them. Their complacency, apparently so solid, was being gnawed away, hollowed out, by doubts and fears. After all, the times were on the move, so they could not help wondering in secret if they were not in danger of becoming out-of-date. Of all the classes under review here, this large section of the upper middle class was the most Victorian in its outlook and values.

This class, having money to spare, was extremely influential: it could buy books or command circulating libraries to buy them; it could afford tickets for the stalls or dress circles of theatres; it bought pictures of a sort for its drawing and dining rooms. It was these people who were the patrons of everything safe and nice, just as it was they who fiercely denounced anything new, unsafe, dangerous, all that poisonous stuff, as we have seen, which could easily rot the whole community and leave it open to German invasion.

I have now accounted for nine-tenths of this upper middle class. What about the remaining one-tenth? The answer is that I prefer to leave this last small section until I have dealt with the *lower* middle class; and this is not unreasonable because the lower middle class has a similar small section, linked with that of the upper middle class. We will come to both of them at the same time, later. Now, as I have already declared, I was brought up a member of this Edwardian lower middle class, so I am at last on my home ground. It was of course a very large class, much larger than the upper middle, probably supplying most cities and towns – and it was chiefly urban – with about a quarter of their population. Most shopkeepers, office workers, superior factory foremen, the less successful professional men, teachers, craftsmen, commercial travellers ('salesmen' to us), owners of small businesses, all were members of this class; but the range is so wide it would be tedious to explore it thoroughly. They earned anything from £150 to £500 a year. Those on the higher level might employ one servant or a regular cleaning woman (a 'char'); their wives did the cooking and, if they lived in the North, baked their own bread too. (Among the people I knew, Thursday was always baking day, Friday a thorough house-cleaning day, and washing day was Monday – and there was no meeting for coffee at 11 a.m. The women were all too busy, even though some of their shopping could be done at the back door, buying fruit and vegetables and fish from carts.) They lived mostly in terrace houses or, more ambitiously, in new semi-detached small villas.

In 1904 my parents bought a new house, one of a row in a suburb. It had a kitchen, where we ate when we were by ourselves; a front room, where we ate when we had company; a smaller and gloomier back

(below left) *Ennui*, *c.* 1913, by Walter Richard Sickert

(below right) Edwardian Interior, *c.* 1901–5, by Harold Gilman

room, where I spent a lot of time playing the piano; a bathroom on the half-landing, two bedrooms, and two attics. The back attic was a lumber room and contained piles of old magazines that I used to read in bed. The front attic was my bedroom from the first, and afterwards, when a tiny gasfire was installed, I transformed it into my 'den'. This house, solidly built of stone, cost about £550. Now it seems an unbelievable bargain.

Between 1904 and 1914 I had a good life in that house, but why I did and how I did I will explain presently. Here I must point out that a large proportion of the Edwardian lower middle class did not have a good life anywhere. Most of these people had *risen* into this class; they were not 'drop-outs' from higher social levels. I knew several 'drop-outs' and they never seemed to be having a bad time. One of them, who, to the best of my recollection, was living with a woman he ought not to have been living with, could have been comfortably-off if he had stayed in the family business, but he preferred to play twice-nightly in a music hall orchestra – the fastest I remember at dodging out for a beer when he was not wanted for ten minutes. Another 'drop-out' was a descendant of a sporting squire, notorious for his eccentricities and extravagance; he was a railway clerk, probably earning 35 shillings a week; a big jovial bachelor who never seemed to be brooding over his social decline and fall. But such fellows, who had shed anxieties instead of acquiring them, were very different indeed from most members of the lower middle class. These people had emerged, often after a hard struggle, from the working class. A contemporary social critic indicated the divergence 'between the frugal, laborious and rather timid assiduities of the lower middle class on the one hand, and on the other the reckless, generous, improvident life of the working peoples'. He was quite right. Just as the upper middle class was afraid of dangerous ideas, the lower middle class lived in the fear of sliding back into the jungles and bogs of the workers. It had achieved respectability and was terrified of losing it. What a sardonic friend of mine used to call the 'shop and chapel people' were respectable at all costs, arming themselves against any raids by the disreputable. There were of course a few genuine puritans in all classes during these years, but the respectability so prized by this lower middle class does not deserve to be called puritanism; it had not the old depth and dignity; it did not wonder what God would think but what the neighbours would think; it could never have followed an Oliver Cromwell or applauded a Milton; it was narrow, suspicious, carping, mean-souled.

Even my father, a very different type, intelligent, brave, public-spirited, could not altogether escape the infection, simply because he too had emerged, not without self-discipline and sacrifice, from a working-class background. We had a deep affection for each other, and the only sharp resentment arrived in my middle 'teens when I began to strike out for myself – coming home too late, wearing odd clothes, being seen out with girls, usually older than myself, and so forth. My father's cry then was, 'What are the neighbours going to think?', a question that did not worry me then and has never troubled me at any time since. But my father, a schoolmaster, in spite of – perhaps because of – his advanced views, had to look respectable, getting up early on Sunday mornings to put on his frock coat for Sunday School (he was superintendent) and chapel, while many of his relatives and mine (on my mother's side, and a feckless lot) were lying in and then going out, dressed anyhow, for beer. This large and ultra-respectable lower middle class had enormous political influence, especially on the Liberal Party. It is chiefly this influence that explains the anomalies, baffling all foreigners, found in the English social scene, in which you could bet large sums by post but not small sums in the pub or down the street, you could drink any time in clubs but had to observe strict licensing laws in taverns, and all but the rich, who had their own ways of amusing themselves, were victims of Sunday Observance. This lower middle class ignored the rich because it felt they were beyond redemption, on their way to perdition anyhow, but it was determined, through appeals and the ballot box, to keep the rest of the country respectable. These people worried about domestic manners and morals and a general style of living; they were not greatly concerned about ideas, as the upper middle class was, because they hardly bothered about ideas. Yet it was from one comparatively small section of the lower middle class that many of the ideas came, to be cherished and spread by other people belonging to this small section.

The author's childhood home in Bradford, Yorkshire

A Liberal poster of 19

My parents belonged to it, and so did many of their friends, and so did I as I grew up. But in other and less important respects we lived as most of the Edwardian lower middle class did. Until I began to earn something (not much), we existed on my father's salary as headmaster of a large new elementary school, and that was about £350 a year. We lived carefully, frugally if you like, but I was certainly well-nourished. Usually we took our main meal in the middle of the day, except when we had company, and then there would be the colossal Yorkshire high tea. And we often had company; my parents had many friends and were very hospitable; I remember uproarious parties, when I laughed myself into a red haze at charades. Between Christmas and New Year there were parties somewhere every night. People then spent more on hospitality and less on presents than they do now. We went away for holidays, always in boarding-houses, never to hotels, not only in August but often at Easter and Whitsuntide too. Books were bought; we attended concerts; found places in the cheaper parts of theatres. On the other hand, no money had to be found for the purchase and upkeep of motorcars, refrigerators, washing machines, package tours to Spain and Italy. Clothes were absurdly cheap – 12s. 6d., just over $2, for a pair of hard-wearing shoes; 30 shillings, say $3.60, for a suit made-to-measure – but even so, my father being so careful in these matters, I

(opposite) Lloyd George and Asquith, 1910

resigned, two years later, Asquith became Prime Minister and Lloyd George his Chancellor of the Exchequer.

Who wants to know about British politics sixty years ago? Who cares? Why bother about Asquith and Lloyd George and the Liberal majority? How can it matter to us now that the Labour Party captured 29 seats in 1906, that there were also 24 seats held by what were called 'Lib-Labs', an important crossbreed, and that in the next elections, in 1910, Labour would be more strongly presented? Why open political graves and cover these pages with old dust? Have I not already suggested that after 1914 we found ourselves in quite a different world, with the era of hopeful debate left behind for ever? So why should we go rummaging in the dusty lumber room of politics 1906–1911?

To these rather brutal questions I offer an answer that may surprise some protesting readers. In spite of the superficial shifting patterns of relations between parties and politicians themselves, some political roots go deep and survive many outward changes in the general style of life. Some of the issues that came to life in Westminster between 1906 and 1911 are still alive today, dividing men sharply. Some of the consequences then, apparently so much old political history, came to loom large in the history of our own time. Let us take one example - the establishment and growth of a separate Labour Party. Without this there would not have been the dramatic victory of Labour in 1945. That victory meant that India could be given its freedom and the peaceful demolition of the British Empire could begin. It created the modern Welfare State. By offering an example of a government of the Left that was not communist, it checked the rapid spread of communism in Western Europe that followed the Second World War. But it was the pensions and insurance schemes of Lloyd George, sixty years ago, that began to lay the foundations of the Welfare State. (Two points often missed must be made here. Britain did not originate these state benefits, which had existed in Germany since the 1880's. Secondly, contemporary Britain is by no means the supreme example of the Welfare State, as many Americans seem to imagine, because the whole process has been carried much further in several Western European countries.) The fundamental arguments for and against state welfare that are heard today were being heard sixty years ago. Moreover, most of the chief issues hotly debated then are still furiously alive today, as I write. For example, there has long been a Republic of Eire, but the old Irish problem, which chiefly involved Ulster, has not been settled yet. Again, Asquith gave South Africa a constitution and dominion status in these years, but South Africa is a hundred times more important in the world view now than it was then. Again, Asquith and Lloyd George ran into trouble with the House of Lords, and now, although it is much changed, as I write today its future is not yet settled. And that is enough. The people who take no interest in politics should remember that politics take a strong and continuing interest in *them*.

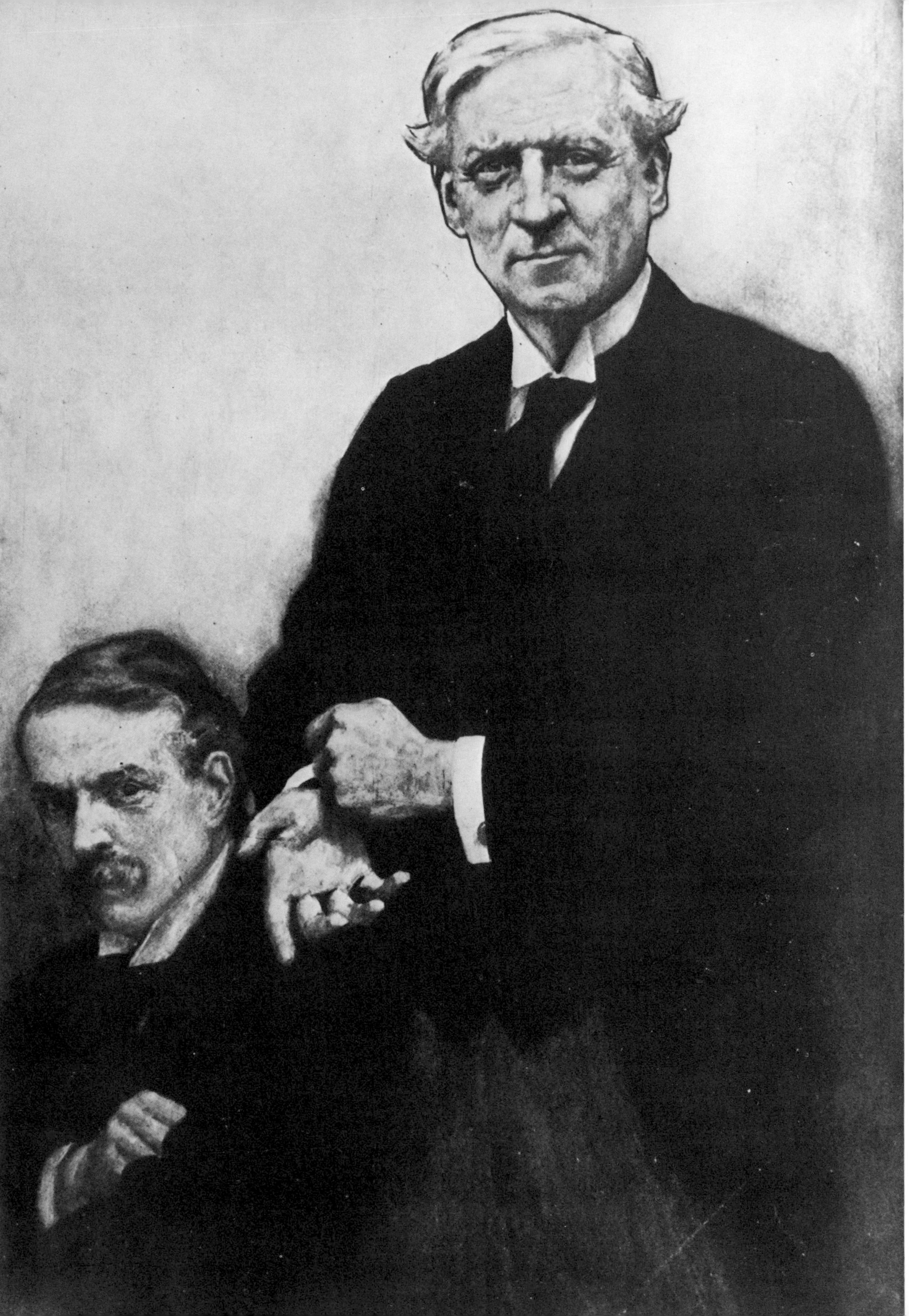

The two men who dominated the later Edwardian political scene, Asquith and Lloyd George, were hardly more alike than a watchdog and a hunting tomcat. Though Liberal leaders, neither was really a Liberal at all: Asquith is best described as a Whig, Lloyd George as a Radical; they represented the two extremes of the Party. While both entered politics from the Law, they came in from two very different sides of it. Asquith left Balliol, Oxford, to succeed as a barrister, an advocate, a merciless cross-examiner of dubious witnesses. He marched into politics like a Roman legion. Lloyd George, a little young solicitor in North Wales, hopped into political life with a torch in each hand, to begin setting it on fire. Though a self-made man, coming from plain West Riding stock, Asquith was somehow aristocratic in temperament and outlook, no more one of the people than a judge in his robes. There was more than a touch of the eighteenth century about him. Lloyd George was not just a man of his time but always a little ahead of it. He was close in type, if not in political theory, to the demagogue-dictators the twentieth century was producing. He and Asquith were an odd pair to be working in harness, and though at this time they complemented each other admirably – Asquith the lucid and massive advocate, Lloyd George the orator and agile tactician; one all solid intellect, the other all intuition and guile rising to wizardry – there can never have been any real sympathy between them. Indeed, within ten years of these Liberal triumphs, when the country was at war, one of them was to destroy the other politically and then go on to ruin the great Liberal Party itself.

It was Asquith, the senior man, who had been chiefly responsible for Joe Chamberlain's failure to rouse the country to support his campaign for Imperial Preference, the abolition of free trade except within the Empire. Chamberlain, a popular and impassioned speaker, had toured the country, and Asquith had followed him, like a tank rolling towards a firework display, flattening his whole argument. 'He talks like an advocate from a brief,' the emotional Chamberlain complained. But that is exactly what Asquith was – a massive advocate-cum-judge. He could not make a crowd stand up and cheer; he did not want to; he had no love of crowds, no desire at all to be one of their idols. He was most at home dealing rapidly but calmly with Cabinet business or suddenly making the House of Commons feel the force of his personality. A. G. Gardiner tells us how on one occasion, when Campbell-Bannerman was premier, Balfour, more effective in opposition than when he was in office, was attacking the government. Campbell-Bannerman said to one of his colleagues, 'Go and bring the sledge-hammer'. And then Asquith entered the House, to destroy Balfour. He was indispensable, being so formidable; he was deeply respected and admired; there was a kind of noble Roman quality in him; but he was felt to be too cold, too aloof, too dryly intellectual, to win any public affection. Now it is possible that he had mellowed and softened by the 1920's, when I knew many of his friends and once had some talk with him myself; but I suspect that from the first he had built up a courtroom and political *persona.* In private there was nothing austere and rigid and icy about him. He enjoyed good living and the company of his friends, men *and* women. Unlike most prominent politicians, he had a wonderful appetite for and relish of solid reading, and talk based on literature. He would have been happy, I think, as a Regency Whig, contributing to the good talk round Lady Holland's dining table.

Lloyd George would not have been happy in the eighteenth century or the Regency; he belonged to the first quarter of the twentieth century, and perhaps better understood his own time than any other politician. He was very much, in Jungian terms, the 'extrovert intuitive', with a nose for what would be important in the immediate future, ready to gamble on his brilliant guesses. Though bristling with energy, masculine decision and virility, he had like most creative and imaginative men a feminine element at the centre of him, and mixed ruthless resolution with immense charm. He had not Asquith's weight and calm judgment but he had a flashing insight that Asquith could hardly begin to understand. So, for example, he *knew* that if the Liberals were to carry out a reformist and welfare programme they could not depend on their majority in the House of Commons, they would have to go to the people, fire public enthusiasm, create pressure on the House from outside. This he did himself by making impassioned speeches, filled with startling metaphors, pathos, and venom for his opponents, in places like Limehouse. He also *knew* – and it was something most of his Liberal colleagues failed to understand – that the small but growing Labour Party might soon threaten the very existence of the Liberals as members of one of the two major parties, and that an immediate appeal to the working class was an urgent political necessity. Certainly there was opportunism here, but even so I think some writers on the Left have been wrong to accuse him of completely cynical opportunism, of being the artful instrument of capitalism. They have confused the Lloyd George of 1910 with the Lloyd George of 1920, when the enjoyment of immense power and a certain weariness of the spirit left him a changed man.

The Lloyd George of these Edwardian years was still a genuine Radical, a man of the people who spoke to and for the people. If he disliked socialism, and he did, it was not because he secretly admired big capitalism and privilege but because he felt that socialism was altogether too theoretical, cold, sternly bureaucratic. (If he had had to spend half a day with the Webbs he would have exploded.) But he was a man of action as well as being an astonishing orator. His son tells us that his favourite word was 'efficiency'. He could tear into a slumbering bureaucracy, abolish this and change that, and almost immediately bring a whole department to life. His mixture of energy, ruthless decision and charm could work magic. He was the inspired Celt, moving like quicksilver among the amazed English, who admired him, followed him, but never quite trusted him. His quick wit at all times was famous. For example, speaking at a meeting of Welsh farmers, he declared, 'We will have Home Rule for Ireland and for England and for Scotland and for Wales'. One farmer, half-drunk, chimed in, 'And for hell'. At once Lloyd George cried, 'Quite right! I like to hear a man stand up for his own country'. On and off the platform, he delighted in living dangerously, all audacity. We know now, for we have had it from his own son, that this pillar of the Liberal Party, supported by the most puritanical sects in the country, was a lecher who continually exploited his sexual magnetism. I suspect he enjoyed the dangerous gamble, the sheer impudence of it all, as much as he enjoyed the women.

I never knew him, much to my regret, and the only time I heard him speak he was past his best and the meeting was in the open air; but even so he was by far the most effective orator I had ever heard, moving easily from quick light humour to moments of passion. Churchill, who wrote his speeches and then learnt them by heart, had weight and occasional fine phrase, but his oratory was a slow military march compared with the full grand opera of Lloyd George, who with a few notes scribbled on the back of an envelope could then do what he liked with an audience. Churchill was the more honourable man, though not above a few sly tricks, but in his great days Lloyd George had a range and depth, a political genius, Churchill could not match.

The actual industrial reforms and the welfare measures of this Edwardian Liberal Party – the attempt to regulate hours and fix minimum wages, the first Old Age pensions (five shillings a week), the Unemployment Benefit, the movement towards National Insurance – seem distant and dim today, just as the sums involved seem pitifully small. But they made great demands on Asquith's cool resolution and Lloyd George's fiery energy, for they were fiercely opposed, especially in the House of Lords, filled with wealthy landlords whom Lloyd George was mocking and denouncing every other night. The Lords retaliated by refusing to pass Lloyd George's Finance Bill, on which his 'People's Budget' was based. This was late in 1909; and early in 1910 Asquith, determined to reduce the power of the Lords, dissolved his government to fight a General Election. The Liberal majority was alarmingly reduced, but Asquith was able to assert the superiority of the Commons over the Lords, preventing the peers from holding up finance bills and reducing their ability to postpone other bills. At the same time, the life of any Parliament, which had been fixed at a maximum of seven years, was now cut down to five years, a limitation of great importance to our more recent political leaders.

However, let us return, with the benefit of hindsight, to the primary welfare measure, the Old Age Pension scheme that would give men in their seventies five shillings a week. It was bitterly denounced. It could

(opposite) Woman seated on a bed, *c.* 1909, by Spencer Gore

bankrupt the country. It could encourage old men, with five shillings in their pockets, to spend their last years in debauchery. We can ignore this last bit of nonsense but not the idea that the country could not afford to indulge in welfare schemes. Though there was no great slump, the large employers and exporters were worried men. They were living in a country committed to free trade because it had to import food and raw materials at the cheapest possible rate. Yet they themselves not only faced increasingly keen competition but also a wall of tariffs – duties ranging from about 25% in Germany to over 70% in America. These men felt that money was tight – and the Navy was costing more and more – and therefore the country could not afford such fancy benefits. An increase in direct taxation might meet the bill, but the tax was already a shilling on unearned income and ninepence on earned income. And indeed, as Labour was quick to point out, when Lloyd George finally introduced his more elaborate National Insurance scheme, it was largely financed by the working class it was supposed to benefit. There was something niggardly and timorous about the whole thing, as there was to be about so many government measures later between the wars. Wells was no great political thinker, but he had his moments of insight, as when once, arguing with Lloyd George, he accused the latter of agreeing with the familiar 'patchwork' economic policy – 'Cutting a piece of the tail of the shirt to mend the hole in the collar,' H. G. squeaked indignantly. Now for the hindsight I promised: there is one situation in which a British Government decides against being timorous and niggardly and indulging in mere 'patchwork', when conscientious but over-cautiou senior civil servants are no longer listened to, when the expenditure of a few more million pounds will not ruin the country – and that is when it is at war. I have sometimes thought that Britain ought to be permanently at war – with Outer Mongolia perhaps.

Labour in general supported the Liberal social reforms, even if it was felt that they did not go far enough and that Lloyd George was no people's hero. But the Labour movement, and the trades unions that were largely backing Labour, gained much from two Liberal decisions. They are worth mentioning here because the issues represented have remained important – not only in Britain but in the whole modern world itself. In 1900 men working in South Wales for the Taff Vale Railway Company went on strike, unofficially at first but shortly afterwards, when the railway found 'blacklegs' to run it, supported by their trade union. The manager of the railway then brought an action against the union for the loss incurred by his company, and when his case finally reached the Lords he was awarded £23,000 damages, which the union had to pay, in addition to the costs of the case, the whole amounting to about £50,000. This Taff Vale judgment meant that any strike, in whatever circumstances, might be ruinous to the union concerned. But in 1906 the Trades Disputes Bill, brought in by the new Liberal Government, included a clause introduced by a Labour member that finally abolished

Bank Holiday, 1912, by William Strang

any legal idea of a trade union as a 'conspiracy' (what an individual had a right to do, a combination of individuals had a right to do), and freed the trade unions from any liability to damages because of financial losses during strikes. So far, so good; but then in 1908 the Labour Party suffered from a disastrous defeat. It had already been largely supported by contributions from trades union funds, but now the Law Lords, passing final judgment on a case brought by one Osborne, decided that the unions were not entitled to divert any of their funds to a political party. This was not officially a government decision – the Law Lords acted independently, as supreme judges – but in spite of constant Labour protests, the Liberal Government was in no hurry to pass an Act reversing this Osborne judgment. (It came in 1913, and the trades unions have been the chief support of the Labour Party ever since.) However, Asquith and Lloyd George felt that the Labour men in the House, on most occasions their necessary allies, could not be allowed to face destitution, so in 1911 they brought in payment for all members of Parliament, each to receive £400 a year.

Two years before, the Liberal Government, with men like Smuts and Botha very much in mind, agreed that South Africa should have a new constitution that would give it self-government. This act was widely applauded in all Liberal circles, and was seen as the beginning of a new and 'truer Imperialism'. Some of the old imperialists, still brooding over the Boer War, condemned such conciliatory sloppy proceedings. Warm in the sunshine of their own and many other people's approval, Asquith and his friends found it easy to deal with these fellows, all out-of-date. But it was rather annoying when some Labour members, and even a few crackpots belonging to their own party, refused to bless a settlement that was a triumph of Liberal benevolent policy, already shaping the new and truer Imperialism. These objectors pointed out that there were far more black men than white men in South African territory, and that the new constitution completely ignored them. Was it not the duty of the Empire to protect the interests of black men as well as white? Asquith brushed this aside, saying that the British Government could not intervene in South Africa affairs: all would go well. But now, after sixty years, staring helplessly at *apartheid*, we know better. Already, however, there were two issues, one old, Irish Home rule, the other new, Votes for Women, that were receiving far more attention than South Africa. But these burning questions came to have more heat and glare in the years immediately before the Great War, so I am leaving them to add more colour and drama to Part Three.

It is impossible to close this political section without bringing in socialism. I may be deceived by my own early memories, but it does seem to me that socialism was more in the air during these years than it was later, when it had acquired definite political force. I shall be told that that was all it was – something in the air, not steadily moving forward on the ground. But what is in the air is very important, contributing to the atmosphere in which we live. We have seen that this was very much an era of hopeful debate, and if socialist belief heated the debate it also enlarged the hope. It is easy to say that the kind of socialists I knew in my youth, rather vague and immensely optimistic, would not have been able to pass any realistic political-economic testing, that they were merely dreaming dreams. But while something was gained later by an altogether more realistic approach, in the cautious Fabian style, something was lost too, except during the summer months of 1945, when young people were demanding the widest possible changes. For while policies must be decided upon and the best methods of carrying out those policies be carefully checked, the whole machinery of political and economic power being meticulously examined and oiled, I feel that there should still be some dreaming of dreams, some huge hopeful vision, otherwise the whole process goes dead. What has been wanted all along, a great and lasting change in the condition, outlook and behaviour of humanity, dwindles and then vanishes. We are often told that this inevitably happens when dreamy theories meet the challenge of enduring human nature, ready to behave badly and wreck any hopeful system. But it is equally part of human nature to reach towards dreamy theories, to want something better all-round, and, as we are discovering to our cost now, to feel frustrated, cheated, and therefore rebellious if no great change is in sight. We may want 'better bread than can be made out of wheat', but we are already dying on our feet if we give up trying.

Except for the comparatively small numbers in the Social Democratic Federation, bossed by Hyndman, and for Bernard Shaw and some of his admirers, this Edwardian socialism was not Marxist. (And none the worse for that.) I grew up in the city where the Independent Labour Party was founded, and in my later 'teens I often contributed to a local Labour paper, but though I agreed or disagreed with all manner of people I never remember arguing with a Marxist. It was after the War – and the Russian Revolution – that Marxism and Communism attracted the younger intellectuals. There was a good deal of uneasiness among Edwardian socialists about complete state control. With the increasing spread and size of trades unions, many theorists of the Left tried to escape altogether from state socialism. There was even an importation from France of Syndicalism, which not only demanded that workers in all industries should be in command of them but also that familiar political institutions, parliaments and all, no longer necessary in the view of good Syndicalists, should be swept away for ever. Less wildly revolutionary, with at least some appeal to commonsense, was Guild Socialism, which for some years, at this time and even after the War, was accepted and warmly advocated by Left wingers of some distinction, though it never had a large following among workers themselves. Yet it offered them, as producers, absolute self-government in their various industries, while at the same time it retained the state as the owner of all means of production and the representative of the consumers. It was an ingenious and attractive system, and I remember Graham Wallas taking it as the subject of one of his lectures at Cambridge, where he was a visiting professor, in (I fancy) 1920. He pointed out that if workers and producers had complete control of their industries, and so were able to resist any pressure from outside, nothing new would ever be attempted, the familiar conservatism of men working in any industry being always triumphant. But then Graham Wallas, whose *Human Nature in Politics* had broken new ground, was one of the original founders, back in the 1880's, of the Fabian Society.

The Fabian Society was not a political party – it was careful to avoid taking sides on many important social issues – and might be considered now a research-and-pressure group. Its leading figures were Beatrice and Sidney Webb. He worked like a demonic mole on statistics and administrative problems while his wife, a handsome bossy woman with a useful private income, arranged little dinner parties (with horrible food) where important people might come under their influence. The Society's best debater and showman was Bernard Shaw. Its aim was to create an entirely rational socialist state. It rejected all emotional appeals and did not turn on propaganda to recruit new members. But after the Liberal victory in 1906 more and more people, with some important authors and journalists among them, asked or were asked to join the Society. Among the authors was H. G. Wells, whose particular mixture of sociology, prophecy (often proved to be right) and scientific bullying, in such books as *Anticipations, Mankind in the Making,* and *A Modern Utopia*, was widely popular. Wells called himself a socialist too, but whereas the Webbs wanted government by highly trained administrators and civil servants, innumerable extensions of Sidney Webb, Wells demanded that scientists should be put in charge of everybody, except creative artists. For them he had a tenderness certainly not shared by the Webbs, who would have been quite happy in a world from which the last glimmer of the arts had vanished. Wells nearly wrecked the Society, not by the notorious love affair he was having and his defence of Free Love, though that horrified the Webbs and the older Fabians, but by his attempt, which nearly succeeded, to take over the Society. (While impatiently demanding that people everywhere should agree and be co-operative, Wells was capable of disrupting any committee in ten minutes.) After giving a Fabian lecture in which he equated marriage with the ownership of private property, Wells only succeeded in giving the Tories some big juicy lumps of anti-socialist propaganda. Though he was still a member of the executive, with a large following among the younger members, he finally resigned, shrugging away the whole Fabian movement. He amused himself afterwards, in his unconvincing political novel, *The New Machiavelli*, by offering his readers extremely malicious but entertaining caricature-portraits of the Webbs as Altiora and Oscar Bailey – two active self-centred people, excessively devoted to the public service.

Hilaire Belloc, photographed by Beresford, 1909

The Webbs in fact did some extremely useful work, as their *Minority Report of the Poor Law Commission*, 1909, testified. But they took colour and feeling out of socialism. They wanted efficiency, not the high glowing dream of the Great Change. Wells had his quirks about the rule of science, the possible abolition of the family, and so forth, but he did bring imagination, a feeling for the arts, and a certain pluralistic breadth, to his sociology. On the other hand, like the Webbs and Shaw he was sharply anti-democratic: they all shared a contempt for the common man, that muddle-headed wistful creature. They and all other advocates of a collective solution were boldly challenged, a little later, by Hilaire Belloc in *The Servile State*, a book so little remembered that it is not even mentioned in a recent dictionary of literary biography. Belloc argued that state welfare and security, while apparently bringing benefits to workers, would not only rapidly increase their regimentation but were in fact reducing their status. From free men making contracts for their labour they were reduced to a semi-slave proletariat that had to be protected just because it had lost its freedom. He applied the same argument to paternalism in industry, then becoming prominent, because the employer who provided living accommodation and various social facilities for his workpeople was already assuming they were in a different category from himself, were not really free and independent fellow citizens. To anybody who doubts this, I must point out that I have visited several towns created entirely for workpeople in which the prejudices of the employers – against drinking, smoking or eating meat – rigidly determined behaviour in those towns. And to my mind this is not simply employing a man but owning him. To check this socially undemocratic trend, Belloc offered his Distributive State, which would turn the majority of men into property-owners of a sort, raising them above the status of a dispossessed proletariat. But here, as often with Belloc, he was thinking in French rather than English terms. Without a peasantry but with an enormous number of industrial workers, how could England begin to distribute property? However, there was something then – and there is something still, I fancy – in Belloc's original argument about the dwindling status of the ordinary worker. Has the fact that he is now probably a member of a powerful trade union really changed the situation? Perhaps, perhaps not.

A final note about the Edwardians and their politics. I offer it tentatively because it depends on what I remember of that time and can hardly be checked by research. Looking back, I find myself believing that the Edwardians were far more inclined to combine other beliefs, prejudices, fads, with their politics than people were later. This was part of the stir and ferment of the era. So there was romantic Toryism as well as the usual financial and social Conservatism. A stern and austere nonconformity, with its bare chapels and long sermons, provided the Liberal Party with its staunchest supporters, though similar types, but without the chapels and the sermons and with much self-education in a severe rationalism, began to join the Labour Party. There were Fabian socialists who shared Shaw's vegetarianism, wore his kind of Jaeger clothing, and delighted as he did in cycle rides and long walks. Among the less severe and vaguer socialists could be found theosophists, devotees of New or Higher Thought, spiritualists, defenders of Free Love on nut cutlets, superior tenants of thatched cottages who did spinning and weaving at home. But some of these later types might prefer to be dreamy bombless anarchists, who read Walt Whitman, Edward Carpenter, Richard Jefferies, loved Nature and were inclined to pantheism and probably refused to vote for anybody. Most of them, being women, would not have had votes and perhaps wanted them so that they could refuse to make any use of them, like Groucho Marx taking out a subscription in order to cancel it. There were even some people who combined Guild Socialism – and this took some doing – with Nietzsche's idea of the superman.

4. Writers

Writers were larger figures in the Edwardian scene than they are now. Newspapers, for example, gave them and their books and their doings an amount of space that seems incredible in these days. I admit that this was largely because films, radio and television were not demanding editorial and public attention then: 'show biz' had not started to bulldoze us. Far more books are published now, but reviewing space, especially in the popular press, has been shrinking and shrinking. All the statistics of publishing, stocking of books, growth of and expenditure on public libraries, show a rapid advance during these Edwardian years. There was not, of course, the immense flood of paperbacks we have now. On the other hand, the Edwardians were able to welcome various series, cheap but reasonably well-printed and bound, of classical reprints, notably Everyman's Library and the World's Classics, and series published by Macmillan, Collins, and other publishers. I still have on my shelves, braving it out among thousands of newer books, Everyman volumes of old poets that I bought after cutting down my lunch to a tuppenny date-and-nut sandwich (an appetite destroyer) and a drink of water from the chained iron cup in the Bradford Central Library.

If I spent more time and money on the older poetry than I did on contemporary poets, that was chiefly because at this time it was prose and not poetry that was creating most excitement. There was a kind of lull between the poets of the 'Nineties and the arrival, in Edward Marsh's anthologies at the end of this era, of the *Georgian Poets*. The contemporary Poet Laureate, Alfred Austin, could not be seriously regarded as a poet at all, and was not much of anything else; it was said that when butlers announced his name nothing came into the room. The obvious choice had been William Watson, but Lord Salisbury would not appoint him because he was strongly anti-imperialist. A conscientious craftsman of verse, Watson comes to life now only in his Epigrams, like that on *Byron the Voluptuary:*

Too avid of earth's bliss, he was of those
  Whom Delight flies because they give her chase.
Only the odour of her wild hair blows
  Back on their faces hungering for her face.

When I say that Watson was the obvious choice, I am assuming that Kipling probably refused the laureateship, for when Austin died in 1913 Robert Bridges, whose *Poetical Works* had appeared the year before, was appointed, though his best-remembered work, done in his old age, was still to come. And it was not until 1918 that Bridges published the poems of his old friend Gerard Manley Hopkins (died 1889) that were to have so strong an influence on young poets. A.E. Housman, whose *Shropshire Lad* was already a classic to Edwardian readers, did not bring out its sequel, *Last Poems*, until 1922, when both his matter and manner were no longer in fashion.

Robert Bridges

Then what about Yeats, recognised now as the greatest of them all? These were the years, described adroitly and not without a sharp seasoning of malice by George Moore in his trilogy, *Hail and Farewell*, when Yeats was battling for the Irish Revival and the Abbey Theatre. He published only two volumes, shorter than usual, *In the Seven Woods*, 1904, and *From the Green Helmet and Other Poems*, 1911. And, as he sang –

All things can tempt me from this craft of verse:
One time it was a woman's face, or worse –
The seeming needs of my fool-driven land;
Now nothing but comes readier to the hand
Than this accustomed toil. When I was young,
I had not given a penny for a song
Did not the poet sing it with such airs
That one believed he had a sword upstairs;
Yet would be now, could I but have my wish,
Colder and dumber and deafer than a fish.

These two slight volumes for the Edwardians, I fancy, have now been dimmed by the audacity and splendour of his later poems; but they do in fact offer us some of his finest love poetry. And I can well recall reading and re-reading them – under cover of the lid of my office desk – when I ought to have been writing to the Leeds and Liverpool Canal Company.

We might remember that one of the most American of American

poets, Robert Frost, lived for some time in this pre-war England. Two of his friends whom I came to know very well afterwards, Walter de la Mare and Lascelles Abercrombie, were equally delightful as companions but very different in their poetic style. There was something desert-craggy, sand-blasted about Abercrombie's poetry that asked for respect rather than affection, unlike the man himself, also an excellent if rather severe critic. It is worth noting that as early as 1908, when he was only thirty-five, de la Mare was given a civil list pension to free him from an oil company's office, proving that somebody in that Liberal Government had eyes, ears and sense. Though finally awarded the Order of Merit, the highest honour a writer can receive, de la Mare always seemed to me to be seriously under-valued by later and much younger critics, both for his poetry and his equally original short stories. On the other hand, Thomas Hardy's poetry – and about half of it arrived during these years – was increasingly admired later, so that ten years after his death, in 1928, it was Hardy as poet and not novelist who was being read, studied, and trotted out in lecture rooms. Living well away from literary circles, he was astonishingly simple, direct, modest, and, as I discovered to my delight, not above writing a friendly note, when at the height of his eminence and in his eighties, to a young essayist.

I feel something ought to be said here about the unfortunate poets who shot up like rockets while still young and then went out in fading sparks. John Davidson was hardly one of them, because he never had too much praise, and his best work, original and good but somehow always promising to be better and never quite succeeding, belonged to the 'Nineties; but it was in the middle of this era that, poor and ailing, he committed suicide. A far better example of the rocket poet turned into a falling stick was Stephen Phillips, cousin of Laurence Binyon, that quiet good poet and fine art critic. Phillips was not only hailed as a *great* poet but also as an equally great poetic dramatist, peer of all the Elizabethans except Shakespeare. The reviews and dramatic notices of his work were rhapsodies, and make strange reading now. Suddenly it all went, as if the critics had been drunk and then stared at him through a hangover. It was the worst of luck, but he did not survive it long, dying in 1915 at the age of fifty-one. Alfred Noyes lived into his late seventies and never fizzled out like Phillips, but he shared some of the bad luck. This was because he was enthusiastically praised and immensely successful while still in his twenties, writing rather like Tennyson in his weaker airy-fairy or patriotic moods. Then later, when he was actually producing more solid work, he went out of fashion, except among fellow Catholic reviewers and readers. Morover, one or two of his worst pieces of dramatic verse were always being recited, quoted – and then parodied. All this left him feeling embittered at heart, though in most respects a friendly man, outwardly amiable enough. In the 1930's, when I had a holiday house on the Isle of Wight, he was one of my neighbours, and we often exchanged visits, to play tennis or to dine. One summer, Hugh

Thomas Hardy, *c.* 1905

(opposite above) W. B. Yeats, *c.* 1905

(opposite below) Walter de la Mare

Walpole was spending a long weekend with Noyes, and he had arranged to come and stay with me on Tuesday morning. But early on Monday I found Hugh on my doorstep, high-voiced and almost quivering, divided between fury and laughter. Late the night before, while the company was indulging in rather idle literary chitchat, Walpole, to make conversation, had said something in praise of Joyce's *Ulysses*. Noyes had immediately jumped out of his role of courteous host, had thundered that he could not allow such talk in his house, and had told Walpole to leave it first thing in the morning. This is what the movement of literary fashion, for ever on the move, could do to an essentially decent kind man. However, it was Noyes, who had an eye for these idiocies, who quoted to me the young critic who had said that what was wrong with Tennyson was that he didn't understand that Nature was 'red in tooth and claw'. As not everybody reads Tennyson these days, perhaps I ought to add that it was the poet himself who gave us that metaphor.

A poet far more fortunate than Noyes was John Masefield, who eventually became poet laureate and was given the O.M. and died only recently, though born in 1878. Yet it was back in 1911, in the days when the *English Review*, to which Masefield contributed, was creating much excitement, that he brought out his narrative poem, *The Everlasting Mercy*, into which he introduced – a novelty then – the ordinary rough language of the streets. His best narrative poem, *Reynard the Fox*, came just after the War, which he described in two prose books; and then shortly after that his *Collected Poems* had an immense sale. Though I admire his little book on Shakespeare, again belonging to 1911, Masefield as poet, dramatist and, much later, storyteller, never quite came off for me. His touch rarely seemed sure. Thus for example, in his enormously popular lyric about going down to the sea again he refers to 'a laughing fellow-rover', and this is far from my idea of a British ordinary seaman. The eminence he enjoyed during the latter half of his long life never seems to me to have been really well-deserved. I would swap all his collected poems for the small lyrical output of Ralph Hodgson, one of those men who seem commonplace when first met but then prove to be completely original both in their work and their lives. After editing a boys' magazine and breeding bull-terriers, Hodgson wandered away to Japan and finally settled down in – of all odd places for an elderly English poet – the town of Minerva, Ohio. Apparently slight and unpretentious, his work has a queer magic, which is what I want from poetry.

If Ralph Hodgson ended up in the American Middle-West, another and very different poet began there, but settled in London in 1908. This was Ezra Pound, who from the first combined scholarship and modernism with the enthusiasm and drive of American salesmanship. It was during the 1920's and 30's that he was such a considerable figure among the *avant garde*, but I remember various poems and translations of his being read and discussed in the years before the First War. With

Two idealized views of the Edwardian woman:

(right) The Cloud, 1901, by Arthur Hacker

(below) The Elf, 1910, by Sir William Goscombe John

Richard Aldington and 'H.D.' he founded the Imagist school, and then moved on – he was always moving on – to Vorticism. But his more important work, about which opinions differ sharply, falls outside the scope of our survey here.

Coming now to prose, especially fiction, I shall enlarge a little the period under review, beginning it in 1904 and ending at 1912. Before bringing in any names and titles, I want to make two points about Edwardian fiction. The first is that although the actual sales (at the time) of many of the novels I shall mention were small, surprisingly small, they were nearly always eagerly discussed, particularly by their younger readers. Their publication was an exciting event. Now and again today, especially in America, sheer audacity and shock tactics, with sex rushed in everywhere, can bring interest to the boil for a short time, but the excited discussions of novels *as* novels, common enough sixty years ago, are rarely heard – or overheard – nowadays. The art of fiction carried a greater charge of electricity for the Edwardians. The second point I want to make is concerned with the range and variety of this fiction, reflecting the peculiar character of the era itself. It is simply silly to announce, as some hasty critics have done, that this was the age of extremely naturalistic and sociological novels. They existed then, but so did novels of a very different sort. If we go back to 1904, we find it gave us, taking it on its highest level, Henry James's last novel, *The Golden Bowl*, Conrad's *Nostromo* and W. H. Hudson's *Green Mansions*, and anybody who can find any common ground here of naturalism or sociology is either much cleverer or more idiotic than I am. If we jump to the other end, to 1911–12, when the new novelists were coming up, we find ourselves with D. H. Lawrence's *The White Peacock*, Compton Mackenzie's *Carnival*, Walpole's *Mr Perrin and Mr Traill*, Gilbert Cannan's *Round the Corner*, to name no others; no lack here of wide differences in subject matter, treatment and temperament.

Certainly there was a large sociological element in H. G. Wells's fiction, and he did rather dominate the scene for some years, with *Kipps*, *Ann Veronica*, *Tono-Bungay*, and *Mr Polly* coming out in fairly quick succession. *Kipps* and *Mr Polly* (in which, I feel, the sociology is an intrusion) are rightly considered his masterpieces, but I have recently re-read *Tono-Bungay* and have enjoyed it far more than I thought I would do. In spite of its very sketchy and rather bogus scenes of high finance, I feel it deserves the high place it once had. *Ann Veronica* was really an early shock-tactics job, as well as being a version in technicolour, with orchestra, of H.G's affair with an ardent Cambridge girl. Perhaps the fuss that followed its publication did more good than harm; but it represents the weaker side of Wells. So, later, did *The New Machiavelli,* which is neither good fiction nor good politics. Wells, a born novelist, really threw away the novel, as a form, because he cared too much about other things. But almost to the end there were flashes of the man who wrote *Kipps*. I have known a good many writers who thought they had literary genius when they hadn't, but only one man, Wells, who really *had* literary genius and didn't care a rap about it – never wanted it mentioned.

After *Nostromo*, Joseph Conrad temporarily abandoned the sea and exotic regions, and *The Secret Agent*, 1907, and *Under Western Eyes*, 1911, are quite different from his earlier novels. (But his reminiscences and meditations in *The Mirror of the Sea*, published in 1906, are very fine.) Conrad at this time had not reached a large public, but certainly in the years just before the War we youngsters were very enthusiastic about him, and I for one continued to devour him greedily for a few years after the war. Then, like so many other readers, I almost forgot him. As I said in *Literature and Western Man:* 'He is one of those writers whose importance we find hard to estimate, just because at some time in our lives we are completely fascinated by them, and then later, because we have already taken so much from them, we miss this first enchantment.' At a guess – and it must be that because I have not re-read him completely – I would say he is best when working on a small scale, and far less good, rather unsatisfying and irritating, when he is more ambitious, complicated, suggesting psychological depths we find we cannot explore – in fact, overdoing it all. But I could be wrong.

Arnold Bennett's *The Old Wives' Tale*, *Clayhanger* and its sequel,

(left) Joseph Conrad, *c.* 1911

(right) Arnold Bennett

(opposite above) John Galsworthy, photographed by Hoppé, *c.* 1910

(opposite below) W. H. Hudson, *c.* 1905

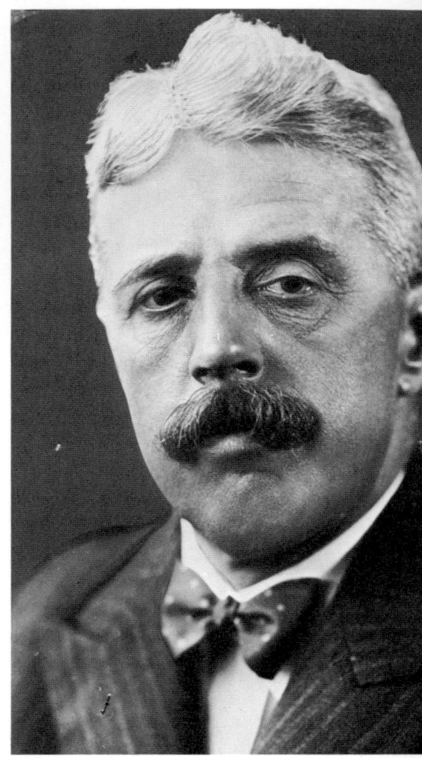

Hilda Lessways, belong to these years, and gave him a reputation he well deserved. After that, though really a rather shy and sensitive man, genuinely devoted to literature and the arts, he acquired a *persona* that recommended him to gossip columnists and head waiters, and he fell under the baneful spell of the rich and smart. Even so, he kept turning up with some occasional good writing, giving what appeared to be ordinary a faint glow of romance, right to the end, which came too soon: he was only sixty-three. In the 1920's, because we shared many friends, I met him fairly often but always in company, where we never really got along. I blame myself now that we never had any talk in private, because he loved to play kind uncle to younger writers, and I never wanted a kind uncle, being too bumptious and pleased with myself.

John Galsworthy I saw less often, though we shared the same publisher. His Edwardian novels were *The Man of Property* (the most important), *The Country House*, *Fraternity*, *The Patrician*. These were received respectfully but enjoyed no great success. It was in the 1920's after the publication of *The Forsyte Saga*, that he went on to reach world fame (as the novelist who explained English life) and the Nobel Prize. To put the Forsyte novels together and call them a *Saga* was not his idea but a sudden inspiration on the part of Charles Evans of Heinemann, his friend – and mine for many years – and a publisher with a flair. And of course, only recently and thirty-five years after Galsworthy's death, his Forsytes have captured the vast television public. He was a con-

scientious writer and a truly compassionate man, but he lacked imaginative depth, was not really a committed artist; he remained instead a Forsyte conducting his own tidy rebellion against the other Forsytes.

Except in social status, there was nothing of the Forsyte in Edward Morgan Forster. His career as a novelist is one of the most curious on record. He produced four novels between 1905 and 1910, did no more until 1924, the date of his masterpiece, *A Passage to India*, and, at this time of writing, has not offered us a novel since. The four Edwardian novels were *Where Angels Fear to Tread* 1905, *The Longest Journey* 1907, *A Room With a View*, 1908, and the most substantial and successful of these four, *Howard's End*, 1910. In my view, he is in these novels anti-Edwardian while yet remaining Edwardian, further proof of this age's extraordinary variety. He is in them, too, the reverse of the solid sociological novelist, with no broad panorama and a large cast of characters. He works in brilliant flashes, sudden revelations of character, mixing satirical wit with a poetic evocation and the symbolism dear to many of our contemporary novelists, probably influenced by him. So *Howard's End*, which might be said to represent the conflict between the majority and minority sections of the Edwardian upper middle class, has some memorable passages together with some episodes that seems to me wilfully unconvincing, almost nonsensical. His fiction is very personal, and if it has been over-praised, that is probably because he is himself a most unusual person, at once highly civilised and endearing.

There was then another Morgan, William de Morgan, who after retiring at sixty-seven from designing pottery and stained glass began writing copious Victorian-style novels. His first, *Joseph Vance*, 1906, was astonishingly successful, and so in the following year was his second tale, *Alice-for-Short*; and he dashed off five others before he had done. He is almost forgotten now. Though he had Dickens too much in mind, there were odd original elements in his earlier novels, which some people might enjoy as a sharp contrast to our contemporary fiction. There were in fact a number of largely forgotten Edwardian novelists who can still be read with interest and pleasure. Among them – and I pick him out because he was a much senior fellow-townsman of mine – was Oliver Onions, a rum wayward man who had very considerable talent. I remember reading his satirical *Good Boy Seldom* in my 'teens, then his trilogy of grimmer novels about divorce, and then re-reading more than once his book of fine creepy short stories, *Widdershins*, not quite in the de la Mare class but on the way there.

Widdershins reminds me that Edwardian writers and readers enjoyed the macabre and at least a suggestion of the supernatural, the kind of story Algernon Blackwood developed with great skill. And what might be called 'the playful supernatural' frequently appears in the fiction of these years: Pan is piping among the reeds in story after story, even Irish leprechauns are wandering on to the scene; and fairies are back, at the Duke of York's Theatre, where Barrie has staged *Peter Pan*.

UNDINE

ILLUSTRATED BY
ARTHUR RACKHAM

(opposite) The blocking design by Arthur Rackham for *Undine* by De la Motte Fouqué, published by Heinemann in 1909

The Edwardian variety of literary interests and abilities can be well illustrated by some mention of the finely-written whimsical tales it has left us, the kind of work later writers have never been able to improve upon or to supplant. I have in mind here Kenneth Grahame's *Wind in the Willows*, now a children's classic; Max Beerbohm's mock-solemn absurdity, *Zuleika Dobson*; and James Stephens's *Crock of Gold*. Perhaps room ought to be made for the funny-cruel short stories of Saki (H. H. Munro), Ernest Bramah's *Wallet of Kai Lung*, which either you don't want at all or keep on quoting for the rest of your life, and Chesterton's uproarious fables, especially *The Man who was Thursday*. And I am ready to include in this class Edith Nesbit's entrancing stories about children, which I read and enjoyed as a child and then, enjoying them all over again, praised in print when I was fully adult – but still fascinated by magic. Again, Edwardian fiction was generous and rewarding in its supply of light but civilised novels and tales, suitable for a train journey or some reading in bed. Many of them found their way into Nelson's red-backed sevenpenny series, of which some older English readers, like me, must have happy memories. These Edwardian writers may have had no high aims, hoping only to entertain us for a few hours, but they took the trouble to write decently – and indeed to behave decently. They might sometimes wander into a sentimental haze, and be rather too snobbish at times. But they did not inject into their tales the raw sex, violence and cruelty, all the sado-masochistic stuff for 'kicks', that our 'thrillers' seem no longer able to do without. After reading them, an Edwardian lad would not want to beat up somebody or a girl be left wondering what it would be like to be raped.

It was a great time, too, for the essay and the literature of travel. The essayists – Chesterton, Belloc, Beerbohm, E. V. Lucas, Alice Meynell, Augustine Birrell, G. S. Street, to name the first that come to mind – might turn up anywhere, sometimes regularly in a popular newspaper, for there was plenty of space for essays, and somehow plenty of time for them to be carefully written and then slowly enjoyed. (I often wonder what we do with all the time we have saved by using time-saving devices – just sit around giggling over gins-and-tonic?) As for the literature of travel, I can well remember generous extracts from H. M. Tomlinson's *The Sea and the Jungle* – one of his two travel masterpieces, the other being *Tidemarks* – appearing in our local morning paper, the *Yorkshire Observer*. Doughty's *Arabia Deserta* had first appeared much earlier and so had much of W. H. Hudson, but somehow, perhaps through reprints, the work was around in my youth, and we read and discussed it. We had the time and the taste for leisurely prose partly because, the world drama not having raised its curtain then, we were not being continuously machine-gunned by the news. The experts on everything had not begun their regular barrage of dubious information and guess-work. Not wondering then when the whole roof of our civilisation might fall in, we could enjoy some quiet reading.

5. Music

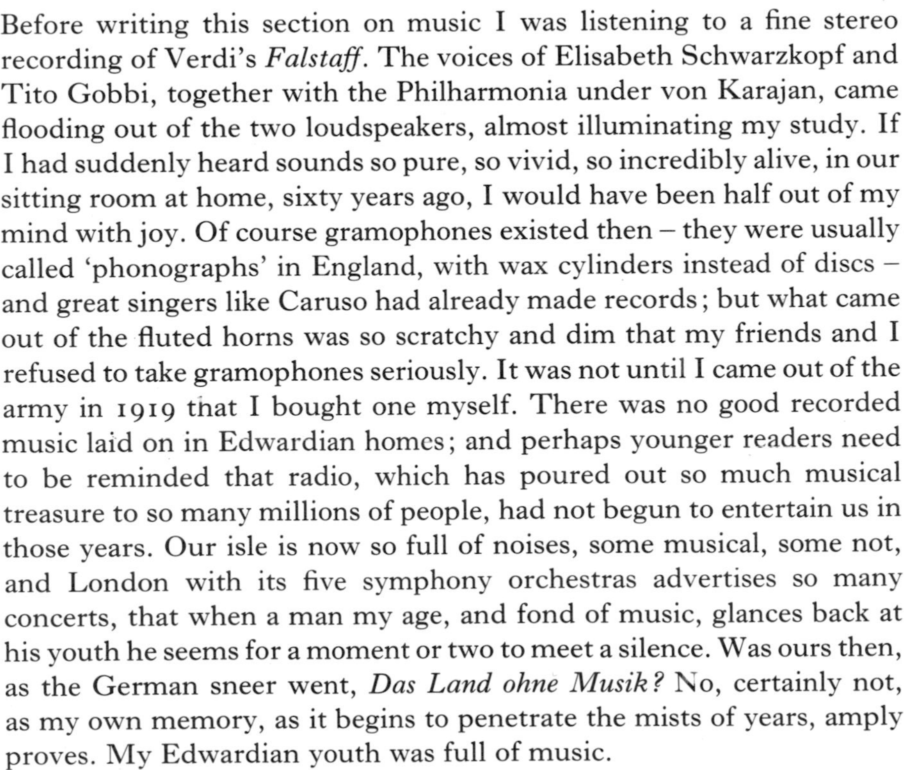

Before writing this section on music I was listening to a fine stereo recording of Verdi's *Falstaff*. The voices of Elisabeth Schwarzkopf and Tito Gobbi, together with the Philharmonia under von Karajan, came flooding out of the two loudspeakers, almost illuminating my study. If I had suddenly heard sounds so pure, so vivid, so incredibly alive, in our sitting room at home, sixty years ago, I would have been half out of my mind with joy. Of course gramophones existed then – they were usually called 'phonographs' in England, with wax cylinders instead of discs – and great singers like Caruso had already made records; but what came out of the fluted horns was so scratchy and dim that my friends and I refused to take gramophones seriously. It was not until I came out of the army in 1919 that I bought one myself. There was no good recorded music laid on in Edwardian homes; and perhaps younger readers need to be reminded that radio, which has poured out so much musical treasure to so many millions of people, had not begun to entertain us in those years. Our isle is now so full of noises, some musical, some not, and London with its five symphony orchestras advertises so many concerts, that when a man my age, and fond of music, glances back at his youth he seems for a moment or two to meet a silence. Was ours then, as the German sneer went, *Das Land ohne Musik?* No, certainly not, as my own memory, as it begins to penetrate the mists of years, amply proves. My Edwardian youth was full of music.

I admit I was fairly well-placed. I might have been better off in Manchester, Birmingham, Liverpool, but my native Bradford, though smaller and without an academy of music or a university, devoted more time, money and attentive appreciation to music than most industrial

(opposite left) Illustration for *The Tailor of Gloucester*, 'Simpkin at the Tailor's Bedside', *c.* 1902, by Beatrix Potter

(opposite right) The Dance in Cupid's Alley, 1904, by Arthur Rackham

(opposite below) Peter Pan, erected in Kensington Gardens in 1911, by Sir George Frampton

towns. There are three reasons for this: it was wealthier for its size than they were; Yorkshire folk take to music; and Bradford taste had been leavened by the German-Jewish merchants, many of them rich and influential, who had migrated there. So before we consider Edwardian musical life in general, allow me to revive my memories and set down what I know, as they say to witnesses, 'of my own knowledge'. To begin with, there was then a great deal of music-making at home. Some of it was not very good, as when, for example, I spent scores of evenings accompanying friends of my parents, with sopranos trilling away at *A May Morning* or basses telling sailors to *Beware*. On the other hand, some of this home music was on a very different level, for some of our amateur vocalists, pianists, violinists, were almost as good as the professionals occasionally engaged to perform in the larger houses. Then we had two tremendous choral societies, magnificent in oratorios (for which I never raised a passion) and capable of sweeping away prizes anywhere. We had too any number of ballad concerts and the like, on a professional or semi-professional level, though I kept away from them unless I was conscripted as an escort by maiden aunts.

Throughout the summer, in the park nearest to us, we had military band concerts every Wednesday and Saturday. Older people sat around the bandstand; most youngsters slowly paraded, two or three of each sex keeping together, at the back and above the seated audience, with the boys staring at the girls, who did not return the stares, having made up their minds already after one lightning glance. The programmes were not entirely made up of cornet and piccolo solos, musical comedy selections, a ubiquitous piece called *In The Shadows*; there were attempts at serious music. At the time our most frequent visitors, the bands of the various Guards regiments, were highly trained, probably at their best; and an old friend of my parents could describe at length the exact difference between the clarinets of the Grenadier Guards and the Scots Guards. Then on Saturday nights during the winter we had concerts by our own Permanent Orchestra, not one of your hundred-men jobs, about half the size of the orchestra Strauss's tone-poems demanded. While the strings were adequate, it was always touch-and-go, for example, with the horns, liable to come in or go wavering out as best they could. Even so, I remember many a pleasant Saturday night spent, in the gallery of our dingy old St George's Hall, listening to the Permanent struggling away, at times dangerously near defeat, at others soaring in triumph.

However, towering above all these worthy efforts were our Subscription Concerts, an imitation originally of a famous old series in Leipzig. Rich families subscribed year after year for what they thought were the best seats – they weren't; the gallery was better for sound, and I often heard it said, 'Diamonds in the circle, scores in the gallery'. Manchester, Birmingham or Liverpool, but my native Bradford, though up there.) There is a sketchy impression, with some names changed, of one of these concerts in my novel *Bright Day*; but the whole feeling, tone, atmosphere, of concert-going at this time, with Bradford exchanged for Manchester, have been best and most wonderfully conveyed by my friend Neville Cardus. His orchestra and ours were no different at all; it was the Hallé, conducted by Hans Richter, the very same Richter who had worked with Wagner preparing his later scores for publication and had conducted the first performance of *The Ring*. There was musical history written all over his broad back as he conducted for us. He was a solid dependable man and he had a solid dependable orchestra.

Then, one astonishing evening, I stared at and was ravished by another conductor and another orchestra: Nikisch arrived with the London Symphony. It was as if electricity had just been discovered in St George's Hall. Richter had always been large, sweeping, majestic. A much smaller man and quite restrained in his conducting, Nikisch yet appeared almost demonic, producing what seemed to me an astounding effect of verve, brilliance, white fire. I fell in love with the London Symphony then, and, after wandering away to other loves for

Miss Evie Green singing to her own voice, 1902

more than half a century, I fell in love with it all over again a few years ago. Intrigued by such an odd month's engagement, I followed the L.S.O. to Daytona Beach, Florida, describing what happened there in a book, *Trumpets over the Sea*; and more recently I attended its 65th Birthday concert and supper party.

In the programme of this Birthday concert there was a frank account of how the L.S.O. came into being, and it is worth quoting because it throws some light on the Edwardian musical scene:

> Sixty-six years ago, the patience of Mr Henry Wood, conductor of the Queen's Hall Orchestra, ran out. He found the deputy system then in vogue intolerable. Instrumentalists scheduled to play for him would at the last moment accept a more profitable engagement elsewhere, send in their place substitutes. Artistically disreputable, it was a practice fostered by the shaky economics of an Edwardian musician's life. Mr Wood's answer was to offer the members of his orchestra a contract of a £100 a year in return for his first call on their services. It made sense but it split his orchestra. Led by three horn players, including the redoubtable Adolph Borsdorf, and one trumpeter, fifty members of the Queen's Hall Orchestra broke away, enlisted ten more, and formed the London Symphony Orchestra. That was in 1903. On 9th June 1904, it gave its first concert in the Queen's Hall, conducted by the illustrious Hans Richter. That was a historic date, not only in the annals of the L.S.O., which is incidentally London's oldest orchestra, but in the artistic life of the whole country.
>
> It was a gamble. Many thought the whole idea impracticable. Jobs were scarcer than now and there was no guarantee of success, still less of security, save in the confidence and talents of those enterprising musicians. But the gamble paid off. A fifteen-year-old Westminster schoolboy, Adrian Boult, was in London at the time of the inaugural concert and was later to write that its 'brilliance staggered all those who knew the London orchestral world at that time'. The L.S.O. started at the top. It has been its proud ambition to stay there. A self-governing co-operative, a republic of musicians, it began by engaging the best conductors of the day . . .

Caruso as Canio in *I Pagliacci*

In 1912 it toured the United States and Canada under Nikisch, and was in fact the first British orchestra to visit America. Incidentally, providence or a guardian angel of music must have intervened at almost the last moment, for it had to change liners – and its original passages had been booked on the *Titanic*.

Those 'shaky economics', rightly complained of, were not without some benefit to us youngsters living in the provinces then. Many London musicians and some in the Hallé wanted to earn money during the summer, so they went off and formed the nucleus of smaller but not negligible orchestras playing regularly, during the summer season, in seaside resorts like Bournemouth and Llandudno and inland spas such as Harrogate. I can remember listening day after day to two or three of these orchestras, while on holiday with my parents, and while

I might have to sit through more and more of *The Gondoliers*, *The Merry Widow*, and *In The Shadows*, I also heard some Mozart and Schubert. However, I never walked through the sparkling summer air of the holiday resorts to hear the great soloists; I was always taking a tram through the winter gloom of Bradford. Usually they took over the evening with their own recitals, but on a few rare and exciting, occasions they came with other masters and offered us chamber music. Curiously enough I cannot recall from that time any piano quartets – later, one of my favourite forms – but I am convinced that I heard then, for ninepence, Kreisler, Casals and Bauer playing among other things Schubert's glorious Trio in B flat, Opus 99. If I am a little uncertain about one or two of the names that follow, it is not because I never heard them but because in one or two instances I may possibly be confusing men I heard just after the First War with those I heard before it. The masters who return to memory include Busoni, Rachmaninov (short-haired, not picturesque), Paderewski, Pachmann (the most eccentric of these virtuosi, wonderful in more delicate Chopin), Ysaye and Jan Kubelik among the violinists, and of course Kreisler, and Casals as 'cellist. And I agree with those elderly concert-goers who have argued that although these men may not have had the sheer perfection of technique (partly imposed upon them by constant recording) of some later pianists and violinists, somehow they brought to the platform larger, more commanding or warmer, personalities. But of course we could not go home then and compare their performances with those on our records.

Henry Wood, *c.* 1905

At no time have I ever been sent out of my mind by voices *qua* voices, songs without thought, exquisite but almost meaningless sounds; and fortunately, at least for me, a number of Edwardians began to welcome those singers who were not all voice but knew how to interpret the great German-Austrian *lieder*, like Elena Gerhardt (with Nikisch in attendance), and how to add colour and drama to any song worth singing. So, while neither Gervase Elwes nor Plunket Greene had particularly remarkable voices, they could compel my attention and then enlarge my experience as none of the golden-voiced types could do. During these years folk-songs were *i-comen in*. There had been some discovery of them during the 1880's and 90's, but it was in 1903 that the eager and industrious Cecil Sharp published the first of his collections. Not only did the more advanced singers take to folk-songs, the younger composers did too, writing new songs rather like the old ones robbed of their ancient certainties, then making use in more ambitious works of English folk themes. This of course enabled them to break away from Central European sources and influences; they could be English enough now; but I am inclined to think – even though I am no more a musicologist than I am a ballet dancer – that this new folk influence did rather more harm than good. True, it can be heard in Delius's fine *Brigg Fair* (first performed in Basle in 1907) and there is

The Queen's Hall, Langham Place

often an echo of vaguer and more melancholy folk-song in his other works, together with some memory of the careless chanting of the coloured men he heard on his Florida plantation. Most of Delius's best-known work came either before or after these Edwardian years. It is worth pointing out, however, that Delius is not the weakly regretful and sentimentally nostalgic composer he is often thought to be. *Brigg Fair* itself, for example, is a work of formidable strength and originality. Beecham's admiration and championship of Delius were unfailing. George Butterworth, a young composer of great promise, would probably have escaped the folk-song influence if he had survived the War. Both Vaughan Williams and Holst started from folk-song but had moved away from it when they achieved their more ambitious and lasting work after the War. And Elgar was never inspired by folk-song.

These years were Elgar's. Between 1905 and 1911 he produced his magnificent *Introduction and Allegro for Strings*, his two symphonies, and the violin concerto. Both his detractors and his admirers, like me, see him as music's Edwardian. I am ready to accept the Edwardian label for him, but then I think people who sneer at him fail to understand either Elgar or the Edwardian age. They take his weaknesses – the brassy pomp, the too obvious *nobilmente* – then blow them up and attach them to a false picture of the age, which did not simply consist of the British Empire still untroubled, garden parties and champagne suppers, and the Guards on parade. Certainly, as we have already discovered, Elgar genuinely admired King Edward. It is easy to understand why he should have done. Apart from his music and all that it involved, Elgar was a modest man, almost naive; he was a self-made provincial musician, who married a woman a few years older than himself, a member of a socially superior family; and though he had the *Enigma* variations and *Gerontius* behind him, he could not help feeling delighted by King Edward's reception of him. (Elgar was deeply devoted to his wife, the daughter of a major-general, and it is more than likely that his tendency to be ultra-conservative and chauvinistic was the result of her influence.) His Second Symphony, the E flat, had at least been sketched out some years before the First, 1908, but was not finished

Edward Elgar, 1911, by William Strang

until 1911, when it had to be dedicated to King Edward's memory. Though the noble slow movement, which explores the depths of grief, is generally held to be an elegy for the late king, we know now that the loss of his friend, Rodewald, back in 1904 when he first began work on the symphony had distressed him terribly. 'O my god; it is too awful', he had written to a friend; and we can catch that cry in certain moments of the slow movement.

Elgar is essentially Edwardian, not because of his pomps and circumstances and his increasing enjoyment – though perhaps, better, his enjoyment of his wife's enjoyment – of the society of important personages and a fine style of living; but because there is in him and his music all the rich confusion of this age, the deepening doubt, the melancholy whispers from the unconscious, as well as all that hope and glory. He is very English in this, just as he is in his characteristic rhythms and cadences. I have heard many great foreign conductors playing Elgar, but it has always seemed to me that they never quite reproduce the right shape and flow of him as conductors like Boult and Barbirolli have been able to do. Over and above his inventiveness and magnificent orchestration, and more important than they are, is something that never fails even now to ravish my ear and catch at my heart. It is the kind of passage, for ever recurring, when strings are quietened and the jagged thunder of his brass has gone, and like a purple-and-sepia sunset suddenly revealing patches of purest cerulean or fading apple-green, it is all different, strangely beautiful as music and catching at the heart because the man himself, no longer masterful, seems to be staring at us out of a sorrowful bewilderment. These moments when the *persona* is dropped are to me the secret of Elgar's lasting enchantment. The musicologists who shrug him away, because he added little or nothing to the formal development of the art, cannot want to find in music any communication from a great fellow man. His *Falstaff* is a glorious feast of sound, but it is not about Falstaff, better suggested by Verdi in his old age. It is a pity that Strauss did not tackle Falstaff, and Elgar Don Quixote. Clamped into his retired-colonel-off-to-the-races *persona*, he outlasted the Edwardian era by nearly twenty years, and his last major work, the 'cello concerto in 1919, is more or less a lament, in which we catch him looking back, not merely with nostalgia but often with anguish, at the Edwardian years, gone for ever.

Preparing to write this section, I re-read among other things the little autobiography of that fine 'cellist, Carl Fuchs, who sent me an inscribed copy in 1942. It is one of those books, rather ingenuous, all smiles and thanks, innocent as an egg, that executant musicians can write and authors would not know even how to begin writing. A passage caught my eye:

> A good many years ago a young man visited me. I did not catch his name. He said he was going to conduct the Hallé Orchestra, and would I play a concerto. I asked him where it was to be.

Sir Thomas Beecham, 1908, by 'Emu'

> 'I suppose you know St Helens,' he said.
> 'Of course I do – St Helens – Beecham's Pills!'
> 'Yes, that is my name,' he rejoined.
> To this day I regret I had another engagement, for that concert was the beginning of the career of a great English conductor. It appeared his father had engaged the Hallé Orchestra for the son to conduct as his twenty-first birthday treat. For days the orchestra talked of the excellent supper after the concert, and of the enormous size of the Havana cigars . . . .

I intend no disrespect – indeed, I offer it as a compliment – if I say that with all the music Tommy Beecham gave us afterwards, some of it incomparable, there was always the suggestion of an excellent supper with large Havana cigars to come. He communicated as nobody else did his enormous *enjoyment* of the music he preferred to play. His concerts and operas were always a twenty-first birthday party. And I do not mean to take away anything from Henry Wood, who toiled day and night, then and later, to keep orchestral playing going, to bring in all worthy new work, if I say that Edwardian musical life owed most to Beecham. He had the means, the enthusiasm, the fine taste; he had tremendous energy and zest; he knew how to pick up first-class orchestral players and how to inspire them. If Covent Garden were not available, he would pounce on Drury Lane or His Majesty's Theatre, and symphonic music, opera, ballet, were all one to him. In 1910 this whirlwind of a man actually put on about thirty operas in twenty-eight weeks. But music, opera, ballet, were all one to him. In 1910 this whirlwind of a man actually put on about thirty operas in twenty-eight weeks. But Beecham's operas did not come my way in those days. We had to be content with fairly regular visits from the Carl Rosa, a gallant company that would have a shot at almost anything, the Moody-Manners, less ambitious, and somebody's – I have forgotten the name – Italian Opera Company, not taken very seriously: I seem to remember its Mephistopheles, too short and stout for the part, stuck in the trapdoor. And there, with the devil not quite in, not quite out, we might leave Edwardian music – except to add, perhaps, that Edwardian playgoers had one advantage some of us sadly miss: they could hear good music, played by excellent resident orchestras, even in theatres producing 'straight plays' as distinct from musicals. Composers like Edward German and Norman O'Neill regularly wrote for such orchestras – *and* conducted them.

6. Artists and Craftsmen

Some art critics and historians write as if they believe that for the last hundred years or so art has been going *somewhere*. So it follows that painters are more important if they are further along the road to that somewhere. But what and where is the goal? At this time of writing it appears to be pop art and op art, which do not appear to some of us to suggest any shining peaks of achievement. But then again, before these words appear in print the fashion may have changed, and genius, talent or mere impudence may be judged by their progress along another road – to somewhere.

An observation by an American critic of Edwardian society (though not himself an art critic) is worth noticing. He has been condemning, rightly too, the academicians who refused to consider the exciting French painters and spent their Chantrey Bequest money on third-rate British pictures, Royal Academy throw-outs. He has also commented on the failure, in 1905, of the show of French Impressionists brought over to London by Durand-Ruel, the Paris art dealer: it was not badly attended but only a few pictures were bought. He then goes on to say: 'The ironic consequence of this insular resistance to modern French painting is that Impressionism was old-fashioned before it was fashionable in England.' This is not in its context a foolish statement. But it is art-talk in terms of movements and going-somewhere and what was 'in' and what was 'out', with a background of meetings in cafés and manifestos rather than one of painters actually at work. (There is no hostile criticism of the French Impressionists intended here: I do not simply admire their pictures, I love them.) Impressionism not as a Movement but as a way of looking at landscapes, persons and things, and as a manner and style of actual painting, did not have to be introduced into England because they were already there, and indeed had been there, to be found in the later Turner and Constable, long before Monet and his friends announced their intentions. Many of the Edwardian painters *were* impressionists, but were nearly always using a very different palette because they were fascinated by blurred London streets and houses and darkish interiors. And if, for example, they were not tempted to imitate *Les Fauves* and compose in the highest possible colour-key, I on my part do not blame them, for though this brief movement had some magnificent painters working in it, they worked much better when it was over. I never remember seeing a single *Fauve* painting I wanted to steal.

There was of course the now-famous Grafton Galleries show in 1910, organised by Roger Fry with considerable assistance from Desmond MacCarthy, as he told us long afterwards in his *Memories*:

> When Roger Fry proposed that I should go abroad and help assemble a representative exhibition of pictures by Cézanne, Matisse, Van Gogh, Gauguin, Seurat, Picasso and other now familiar French painters (incidentally he promised me a few days bicycling in France), I don't think he chose me because he had special trust in my judgment.
>
> Hearing that the Grafton Galleries had no show between their usual

(opposite) The Fabian Window at the Beatrice Webb House, Leith Hill, Surrey. The large figures *(left to right)*: Edward Pease, Secretary to the Fabian Society, Sidney Webb and George Bernard Shaw. The kneeling figures, all Fabians, include H. G. Wells, thumbing his nose, at the left, and Caroline Townshend, who made the window, at the extreme right. The books composing the altar include works by Shaw and the Webbs and *Fabian Tracts*. The window was commissioned by Shaw in 1910

EMOU LDIT NEARER TO THE HEARTS DES
F. S.
PRAY DEVOUTLY HAMMER STOUTLY
MINORITY REPORT ON THE POOR LAW
INDUSTRIAL DEMOCRACY
HISTORY OF TRADE UNIONISM
ENGLISH LOCAL GOVERNMENT

London Season exhibition and the new year's, he proceeded to convince them that they might do worse than hold a stop-gap exhibition of modern foreign artists . . . It was all settled in a tremendous hurry. I had just time to interview the director of the Galleries. He apologised for the smallness of my fee (a hundred pounds). But if – he added, with a pitying smile – if there were profits, I might have half of them. Neither the committee of the Grafton Galleries nor Roger Fry thought for one moment that the show could be a financial success . . .

On my return to London I reported that several hundred interesting pictures were available (transit insurance probably £150) . . . What was the exhibition to be called? That was the next question. Roger and I and a young journalist who was to help us with publicity, met to consider this; and it was at that meeting that a word which is now embedded in the English language – 'post-impressionism' – was invented. Roger first suggested various terms like 'expressionism', which aimed at distinguishing these artists from the impressionists, but the journalist wouldn't have that or any other of his alternatives. At last Roger, losing patience, said: 'Oh, let's just call them post-impressionists; at any rate, they came after the impressionists . . .'

Soon after ten the Press began to arrive. Now anything new in art is apt to provoke the same kind of indignation as immoral conduct, and vice is detected in perfectly innocent pictures. Perhaps any mental shock is apt to remind people of moral shocks thay have received, and the sensations being similar, they attribute this to the same cause. Anyhow, as I walked about among the tittering newspaper critics busily taking notes (they saw at once that the whole thing was splendid copy) I kept overhearing such remarks as 'Pure pornography', 'Admirably indecent'. Not a word of truth in this, of course . . . . The Press notices were certainly calculated to rouse curiosity. And from the opening day the public flocked, and the big rooms echoed with explosions of laughter and indignation . . .

It is bad enough trying to enjoy pictures you already like if the rooms they are in are crowded and noisy. It is hopeless if the rooms are very crowded and very noisy and the work displayed in them is quite new to you, original and challenging.

I have quoted MacCarthy at length because he offers us, characteristically, a sensible cool look at an event that encouraged almost every form of wild exaggeration. (Well worth reading too is Virginia Woolf's account of it in her affectionate biography of Roger Fry, a character deserving Virginia Woolf's or anybody else's affection and admiration: we are all deep in his debt.) We know about the hoots of laughter and the sudden blaze of fury – one elderly man had to be taken outside to cool off. Old Academicians, suspecting anything French anyhow, were bound to denounce the whole thing and see it as yet another attempt to contaminate and then ruin the young. They were one extreme glaring at the other extreme. They were angry at these impudent daubs because they saw in them not only a challenge to their ideas of painting but a deeper challenge to their whole idea of how life should be lived: it was

Gauguins and Connoisseurs at the Stafford Gallery, London, *c.* 1911, by Spencer Gore. The visitors include, extreme left, Walter Richard Sickert, below left, Augustus John; John Neville of the Stafford Gallery in the middle biting his thumb, and on the right with no hat Philip Wilson Steer

Caricature of Roger Fry, 1913, by Max Beerbohm: 'We needs must love the highest when we see it'.

(opposite above) Crows over a wheat field, 1890, by Vincent van Gogh, exhibited at the Grafton Galleries, 1910/11

(opposite below) The House of the Hanged Man at Auvers-sur-Oise, 1873, by Paul Cézanne, exhibited at the Grafton Galleries, 1910/11

like a death sentence coming out of the unknown. The huge rush of anger is significant; there is always deep-seated fear behind it. Some of us now are always being asked, not only in dealers' galleries but also on television, to admire new work, perhaps abstract painting reduced to a couple of blobs or sculpture welding together motorcycle parts, that we do not feel inclined to admire; but if we do not find our blood pressure rising, do not roar out tremendous indictments, that is because we do not feel, as so many belated Victorians did in 1910 at the Grafton Galleries, that our whole world is being undermined and may crumble at any moment. Incidentally, though it is impossible not to admire Roger Fry's taste, enterprise, courage, his tactics in this campaign are open to criticism. He brought in too much all at once; he did not make sufficient allowance for the influence of the popular press, first into the show and therefore able to strike the first blow against it.

In point of fact, there was some sensible press criticism and it was not all silly. And though some of the older painters, not themselves last-stand academicians, merely shook their heads and kept out of the brawl, others were sympathetic if not always enthusiastic about everything. After all, some of them had lived and worked in France, even though they were not painting like Van Gogh, seeing visions in the blazing sunlight of Provence, or like Gauguin, working far away in the South Seas. (By the way, it was after I had spent some weeks in Tahiti and Moorea, early in 1931, that I realised that the charge against Gauguin of being an impudently wilful colourist was unfounded: his decorative forms and pattern-making might be his own, but the strange lights and shadows were there in the islands.)

I think too it was a pity that Roger Fry could not have sent at least part of his exhibition touring the country. Of course public taste – and I mean by that something already formed, not untutored natural reaction

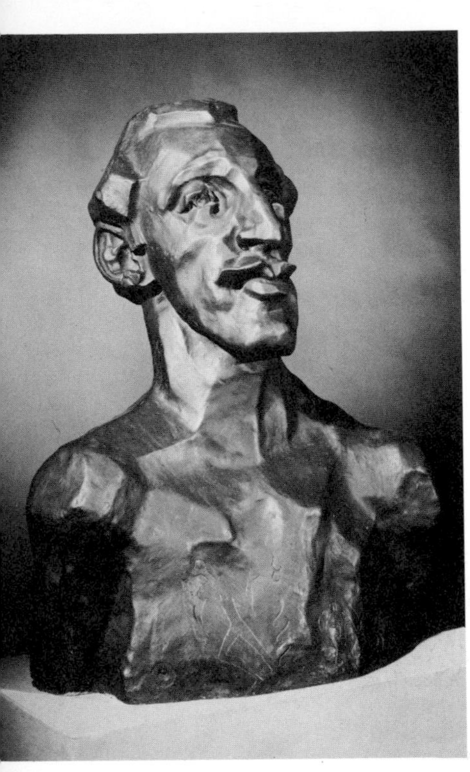

(above) Horace Brodzky, died 1913, by Henri Gaudier-Brzeska

(opposite, above left) The eldest daughter of Mrs William K. Vanderbilt, 1910, by Prince Paul Troubetzkoy

(opposite, above centre) Putting the weight, 1913, by Reginald Fairfax Wells

(opposite, above right) Orpheus and Eurydice, *c.* 1905–7, by Charles Ricketts

(opposite, below left) Nan the Dreamer, 1911, by Jacob Epstein

(opposite, below right) Bathsheba, by Charles Holroyd, exhibited 1912

– was dreadful. I had a brief example of it about 1911, when I kept on deciding that a wool office was not for me. I went to see one of Bradford's art dealers who, to try me out, sent me off one evening to one of his tougher customers with a fairly large, darkish-brown painting of some vague cathedral front. I argued as best I could the merits of this highly undistinguished painting, but the patron, a small elderly man, hard as a walnut, would have none of it. 'Not enough figgers', he declared. 'Ah like plenty o' figgers'. If Fry could have toured part of his exhibition, it might have cut through public taste to reach those people – and though there may not be a lot of them, they exist everywhere except in the vicinity of West End galleries – who do not know what is fashionable or not fashionable, what can be accepted or not accepted, but depend entirely on their own natural reactions. Fry himself knew this, as he knew so much else, but he was not able then to act on his knowledge.

If I have given so much space to the 1910 Grafton Galleries show, it is because others, describing the Edwardian art scene, have given it far more space – and even more significance. I do not blame them for seeing it as a raid before a triumphant invasion, with Cézanne's mastery of form as a secure base and Picasso's restless genius leading the raiders. But I deplore the tendency to diminish the contemporary English painters into dwarfs working in the dark. There was some good art being created during the time when Henry Tonks, severe and sarcastic but another lovable English character, taught drawing, with passion, at the Slade. Some giants, of course, were his friends, not his pupils. There was the great Sickert, who had worked under Degas years before, now very much an English painter, in spite of his Danish-German family background, and one whose work, if it had had the international backing the French painters have had, would now be reaching those fantastic figures at Sotheby's and Christie's. (I have owned a number of Sickerts, some of them theatre pictures too dark for a modest private house, and I still own a few.) Though he went back to Degas and Whistler, there is to my mind something tremendously Edwardian about Sickert, and most of the best younger painters looked to him. There was the placid and massive Wilson Steer, beginning to turn to the watercolours that some of us now prefer to his elaborate oil landscapes. Augustus John was much younger, but his natural genius for drawing and his brilliant portraits had given him giant-size. In portraiture generally Orpen had now taken over from Sargent: his two very successful group pictures, *Homage to Manet*, with George Moore and his friends, and his *New English Art Club Jury*, deciding what should go into the next show, are almost illustrated guides to Edwardian artistic life. The New English was founded back in the 1880's and still had authority, but just as it had broken away from the Academy, so now many younger painters were dissatisfied with it, feeling they had had enough of the New English manner, style and repetitious subject matter. Without being wildly rebellious, the better

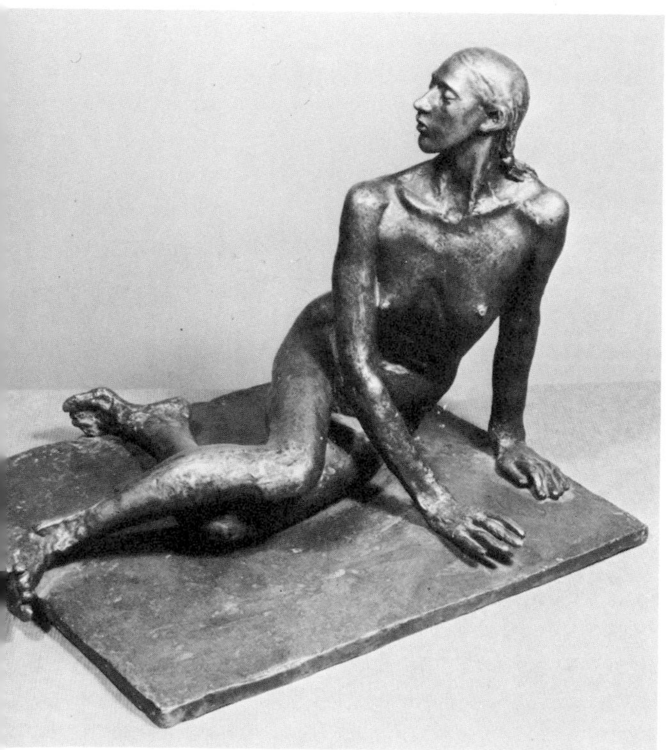

Edwardian painters were always moving steadily away, first from official Establishment picture-making and then from the rather routine painting of the New English. Without being amateurish, and with a few aesthetic theories of their own that they made no fuss about, these Edwardians strike us as being very private artists – and very English.

Some collectors would want to go back to the 'Nineties, others to go forward to the 'Twenties, but I know I could have been very happy, *if* I had been a real collector, with some share of this Edwardian spoil. There could have been a few little masterpieces by Gwen John, eccentric and highly gifted sister of Augustus. I might have acquired some early Henry Lambs, running off with his inspired painting of Lytton Strachey, which Lamb kept so delicately poised between portraiture and caricature. (There was around then plenty of Max Beerbohm's work, often delicately poised between caricature and assassination.) Then what about a still-life or two from William Nicholson, not a great artist toiling up Olympian heights, but a man-and-a-brother who shares with us his delight in painting? At a Cézanne you stare and wonder, begin to comprehend and then retreat respectfully, but one look at a Nicholson and you want to rush off and find canvas, brushes, paints. Finally, there is the work I wish I could have grabbed and 'cornered'. It belongs to the Camden Town Group, which Sickert, not at all a movement-and-manifesto man but a good host with a very perceptive eye, brought into being in 1911. It included among others Spencer Gore and Harold Gilman, who both died too young, and Ginner, Bevan, and Lucien Pissarro, son of Camille. There is in their best work a little magic, impressionistic and post-impressionistic, subtly illuminating what other people saw as drab London scenes or commonplace provincial places and persons. I may be over-indulging my own taste and temperament, but it does seem to me that a great deal of satisfying art came out of this era.

Its sculpture, architecture, decoration, I propose to leave to our illustrations, which offer the best chance of a quick sure judgment. But there is one small point I should like to make as I hurry on. I have felt for a long time that the Edwardians, whose taste and style in public decoration have often been challenged and condemned, were in fact extremely adroit in creating an air of vague luxury. In their hotels, restaurants, cafés, liners' saloons, there was nothing in particular to catch and hold the eye and then raise questions. For my part I do not want to dine facing emphatic works of art: if I feel they are good I do not want to be spooning soup in front of them, and if they seem to be bad I would rather they were removed. There are times when most of us like to feel rich, idle and luxurious – rare times if we are sensible; too much of this could be hell – and it seems to me the Edwardians were supremely successful in creating the appropriate atmosphere.

However, I have space enough left in this section to squeeze in some mention of a book published in 1908, now long out of print, that deserves

(opposite) Homage to Manet, 1909, by Sir William Orpen. *(Left to right)*: George Moore, Philip Wilson Steer, Henry Tonks (holding a cane), Sir Hugh Lane (hand to head), D. S. McColl, Sickert (hands to lapels). The room is in a house in South Bolton Gardens which belonged to Lane and later to Orpen. The painting on the wall is Eva Gonzales by Manet

(opposite above) Marsh Court, Stockbridge, Hampshire, 1901, by Sir Edwin Lutyens

(opposite below) Home Place, Kelling, Norfolk, 1904, by E. S. Prior

(right) Hill House, Helensburgh, Dunbartonshire, 1902–3, by Charles Rennie Mackintosh

(below right) Liverpool Cathedral, 1903, by Sir Giles Gilbert Scott

to be re-printed together with suitable comment by a sociologist or social philosopher. This is *Craftsmanship in Competititive Industry: being a Record of the Guild of Handicrafts, and Some Deductions from their Twenty-One Years' Experience*. It is by Charles Robert Ashbee (1863–1942), architect, craftsman, town planner, an extraordinarily energetic, enthusiastic and rather impatient man, who during a long life turned up and worked in all manner of places, including Jerusalem and the lecture-tour cities of the American Middle West. Inspired by Ruskin and Morris and forming a small limited company to finance the Guild of Arts and Handicrafts, he led an exodus of craftsmen and their wives and families from London to Chipping Campden in Gloucestershire, still one of the most delightful little towns in England. This was in 1902, and by 1907 the Guild had lost money and could not raise any more, though a few thousand pounds could have saved it. But, as Ashbee points out, it had done a great deal. It had produced a high standard of craftsmanship in a variety of different crafts. It had trained and developed a body of workmen with a higher standard of life. It had changed Campden from a decaying village into a lively little town, had built clean new houses and workshops, laid out gardens and allotments. and had established a School of Arts and Crafts for some three hundred men, women and children. In his introductory chapter Ashbee declares that this movement

> is not what the public has thought it to be, or is seeking to make it: a nursery for luxuries, a hothouse for the production of mere trivialities and useless things for the rich. It is a movement for the stamping out of such things by sound production on the one hand, and the inevitable regulation of machine production and cheap labour on the other. My thesis is that *the expensive superfluity and the cheap superfluity are one and the same thing*, equally useless, equally wasteful, and that both must be destroyed. The Arts and Crafts movement then, if it means anything, means Standard, whether of work or of life, the protection of Standard, whether in the product or in the producer, and it means that these two things must be taken together.

Very well, it is all a bit hot-headed, too idealistic, old-fashioned in tone and outlook, so that today we need not take it seriously. A lot has happened since 1908. But in fact what is happening now, when the young do not know where to go, except into the streets to parade their despair, should make us think hard about what Ashbee was saying more than half a century ago. What he was denouncing then is now *very much worse* – and, whatever we may pretend, we all know it.

A gathering of habitués in the now vanished Domino Room at the Café Royal, 1912, by Sir William Orpen. *(Left to right)*: Sir William Nicholson, unknown man, Nina Hamnett, James Pryde, self-portrait, unknown man, waiter, Augustus John and George Moore

(opposite) The Jester (W. Somerset Maugham), 1911, by Sir Gerald Kelly

(overleaf) The London Hippodrome, 1902, by Everett Shinn

So it would be one of George Edwardes's Gaiety shows or one of those Viennese things, with all the waltzes, at Daly's; or a farce 'adapted from the French' and just missing being 'a bit too near the knuckle'; or one of those adorable laughter-and-tears pieces – Monica's and Aunt Kate's first choice – by Barrie; or another light comedy, very funny but just a wee bit sharp at times, by that very successful chap, Somerset Maugham. The latter was so successful at this time that somewhere about the middle of it he had four plays running together in the West End. This would be a feat even now. In those days a production with a comparatively small cast and not too many scene changes had a very modest 'get out' or running cost. It could carry on comfortably even if the theatre on an average was only half-full, particularly if the stalls – ten shillings and sixpence then – were not the emptiest part of the house. Moreover, Maugham made clever use of 'the star system', often specially writing parts for particular leading players whose names were valuable to the box office. These years saw the emergence of new star players, of whom Gerald du Maurier (a brilliant performer) was an example, who were increasingly disinclined to go touring, unlike the older actor-managers who had gone round the provinces for years and still continued to do so. This disinclination finally drove a wedge between the theatrical West End and the provinces, and partly explains the rapid growth of the cinema in the 1920's.

I was very much the constant playgoer during my 'teens in Bradford. I could enjoy anything if it was fairly good of its kind, from *Our Miss Gibbs* and *The Count of Luxembourg* (and the Number One tours of such musicals then were carefully produced and had excellent casts) to Martin Harvey's *Oedipus Rex*, based on Reinhardt's production, or Penelope Wheeler's rather too ladylike tours of Euripides, in Gilbert Murray's versions. These last were performed in some hall, but all the others and anything else worth seeing took me to our Theatre Royal, smaller than most of the leading provincial playhouse and having rather more charm. Regular visitors to the Theatre Royal included F. R. Benson with his repertoire of Shakespeare (and cricket), and the (eighteenth-century) Comedy Company of Edward Compton, father of Compton Mackenzie the novelist, a troupe for which I had a special affection. Our other theatre, the Prince's, offered nothing, apart from an annual pantomime, but popular melodramas, such as *The Face at the Window* and *A Royal Divorce*, which we superior 'teenagers occasionally patronised, for a giggle. These pieces were played in an old-fashioned, full-blooded style, and they could still lure away from our two music halls attentive working-class audiences, which would soon, after the War, drift away to the new cinemas. But we had nothing to rival the serious repertory theatre created in Manchester by Miss Horniman, and no local dramatists like the Lancashire Stanley Houghton, whose fourth play, *Hindle Wakes*, can still hold an audience. Dying in his early thirties, Houghton was one of a small group of new Edwardian play-

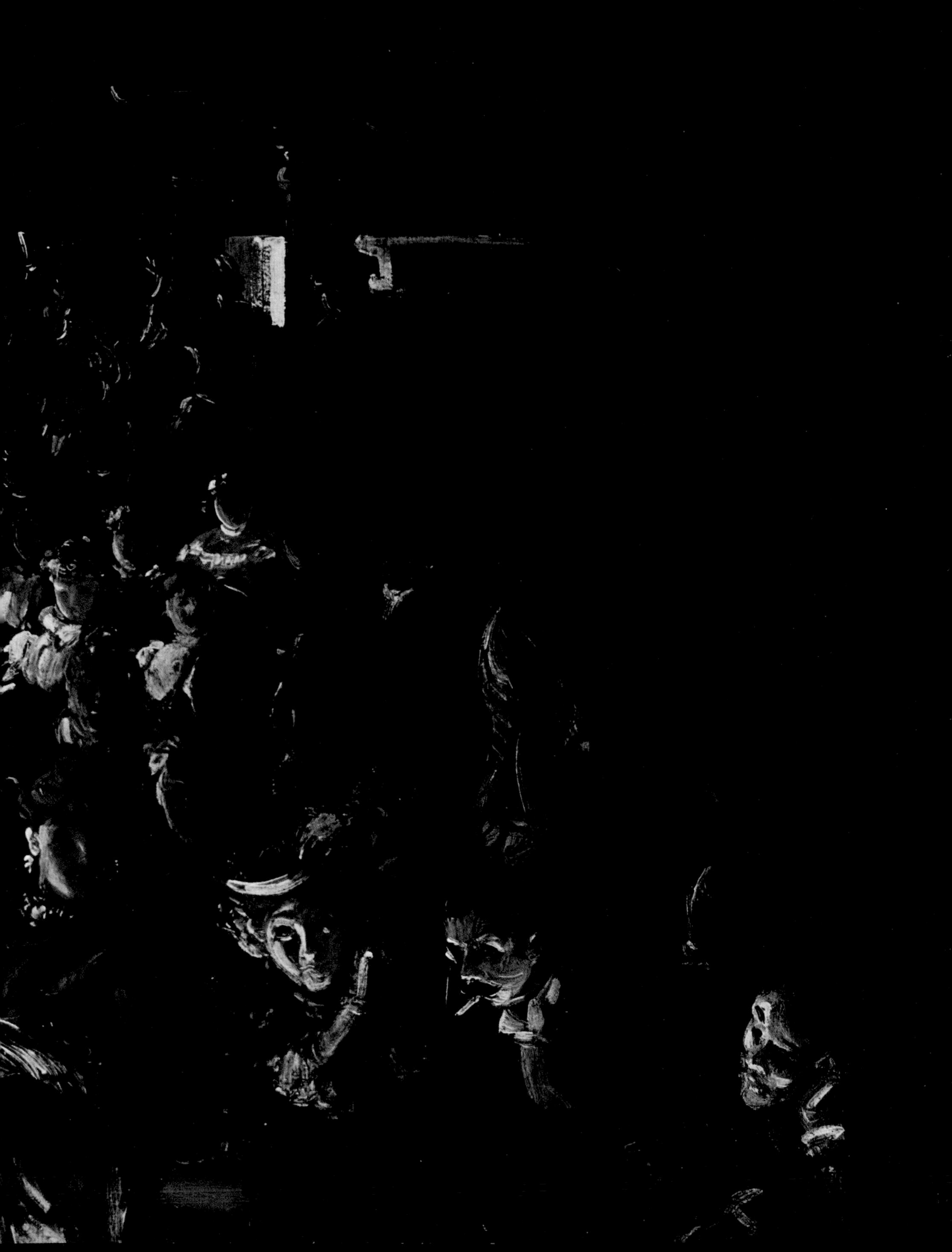

D A & S., LTD.

A SOUVENIR OF . .

"A ROYAL DIVORCE"

With the Compliments of W. W. KELLY

THEATRE ROYAL, SMETHWICK.

A SOLDIER'S HONOUR

BY MRS F G KIMBERLEY

"TAKE HIS SWORD AND KILL ME RATHER THAN BRING DISGRACE UPON MY FATHER"

MONDAY, JANUARY 6th, - - SIX NIGHTS.

wrights, producing sharply-observed wry comedies, who vanished too soon. What we did have in Bradford was an enterprising Playgoers' Society that gave play readings of drama not to be found in the Theatre Royal, including a good deal of Shaw, a dramatist who suffers very little from play reading if it is done intelligently. As there must have been similar groups elsewhere, many of Shaw's best plays were becoming known and appreciated long before they were seen on the stage.

However, we must return to London and go back a few years. What the Theatre offered was done well – the musical shows, the faintly satirical or sentimental comedies, the costume-and-rapier 'tushery' – with a high standard of acting, very strong in superb character actors. But intelligent persons who wanted to be engrossed and not simply amused must have begun to feel they had been rather better off in the 'Nineties. Now they had to content themselves with occasional performances by the Stage Society, which existed to give critics and a few members of the public at least a glimpse of plays the actor-managers and commercial managements did not want. There was an astonishingly clever young man, still in his twenties, who had done some acting and directing for the Stage Society, and now, in 1904, he formed a partnership with Vedrenne, manager of the rather small and unfashionable Court Theatre in Sloane Square, not quite in the West End. He was Harley Granville-Barker (1877–1946), and to my mind the most important figure in the Edwardian Theatre. With Shaw, a close friend, on hand to supply plays and beat the big drum, he directed for three years, on very slender financial backing, the so-called Vedrenne-Barker seasons that made theatrical history. Their range was wide: it ran from poetic drama, including Euripides, and fantasy like Maeterlinck's to Galsworthy's rather flat but compassionate naturalism and cool cynical comedy by St John Hankin (an extremely clever but neurasthenic man who committed suicide in 1909). Altogether thirty-two plays were produced and these included no fewer than eleven by Shaw, among them *You Never Can Tell, John Bull's Other Island* and *Man and Superman*, three of his strongest plays and a great help to the box office, all too often in need of help. In return the Vedrenne-Barker partnership established Shaw as a dramatist who had his own enthusiastic public, after casting and rehearsing his plays with a care they had hardly received before.

For the autumn season of 1907, with several good new plays ready for production, Granville-Barker moved to a larger and more fashionable theatre, the Savoy, but too much money was being lost, there were troubles about casting, and his own new play *Waste* had been banned by the Lord Chamberlain's office. So 1908 found him without a 'season' and permanent company, not able to give the new plays he had accepted anything but occasional performances. However, his reputation as a director had reached New York, and he was asked to take over the new so-called Millionaires Theatre (afterwards the Century) but refused because he found the theatre far too big. Then in 1910 another and

Five postcard throw-aways advertising Edwardian melodramas

(left) Martin Harvey as *Oedipus Rex*, Covent Garden, 1912

(right) Lily Elsie and Bertram Wallis in *The Count of Luxembourg*, Daly's Theatre, 1911

(opposite, above left) Annie Horniman, the founder of the Manchester Repertory Company

(opposite, above centre) Postcard throw-away advertising the Duke of York's Theatre

(opposite, above right) J. M. Barrie (detail), 1904, by Sir William Nicholson

(opposite below) The poster for *Man and Superman* by George Bernard Shaw, Criterion Theatre, 1911

better offer came from New York. Among the managers there was one who combined commercial success with good taste and genuine enthusiasm, Charles Frohman, who was Barrie's manager (and friend) both in New York and London, where he had the Duke of York's theatre always at Barrie's disposal, until May 1915, when the *Lusitania* was sunk and Frohman went down in her. At Barrie's suggestion, Frohman agreed to a repertory season at the Duke of York's, with Granville-Barker and Dion Boucicault as joint directors. It lasted for three months, producing among other things Galsworthy's *Justice*, a notable success, and Granville-Barker's own more difficult and less successful play, *The Madras House*. Three months were all that could be afforded, repertory proving hugely expensive and the Duke of York's not being suitable in size and capacity for this kind of experiment. But Granville-Barker was kept busy, and was on the whole very successful, directing all manner of plays worth directing right up to the outbreak of war. Most important, however, were his Shakespeare productions, first *The Winter's Tale* and *Twelfth Night*, later *A Midsummer Night's Dream*. In these he was entirely revolutionary, conscientiously faithful to the speech but using a stylised imaginative *décor* far removed from the tasteless and absurd realism of producers like Beerbohm Tree, who had even had real rabbits in his Shakespearean forests. Our contemporary productions of Shakespeare owe an immense debt to Harley Granville-Barker.

At the risk of wandering too far from the Edwardian era, I must say

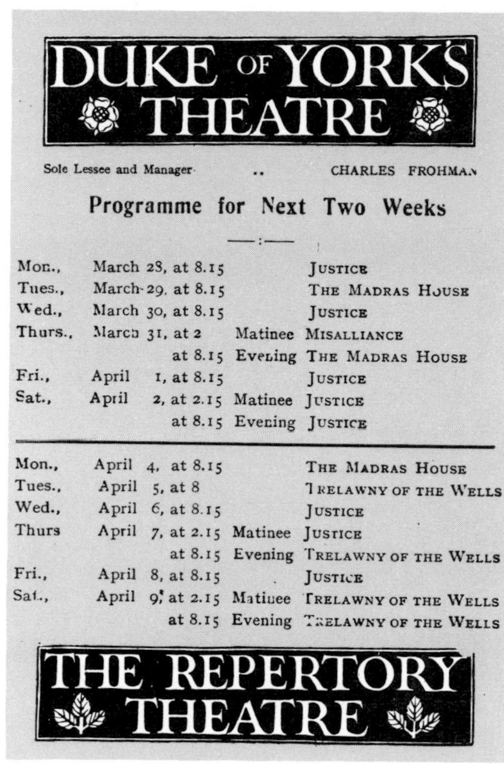

DUKE OF YORK'S THEATRE

Sole Lessee and Manager .. CHARLES FROHMAN

Programme for Next Two Weeks

Mon.,	March 28, at 8.15		JUSTICE
Tues.,	March 29, at 8.15		THE MADRAS HOUSE
Wed.,	March 30, at 8.15		JUSTICE
Thurs.,	March 31, at 2	Matinee	MISALLIANCE
	at 8.15	Evening	THE MADRAS HOUSE
Fri.,	April 1, at 8.15		JUSTICE
Sat.,	April 2, at 2.15	Matinee	JUSTICE
	at 8.15	Evening	JUSTICE
Mon.,	April 4, at 8.15		THE MADRAS HOUSE
Tues.,	April 5, at 8		TRELAWNY OF THE WELLS
Wed.,	April 6, at 8.15		JUSTICE
Thurs	April 7, at 2.15	Matinee	JUSTICE
	at 8.15	Evening	TRELAWNY OF THE WELLS
Fri.,	April 8, at 8.15		JUSTICE
Sat.,	April 9, at 2.15	Matinee	TRELAWNY OF THE WELLS
	at 8.15	Evening	TRELAWNY OF THE WELLS

THE REPERTORY THEATRE

something more about this extraordinary man, whose later years were as odd as his earlier years were sensational. Married in 1905 to his handsome leading lady, Lillah McCarthy, he made a second marriage in 1918 to a wealthy American woman. She did not want him to return to the Theatre and disliked Shaw and most of his theatrical friends; and, perhaps soured by the obvious decline of the Theatre during the war, he submitted, assumed the role of a scholarly country gentleman, and when I met him, years afterwards, this dazzling prodigy of the Edwardian Theatre seemed a disappointingly dull and rather donnish figure. (Though it is only fair to add that his *Preface to Shakespeare* and his lectures have considerable value.) As if burnt out by the blazing creativity of his early years, he could spend his time translating Spanish plays that were not as good as his own. For while he was doing so much else, in his late twenties and earlier thirties, somehow he was able to turn himself into one of the most original and intelligent English dramatists of this century. His three major Edwardian palys, *The Voysey Inheritance* (theatrically the most effective, so most often revived), *The Madras House* and *Waste*, are quite remarkable, looking at first like work influenced by Shaw but then turning into something quite different. But then these plays are odd too, as odd as his own strange career. We expect a famous director to write plays tightly constructed and with a minimum of characters and scene changes. But Granville-Barker's plays might have been written by a novelist – let us say, George Meredith – brilliantly

clever but not quite at home in the theatre. They would even gain artistically by some pruning of scenes and characters. They are expensive to produce and keep running just because they make such heavy demands. I have never been able to understand this, just as I have never really understood why a director with such great gifts, a marvel as a young man, should have decided (wife or no wife!) to turn his back on the Theatre.

I have already mentioned that Granville-Barker's *Waste* was banned from any public performance. It is about a politician of great promise whose career is ruined by a brief but tragic affair with a woman. Its combination of politics and sex was altogether too much for the Examiner of Plays who advised the Lord Chamberlain what new plays might be given a licence. From 1907 onwards all the leading dramatists, supported by other writers, made strong public protests – almost entirely in vain – against the rigid censorship imposed on the Theatre. Readers who would like a careful American account of these tragi-comic battles should try the chapter 'The Theater and the Lord Chamberlain'

(opposite above) Harley Granville-Barker, *c.* 1907

(opposite below) Lillah McCarthy and Granville-Barker in *Man and Superman*, Royal Court Theatre, 1905

(above) Norman Wilkinson's stylised *décor* for Granville-Barker's *Twelfth Night*, Savoy Theatre, 1912

(centre) *The Whip*, 1909, one of many grand scale melodramas produced at Drury Lane

(below) Frank Benson as *Richard III* at the Shakespeare Memorial Theatre, Stratford-upon-Avon, 1906

in Professor Samuel Hynes's study of these years, *The Edwardian Turn of Mind*. (My one complaint is that while Professor Hynes stresses the fact that the defenders of censorship were very Edwardian and English, he tends to forget that the people who protested and tried to defy it were also Edwardian and English.) The Lord Chamberlain's office might be described as a strong point supporting a Victorian rearguard action. Its Examiner of Plays, first an ex-bank-manager named Redford, treated the Theatre as if it were an upper-class dinner-party, possibly with a bishop and a judge among the guests; there was to be no discussion in it of religion, politics and sex. Then, politicians and peers belonging to either the government (compelled to appoint a committee or two to settle this question) or the official opposition, could not help remembering that a number of these protesting dramatists were either socialists or fiery radicals. Some senior politicians – Asquith is the type – who would soon have swept away any censorship of books were not prepared to risk offending a large section of the electorate just for the sake of the Theatre, because at heart they did not take the Theatre seriously. Why be denounced for not allowing public performances of Ibsen's *Ghosts* when they did not want to spend an evening with it themselves? Besides, while round robins of protest looked impressive in *The Times*, there was no great public clamour behind them.

Moreover, theatrical managers themselves – and the Lord Chamberlain's office dealt with them and not with the authors – insisted there should be no abolition, not even any drastic curtailing, of censorship. So on this issue the Theatre itself was divided, especially as many leading actors went along with the managers – and indeed some of them *were* managers. They were wrong, of course, and deeply wrong when they defended censorship out of a dislike for the kind of plays, intelligent, courageous, not aiming at easy amusement, that were being banned. On the other hand, in the circumstances of the time they had a case that was not entirely unreasonable. When a play had been licensed by the Lord Chamberlain, no public performance of it could be in legal jeopardy because some people happened to dislike it: theatres could not be suddenly invaded by the police and their actors swept into custody, something that occasionally happened in other countries, including America. The real question was – did the taste, judgment, general behaviour of the Lord Chamberlain's Examiner of Plays, who could decide the fate of any new play, truly represent a large body of playgoers, in danger of being shocked and disgusted? The authors' answer was that they did not, and it was quite right. The Examiner was absurdly narrow and rigid. So plays that were careful dramatisations of novels that had been well reviewed, on sale sometimes for years, were denied any public performance.

The protest flared up again, bringing with it more irony, when in 1911 Examiner Redford retired and his place was taken by Charles Brookfield. Certainly Brookfield came from the Theatre and not from

(opposite) Marie Tempest, 1908, by Jacques-Emile Blanche

a bank manager's office. He was an experienced if not greatly admired actor (Fred Kerr in his reminiscences called him 'amateurish'); and he had written a number of plays himself. But these were *risqué* farces, often adapted from the French, *Dear Old Charlie* and so forth, exactly the kind of stuff allowed to pass a censorship that would not tolerate any serious treatment of sex. And Brookfield promised to be even more intolerant about plays of ideas than Redford had been. (He was not, I fancy, a very pleasant person, and had been notorious earlier for his pathological hatred of Oscar Wilde. There is further irony here in the fact that he was the son of Thackeray's adored, delicate and over-angelic Jane Brookfield.) To be judged now by the author of *Dear Old Charlie* and the like, a man who could write an article declaring his contemptuous disapproval of the new serious drama, was too much for the dramatists and their friends: they boiled over, with Shaw delightedly capering in the steam. Again the government had to appoint a committee, chiefly consisting of elderly Establishment men who probably never went near a theatre. The authors petitioned the new king, only to have the Society of West-End Theatre Managers send a counter-petition in favour of censorship. The result was that the idiotic system remained, though the death of Brookfield, the dramatists' worst enemy, somewhat eased the situation; but plays intended for the British Theatre continued to be written in the shadow of the Lord Chamberlain for more than half-a-century to come.

So far as there was any movement at all in the Edwardian Theatre, what was central, creative and influential in it moved from the actors' to the authors' Theatre, from 'vehicles' for star performers to plays of substantial merit to which directors and their players devoted themselves: in short, what the author had written came first. Out of these years came dramatists – notably Shaw, Barrie (though at his best later), Galsworthy, Granville-Barker, Houghton – whose work was to occupy innumerable stages. (And one masterpiece from Dublin's Abbey Theatre – Synge's *Playboy of the Western World*.) Moreover, serious amateurs were already at this time taking hold of this work: I remember an impressive performance by amateurs, of Galsworthy's *Silver Box*. Some of the best younger professionals were already sacrificing West End salaries and prospects to join the repertory movement. Basil Dean went from the Horniman Company in Manchester to direct a similar company at the Liverpool Playhouse, and then helped Barry Jackson to establish his Birmingham Repertory Company, which did magnificent work after the war, especially in Shaw. There were new repertory companies in Glasgow and elsewhere. Strictly speaking, however, these, together with countless others founded later, were not really repertory companies at all. They were 'stock companies' producing a series of plays for short runs, perhaps two or three weeks; they could not afford to have a true repertoire and offer several different plays in one week. The old touring companies, playing Shakespeare or

Seated Nude: The Black Hat, *c.* 1900, by Philip Wilson Steer

(below left) Mrs Patrick Campbell, *c.* 1901

(below right) Ellen Terry, *c.* 1903

the eighteenth-century comedies at our Theatre Royal, could do this because they still used the old-fashioned painted cloths, backdrops and wings, which could be hauled up to 'the flies' in a few minutes, and at the same time took care to use the barest minimum of furniture. But the 'box sets', taking the place of the conventional (and very conventional) old scenery, which might be elaborate replicas of over-furnished drawing rooms, made enormous and very costly demands on the stage managers and their staffs; and to this day only heavily subsidised companies can afford genuine repertory. As a youthful Edwardian playgoer, I would stare down one week at some imposing set that might have been lifted straight out of Mayfair or some country mansion, with every detail in its place; and the next week I might be faced with faded old backcloths and wings, offering nothing to the eye, a world away from realism, but bringing into high relief the words, the gestures, the acting. Within eight days, Monday night to Monday night, two extremes of theatrical production could be encountered. But then – wasn't I living in an era of extremes, being at that time an Edwardian?

(right) A Viking costume design by Gordon Craig for Ibsen's *The Vikings*, Imperial Theatre, 1903

(far right) Portrait by Gordon Craig of (?) Ellen Terry as Mistress Page in *The Merry Wives of Windsor*

(below) Costume design for W. B. Yeat's *The King's Threshold,* 1904, by Charles Ricketts

Gladys Cooper, photographed by Bassano, 1910

(opposite above) Lewis Waller as *Monsieur Beaucaire*, Comedy Theatre, 1902. He was the first man to have a 'fan club' and the members wore buttons inscribed 'K.O.W.' – 'Keen on Waller'

(opposite below) Paul Cinquevalli

8. Music Hall and Vaudeville

The music hall of those years, often called 'Variety' in Britain, 'Vaudeville' in America, is no new subject. But there is one very good reason why I cannot ignore it here. Almost every account of Edwardian music hall entertainment describes it in terms of London's West End, taking the reader to its famous variety houses, the Empire and the Alhambra, the Palace and the London Pavilion and the Tivoli, all within a short walk of Piccadilly Circus. But for every single music hall in the West End, there were then about fifty, of varying size and quality, in the provinces. Nor is it just a matter of numbers. Unlike the musical comedies and the straight plays, the variety show had not originated in London and then been taken to the provinces. On the contrary, it first took shape in the provincial industrial towns, where the larger mid-Victorian taverns had 'singing rooms', in which vocalists and comedians took turns to amuse the customer. What began in Coketown finally triumphed close to Piccadilly Circus. And what the big West End variety theatres did, more especially in the Edwardian era, was simply to add dancers, spectacular scenes, 'sketches' or half-hour plays (Barrie wrote several), to a number of 'turns', solo performances lasting about ten minutes, that may have been touring the provinces for years.

Though the flourishing Edwardian music halls, scores of them controlled by the same managements and agents, saw plenty of performers, together with crowds of patrons, from the middle classes, Variety came from the industrial working class and never really moved a long way from it. (So rustic or very genteel acts always seemed bogus.) Music hall humour and sentiment were always at heart working-class humour and sentiment. It was suicidal for a performer, generally referred to as 'a turn', to play down to the audience in the *fauteuils* (as they were often grandly called) and not up to the people packed into the fourpenny balcony and threepenny gallery. These are what we had at our local Empire – and though I never risked the threepenny gallery I often squeezed myself into the fourpenny balcony, from which I recognised and applauded some great talent. The sentiment, which I never cared for, was broader and more stereotyped than the humour. It offered those time-old themes that labouring men and soldiers like to sing about when they are half-drunk – lost wonderful mothers, the death of pure young girls, faithless sweethearts, and 'the Boys of the Old Brigade'. The humour ranged from the wildly incongruous, which appealed to some natural incongruity in the working-class mind (and gave the intellectual a sudden holiday), to the dry and sardonic, developing the irony that poor hard-pressed men can so often appreciate. The old music halls had a fine radical atmosphere: they were always for the poor against the rich.

Variety itself, with its extravagant jumble of acrobats, jugglers, conjurers, singers, comics of all kinds, could be sufficiently fascinating

to men and women who worked long hours with machines and returned to little back-to-back houses down mean streets. Some variety was what they needed. Then the better provincial halls, the big Empires, however hard the cheap seats might be, did suggest a certain luxuriousness, a heightened exciting style of living, together with an air of cosiness, for they had splendid velvet curtains, cheerful brassy orchestras, coloured lights cutting through but partly tinting the smoke of the auditorium, and 'turns' getting £150 a week, money out of the Arabian Nights, yet depending on your goodwill. The performances were twice-nightly: the 'first house' was sedate, not always well-filled, and rather despised, I suspect, by the performers; whereas the 'second house', my own choice whenever possible, was packed, noisy until dominated, uproarious if pleased, and certainly never despised. It was possible still to enjoy the general atmosphere even when many of the acts on the stage seemed tedious. And I must confess that a great many of them did bore me: nearly all the acrobats; most of the jugglers, though not the great Cinquevalli; any conjurers and illusionists who were far below the level of David Devant (the best I ever saw, and he was stricken with *paralysis agitans*, like a Beethoven going deaf); all bogus-refined musical acts, with dear old Dad and his two daughters in a drawing-room set with shaded lamps; and the 'male impersonators' such as Vesta Tilley, who never looked or sounded like the soldiers and sailors they pretended to be, and suffocated me with boredom while all around me were enraptured. Alas, I never saw Marie Lloyd, who was more popular in London, but was always captivated by a twinkling little redhead called Maidie Scott, who used to sing –

> For you don't know Nellie like I do,
> Said the naughty little bird on Nellie's hat.

Many of the soubrettes took the 'naughty but nice' approach in those days. As for some of the most popular comic songs, Freud could have revealed their symbolism and significance in under two minutes. The women in the audience were quicker than that: they always laughed first – and louder.

I was not very fond of the so-called 'eccentric comedians' who came rushing on, in the weirdest costumes, and bawled out nonsensical ditties. There was about them too strong a suggestion of lunacy; and indeed two of the most popular eccentrics committed suicide. But I doted on the great drolls, no matter if they gave solo performances like Little Tich, who contrived somehow to combine furious energy with a certain detachment; or if they had a partner, like the wonderful Grock, who seemed like a serious but bewildered being from another planet; or if they surrounded themselves with infuriatingly daft creatures, like the perpetually amazed and indignant Harry Tate, always the self-important sportsman in a world drifting away from sense and logic, cause and effect. Sketches like Tate's, feasts of unreason, were

(left) Vesta Tilley

(right) Marie Lloyd

(opposite above) Little Tich ('The Droll Dancer') by Alick P. F. Ritchie

(opposite, below left) Harry Tate in his 'Golfing' sketch

(opposite, below right) George Robey as Mother Hubbard in Pantomime

always arriving in the Edwardian music hall, offering us, to our joy, off-beat, surrealist and even *black* humour sixty years ago, perhaps a gift to the rest of society from the hard-driven industrial working class. Its comedians and saucy soubrettes were the last specimens of English folk art. And they travelled far, finally into the new world of films, Charlie Chaplin and Stan Laurel finding their way to Hollywood. Indeed, Fred Karno and other showmen continually sent on tour elaborate clowning acts in dumb show, all superbly timed because they had to capture two audiences a night for months on end; and it was from these acts, because they were very funny and needed no speech and were all happening in a lunatic world, that the early slapstick films, now so much admired by solemn young historians of the cinema, took their method, their style, their inspiration.

The final act in most of these variety shows when all the glory of the programme had vanished, was a few minutes of jerky film, generally called 'Bioscope'. But we rarely stayed to discover what the Bioscope was offering us. Now that we have so many accounts of the early history of films, we know that men in various places were taking them very seriously indeed. But that was true of very few people. My friends and I waved them away. Apart from halls where films were occasionally shown, I seem to remember – as my first genuine cinema – a certain *Theatre-de-Luxe*, where for sixpence you were given an hour or so of short films, a cup of tea and a biscuit. I tried once, and once was enough. Not until the First War, when I was in the army, did I begin to look for films, not simply to take girls into the back rows for canoodling, but in search of the early Chaplin shorts that were arriving then. Before that, in the Edwardian years, like most other people I spent very little time

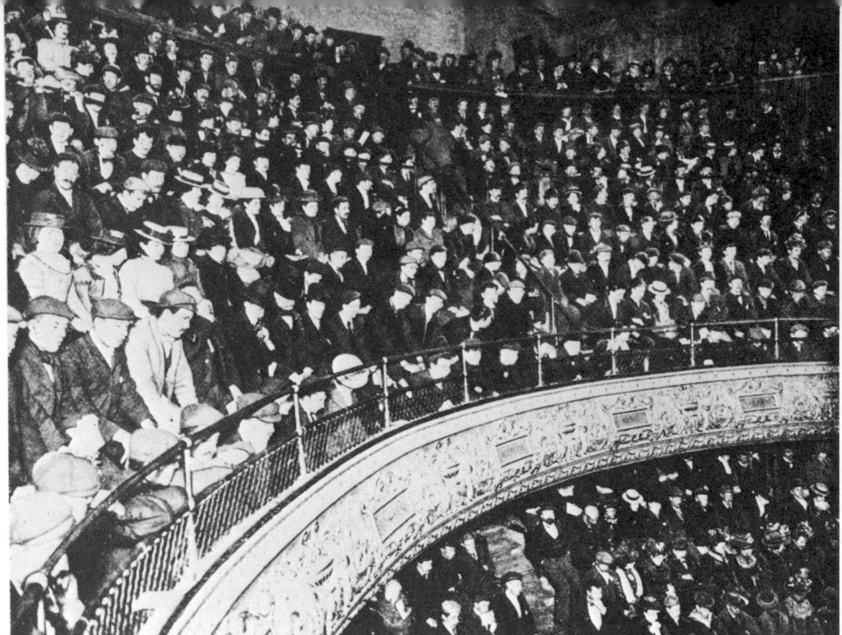

(above left) A music hall gallery, *c.* 1902

(above right) Advertisement for the Biograph, 1905

looking at films, which were just so much prolonged 'Bioscope'. And for that reason I shall spend no more time with them here, leaving them to flicker away, a final disregarded item in the great gaudy programmes of the music hall.

9. The Press

In 1905, Alfred Harmsworth, who had been a baronet for two years, was raised to the peerage and became Lord Northcliffe, which is what I shall call him. With his brother Harold, afterwards Lord Rothermere, who had a flair for big finance, Northcliffe in ten years had made a fortune out of popular journalism. He knew what the big new reading public wanted because he was really one of them himself. He was also a born journalist, ready at any time to turn out a column or to suggest some promising news stories. His *Daily Mail*, which first appeared in 1896 as a halfpenny morning paper, was the revolutionary parent of all popular English journalism. There was a touch of genius in it. He knew – what other proprietors and editors had failed to realise – there was a huge new public as impatient with the old, heavy, long-winded journalism as he was. People wanted something easy to read, bright, exciting, as attractive to ordinary women as it was to their men. But, oddly enough, when he first brought out, in 1903, the *Daily Mirror*, it failed because it was a woman's paper, only succeeding later when it became an even briefer, brighter, more pictorial version of the *Daily Mail*. Meanwhile, he had built up a kind of empire of popular periodicals Then, in 1908, he arrived at what was probably the peak of his ambition as a journalist-proprietor by acquiring a controlling interest in *The Times*. He had a genuine respect for the tradition and prestige of this

Charlie Chaplin 'snapped' aboard the liner *Cairnrona* on his way to America with Fred Karno's *Mumming Birds* in 1910

famous newspaper, but he knew that it was now a financial liability and badly needed new management and a sharper editorial policy. Even so, Northcliffe did not immediately fill *The Times* with his own lively and irreverent young men; he kept on most of its old staff.

In his *Prophets, Priests and Kings*, A. G. Gardiner, a well-known Liberal journalist during these years, wrote:

> Lord Northcliffe is the type of 'the man in the street'. There is no psychological mystery to be unravelled here, no intellectual shadow land. He is obvious and elementary – a man who understands material success and nothing else. He has no other standard by which to judge life. Napoleon's question was 'What have you done?' Lord Northcliffe's question would be 'What have you got?' For he not only wants success himself; he admires it in others. It is the passport to his esteem. It is the thing he understands. If you will watch his career you will see that, as far as he has any philosophy at all, it is this, that merit rides in a motorcar. You become interesting to him, as Johnson became interesting to Lord Chesterfield, immediately you have succeeded . . .

But if we accept this, it raises a curious question. Conducting his halfpenny *Daily Mail*, to appeal to a mass audience, Northcliffe employed some very good writers, unknown before to that audience. Moreover, a few years ago when I saw a facsimile of the *Daily Mail* leading news page for a day in 1908, I noticed that the whole column on the right-hand edge was devoted to an account of Elgar's First Symphony. Now no popular newspaper today would give so much space to a new piece of music. And I do not think editors of mass-circulation papers today would have any use for the very good writers that Northcliffe employed. So where are we? Did Northcliffe himself enjoy symphonic music and superior prose? Or did he feel that a fair proportion of his halfpenny-paper readers liked such things? Or was he compelled to believe, no matter how far he went to please and flatter 'the man in the street', that he had a certain duty towards his readers, so that he could not altogether ignore a major work by Elgar or good writing? (Which is what his successors have done, without a blush.) I cannot be certain, because I never knew Northcliffe, but I am inclined to think that round about this time, say 1908, when he was still only in his early forties, he was not yet entirely without what we might call a sense of cultural responsibility. I think too that his attitude towards *The Times*, after he took it over, confirms this. It also suggests that Gardiner's account of him, quoted above, is too severe.

I am not ready yet to dismiss Northcliffe; he is the key figure in the development of the Edwardian popular press. I shall pay him no further tributes because he illustrates – and is indeed largely responsible for – what went wrong with it, not only in England but in many places elsewhere. (I am not forgetting an earlier impudent pioneer, Gordon Bennet in New York.) And we can add – what has now gone wrong with mass media everywhere. Northcliffe felt that a newspaper intended for mass readership had to be exciting every morning. You could not say in effect, 'Not much news today so we'll write about something else'. If there was nothing sensational to announce, then you invented something sensational to announce. The Northcliffe style of journalism, original then but now common form, not only reported news but *created* news. Not only were little things blown up into big things, his *Daily Mail* could be sensational about itself. Some mornings, a reader bought the paper to read about the paper: anything to keep up the excitement – stunt races and competitions, chances of large prizes, and, what was far more dangerous, impassioned challenges, revelations, campaigns for sudden irrational 'causes'. Though a lot of male readers turned straight to the sports pages while their wives and daughters searched for fashion and gossip, the huge headlines and the placards everywhere had their effect. The final irony here – and I believe it to be largely true of all the mass media today – is that the greatest effect was not upon the hundreds of thousands of ordinary readers, who often just stared and yawned, but upon the politicians and their advisers, the solemn students of public affairs, the popular opinion experts.

No doubt the circulation of his papers and the money they brought him helped to swell Northcliffe's ego, but I suspect that what really took him into megalomania, an occupational hazard of press lords, was the increasing attention, arriving at serious respect, given him in high political circles. Here, it was felt, was the voice of the public. But what was really being heard was the voice of Northcliffe through a dozen different megaphones. And Northcliffe was always changing his mind, never following any steady course. Lloyd George once said that a conversation with him was 'like taking a walk with a grasshopper'. Alfred Harmsworth had made a great contribution to popular journalism, but as Lord Northcliffe he began to make an even greater contribution to the confusion and bewilderment of the times. Other newspaper proprietors imitated the Northcliffe style; their editors demanded brisk and brief news items that need not be accurate so long as they were easy to read; leader writers had not to feel too responsible but had to keep punching hard; there had to be something sensational every morning and evening; it was all rather like playing with thunderbolts at a children's party.

However, there were many educated men in the provinces who never read a London newspaper. My father was one of them. He read the *Yorkshire Observer* and occasionally the *Manchester Guardian*, then, under Scott, probably at its best – filled with accurate reporting, civilised opinion, and good writing on all subjects. The standard of the best provincial journalism was such that the *Birmingham Post* had on its staff as music critic no other than Ernest Newman. What we missed, though I did not realise it then, were the London evening papers, not the halfpenny *Star* and *Evening News*, which had large circulations, but the more intelligent and diversified penny evening papers, the *Evening Standard*, *Pall Mall Gazette*, *Globe*, *Westminster Gazette*. These performed a service not only for readers but also for younger writers, needing an outlet for witty comment and sketches of London life and the odd guinea their contribution brought them. The costs of these papers were low, but even so they led a precarious life and were nearly always subsidised, and clearly they were doomed to vanish sooner or later, but for intelligent readers and writers alike they added a variety and sparkle to Edwardian London. Now we have enormous costs, a complete dependence on advertising revenue, more efficiency in all departments – more monotony, less fun.

What we did not miss, for I can well remember how we got hold of them somehow (possibly at the library) and compared them, were the serious weeklies, so many of them then that I may easily leave out one or two. There were the *Spectator*, *Nation*, *Athenaeum*, *Academy*; then Orage's bold and brilliant *New Age*; and later the *New Statesman*. Again, here were opportunities for young writers either as essayists and reviewers, opportunities that could only exist because it was possible to run a weekly review on a very modest budget. Others, such as the *British Weekly*, very popular among men who wanted to feel serious without making too much of an effort, or *Punch*, which by 1908 had reached the 80,000 mark and was steadily increasing its circulation, were far more substantial commercially. The *Illustrated London News* went on and on, but now it was joined by other pictorial weeklies, like the *Sketch* and the *Sphere*. There were more monthly magazines than I can remember, though I can recall the *Windsor*, *Cassell's* and *Pearson's*, but the best of them was still the *Strand*, which could serialise H. G. Wells, persuade Conan Doyle to bring back Sherlock Holmes, and offer us E. Nesbit's wonderful children's stories. The *Strand* sold about 400,000, and it seems to me that this says something for the taste of the Edwardian middle classes. Here too was the era's rich variety.

10. The King Dies

'We are living', King Edward had noted, 'in difficult times'. He may have been thinking then of events in Central and Eastern Europe and the worsening relations between Austria and the Slavs. But in 1909, when Lloyd George brought in his Budget at the end of April, there were difficult times at home. Extra revenue had to be found to pay for Old Age Pensions and a more powerful navy. Lloyd George announced that on earned incomes over £3000 and on all unearned incomes the tax would be raised from 9d. in the pound to 1s. 2d., that incomes over

Mrs Keppel was called by Queen Alexandra to the dying King's bedside

(opposite) Edward VII and Queen Alexandra, 1905

£5000 would be liable to a super tax of 6d., that 'unearned increment' in land values would be taxed at 20%, that there would be higher duties on spirits and tobacco and that people engaged in selling 'intoxicating liquor' would find themselves facing stiff extra taxation. All this looked like red revolution to the landowning and brewing peers in the House of Lords, which would be called upon to pass the Finance Bill carrying these dreadful proposals. But if there was to be a war between the Commons and the Lords, the government could end it by flooding the Lords with newly-created peers. This conflict and its possible solution greatly disturbed the King, who felt that the Crown itself might soon be involved. Difficult times indeed! But there was something else, which he tried to treat lightly, as if it might disappear if not regarded seriously. This was his own health. He was a corpulent man, still in his sixties but ageing rapidly; he was having more and more bronchial trouble; and while enjoying one of his large cigars, which he refused to abandon, he would suddenly embarrass and even frighten the company by long fits of coughing. On an official visit to Berlin in 1909 he had to wear a Prussian uniform that nearly choked him, and he collapsed. The sharp attacks of bronchitis were putting a strain on his heart. Unfortunately he made such quick recoveries that he ignored all suggestions that he should consider himself an invalid, insisting more and more, often with a show of temper, that he should carry out his familiar elaborate programme, both of official business and of pleasure.

In April, 1910, he set out as usual for Biarritz, breaking the journey at Paris. In his entertaining French account of Edward and the Edwardians, Phillipe Jullian tells us that the King was determined to see Lucien Guitry in *Chantecler*. As the actors were smothered in feathers, the director of the theatre had been keeping it under-heated; but when Guitry warned him that the King would be there and would not enjoy sitting in chill discomfort, the director in his enthusiasm almost turned the place into a Turkish bath. The King was seen to be very flushed as he left, and he was then kept waiting for his car. Bronchitis followed the cold he caught; he refused to return to London and went on to Biarritz, where he spent much of his time in his room reading newspapers and probably shaking his head over them. (Among the speeches they reported was one by Winston Churchill even criticising the Crown.) He looked rather better when he left Biarritz, but in London and at Sandringham people noticed that he was slowing up, neither laughing nor damning anybody, a tired man. By May 3, though he was still attending to state business and giving a few audiences in Buckingham Palace, one or other of the three royal physicians was on hand, and urgent messages were being sent to Queen Alexandra, who had been cruising in the Mediterranean, and various members of the royal family. But at his own request no bulletins were being issued, and the secret of his grave condition was not let out until late on May 5. Then, although he persisted in staying up and carrying on with his duties,

(right) Edward VII walking with Colonel Holford, Equerry-in-Waiting, during his last visit to Biarritz in 1910

even between fainting fits and administration of oxygen, he began to lose consciousness on the afternoon of May 6. Anxious crowds now gathered outside the gates of the Palace. (By a strange coincidence, the Church of England service for that evening included Psalm 33: *There is no King that can be saved by the multitude of an host; neither is any mighty man delivered by much strength.*) He died at 11.45 that night. It was one sign of a rapidly changing world that passengers on the larger liners, now equipped with wireless, knew of his death before people living in London suburbs.

Having compelled myself to read some twenty pages of close print in double columns, under the title *A World In Mourning*, I can testify both to the number and to the eloquence of the tributes to Edward.

Black Ascot in mourning for Edward VII, 1910

The greatest of republics was as quick to respond as any of the monarchies. President Taft sent a long cable of condolence to Queen Alexandra; the House of Representatives passed a resolution of sympathy and then adjourned as a mark of respect; the American press told its readers how great a loss this was ('There is no other monarch', cried the *New York World*, 'whom the civilised world could not better have spared'); the stock exchanges of New York, Philadelphia, New Orleans, Chicago and Baltimore suspended business for the day; Broadway theatre orchestras played *God Save the King*; flags flew at half-mast in New York, and the offices of Pierpont Morgan were draped in black. There was genuine sympathy here, even if it were mixed with confused worry in financial circles, no longer sure about the boom in rubber and oils, or, as the *New York Tribune* gravely indicated, 'the negotiations pending for the placing of various issues of American railway bonds abroad'.

There is ample proof that the affection for 'Good old Teddie!' had never waned. Immense crowds, with thousands flocking from the East End, assembled before dawn and then waited for hours to catch a glimpse of the royal coffin on its way to burial at Windsor. Then, weeks after all the imperial funeral pageantry had passed, after all the foreign but related royalties had returned home to resume more cheerful duties, there was a last odd tribute that Edward himself would have appreciated. The ladies going into the Royal Enclosure for the races at Ascot, always an occasion for sharp competition in new finery and frippery, all wore dead black feathers, ribbons, bows. It was known as 'Black Ascot'. I like to think that Edward, somewhere behind the veil, heard about it and began laughing and coughing over an imaginary cigar. What is certain is that he had vanished from the immediate scene but that the Edwardian era had not vanished with him. It still had a few years to run before it too vanished in August 1914. These years from Edward's death in 1910, crowded and rather strange years, gathering colour and drama, noise and heat, await us in Part Three.

1. Winds of Change

Following his father's death, the new king, George V, wrote in his diary:

> At 11.45 beloved Papa passed peacefully away & I have lost my best friend & the best of fathers. I never had a word (i.e. angry word) with him in his life. I am heartbroken & overwhelmed with grief, but God will help me in my great responsibilities & darling May will be my comfort as she always has been. May God give me strength & guidance in the heavy task which has fallen on me . . .

The style and manner of this entry, old-fashioned in its wording even for 1910, may suggest to some younger readers that the man who wrote it, then aged forty-four, was something of a softie. But he was not. He had gone through the full training of a naval officer, working as hard as the next man, probably harder than most. In January 1892 his elder brother, the Duke of Clarence, had died of pneumonia. This left George next in succession to the Throne. Later in 1892 he was created Duke of York and was given a suite of apartments in St. James's Palace and a small house, long his favourite residence, in the grounds of Sandringham. A year later he married Princess Mary (May) of Teck, whose engagement to the Duke of Clarence had been announced only about seven weeks before his death. This quick transfer from one brother to another looks anything but romantic, a cold-blooded business, but in fact, as the entry in the diary tells us, George and his May were an extremely devoted pair, always happy when they could

Buckingham Palace as it was before the façade was altered in 1911

lead a quiet life together. Queen Mary, as she now became in 1910, had not the beauty or the high spirits of her mother-in-law, Queen Alexandra, but was a very good wife, mother and queen. Though not until her last years as widely admired nor ever quite as popular as Alexandra, she was a better-educated and more intelligent woman.

Not long after the accession of Edward VII, George as heir had been created Prince of Wales. His London residence was now Marlborough House, and he was given places of his own at Windsor and near Balmoral, but whenever possible – and I mention this because it throws a light on his character – he returned to live quietly at the modest house at Sandringham. Unlike his father he took little pleasure in European travel, but on the other hand he enjoyed long voyages to distant parts of the Empire, visiting Australia, New Zealand, Canada and, later,

India. A note he made on his Indian tour is worth quoting: it seems to me to throw more than one light:

> No doubt the Natives are better treated by us than in the past, but I could not help being struck by the way in which all salutations by the Natives were disregarded by the persons to whom they were given. Evidently we are too much inclined to look upon them as a conquered & down-trodden race & the Native, who is becoming more and more educated, realises this. I could not help noticing that the general bearing of the European towards the Native was to say the least unsympathetic. In fact not the same as that of superiors to inferiors at home.

There is about that an air of innocent commonsense rarely found among very important personages. But then George V, though not indifferent

George V and Queen Mary, *c.* 1911

to regal dignity, was not an important personage to himself. Certainly during these first years, before the war heightened his stature and popularity, he was modest, shy, anxious, knowing only too well he could not fill the space his father's death had left empty. He had not Edward's impressive physical presence, nor his worldly experience, tact, charm, robust bonhomie. When a character in *The Edwardians* declares 'And now, of course, the Court will become as dull as ditch-water', she is only saying what so many members of Edward's rich smart set must have said. There would be no more glamorous royal weekends, no more evenings of champagne, bridge, naughty gossip. From the other end of the social scale there would be no cries of 'Good old Georgie!' The middle classes might be glad that now a quiet respectable family man wore the crown, but it would be some time yet before he became a familiar figure, to be regarded with affection. Even the political leaders were at first barely acquainted with him.

In his strictly private life, in his tastes and favourite pursuits, King George was not very different from many another naval officer who had left the service to settle down as a country gentleman. He enjoyed various sports, and when he and the Queen could get away to their little house at Sandringham (the big house now belonged to Queen Alexandra), he liked nothing better, after a day in the open and a sensible dinner, than to sit at ease with his wife and do some reading aloud. (In one respect he was better equipped than his father had been, for he had an exceptionally good voice and delivery, a great asset later when radio came along.) Among his pursuits, he had three passions: shooting, yachting, and stamp collecting; and it is only fair to add that he was a crack shot, an expert yachtsman, and renowned among the world's philatelists for his superb collection. Moreover, though modest, anxious, rather bewildered during these first years, he was no cipher in private, no shrinking milque-toast: he could lose his temper, suddenly let out a quarter-deck roar. Without any temptation to initiate diplomatic moves abroad, as Edward had done, he was continuously and deeply concerned about home affairs, in which he saw his own rôle as that of a conciliator, doing what he could to restore harmony. He had no desire to overplay the rôle, and while conscientious enough in the performance of his official duties he was always hoping to escape for a day's shooting or yachting, to return to the stamp albums and the reading aloud. The irony of his situation was that, after the lull following King Edward's death, King George V would soon be called upon to face more crises than his father had ever known. He was rather like a man who, leaving a noisy party upstairs, goes for a quiet smoke in a basement crammed with gunpowder.

1909 had been noisy and disturbing, with its dramatic and challenging Budget and sharper political divisions, its 'Votes for Women' demonstrations, its signs of growing social and industrial unrest; and at first 1910 seemed comparatively calm, a good time for one king to succeed another, far more experienced, far more popular than himself. But 1910 was deeply deceptive: the gunpowder had gone down into the basement. It was – to change the metaphor – as if unknown to everybody a page had been very quietly turned. What had been noisy and disturbing before would soon be clamorous and distressing. Divisions of opinion were already widening and deepening: men who had agreed to differ for years would soon begin to insult one another. It was as if the curtain had risen on the first act of a cunningly-constructed play, in which so many things were to go terribly wrong. Matters taken easily now might be almost forgotten, only to return much later, wearing a mask of dread or anguish.

So, for example, in June of this year, 1910, Robert Falcon Scott, late of the Admiralty, could slip away in the *Terra Nova* to go back to the Antarctic; and it would not be until February 1913 that people would know that Scott, Wilson, Oates, Bowers and Evans would never sail home, and that between them these men had shaped an epic of the ice that even today can hardly be read dry-eyed. It was that kind of time, the page of history having been secretly turned, with a strange rise in the social temperature, with everything moving faster, bitter drama on the way. Even the London streets looked different, for motorcars were no longer the extravagant toys of the rich, there were fewer and fewer

Review of the Home Fleet by George V shortly after his succession

horses to be seen, and more and more taxicabs and motor buses. An exhibition of pictures from Paris – for this was the time of Roger Fry's show at the Grafton Galleries – could not come and go quietly but had to explode like a bomb. And from Italy, of all places, came the roaring manifesto of the 'Futurist' Marinetti – he and his followers, if he had any, were 'young, strong, living' and the Past was only so much balsam for prisoners, invalids, men on their deathbeds . . . they would chant the praises of arsenals and workshops, adventurous liners, locomotives and aeroplanes . . . and finally and fatally, Futurism was 'out to glorify War – the only health-giver of the world – Militarism, Patriotism, the Destructive arm of the Anarchist, Ideas that kill, Contempt for Women' – and more imbecilities to the same effect.

I am not pretending that Edwardian England was much disturbed by this heady uproarious-café nonsense. (I can personally testify that the influence of Marinetti and his friends was nil in one part of the West Riding.) But a hottish wind was blowing, the temperature rising. Where there could be differences and quarrels – and the area of them was rapidly widening – the differences would soon be deeper, the quarrels sharper and conducted with a new bitterness. Compromise was being rejected: militancy was in the air. There was a growing if largely unconscious desire for public drama, hot news from a press that asked for nothing better; and the drama arrived, in one department of public life after another, and the newsboys went shouting along the streets. If George V valued his role as conciliator, he would not be without opportunities to play it. But if what he wanted most was a quiet life, surrounded by his subjects who were leading quiet lives too, he was running out of luck.

Lieutenant Shackleton who attempted to reach the South Pole in 1908

2. Constitutional Crisis

In the summer of 1910 the new King, still twelve months away from his own coronation, found that he had inherited a constitutional crisis that had darkened the last days of his far more experienced father. And if Edward had felt deeply disturbed and baffled, King George, who had not been acquainted with every secret move, now felt completely bewildered. What added to his bewilderment was that he had to cope now with minds very different from his own: that of his prime minister, Asquith, who could make massive plain statements and yet be a master of political ambiguity; and that of the leader of the opposition, Balfour, whose languid manner partly concealed a most subtle intellect and an unusual power of debate. New and almost entirely inexperienced, King George – though I cannot believe this ever occurred to him – must have felt like Alice in Wonderland.

Captain Scott and his comrades reached the South Pole on January 18, 1912 to find that they had been beaten there by the Norwegian explorer Amunsden. *(Left to right)*: Captain Scott, Captain Oates, Edward Wilson and Petty Officer Edgar Evans. The photograph was taken by Lieutenant Bowers

The political situation was extremely complicated, and to avoid tedium I must risk over-simplifying it. Late in 1909 the House of Lords had rejected Lloyd George's Budget. The fight was on now between the Liberal Government and the Lords. Asquith appealed to the country and in January 1910 there was a general election. Curiously enough, in view of the fact that theirs had been a People's Budget, the Liberals had lost over a hundred seats and now, to have a good working majority in the House, they had to depend on the constant support not only of Labour members but also of the far more numerous Irish nationalist members, who were there to secure Home Rule. The Opposition taunted the Liberals as being so many prisoners of the Irish. The Lords were even more inflexibly opposed to Home Rule than they were to people's budgets, higher taxation and the rest. Indeed, the Tory party to which they belonged, for the most part, had for years called itself 'Unionist' – to show its opposition to Home Rule and any attempt to dissolve the union between Great Britain and Ireland – and if I have not used this term, preferring 'Tory', it has been simply to avoid confusion. It was now urgently necessary, both to the Liberals and the Irish members, that the Lords should not be able to reject measures already accepted, after the required three readings, by a majority in the Commons. So in April Asquith introduced the first reading of the Parliament Bill, which drastically reduced the power of the Lords. It was in effect a re-shaping, long overdue, of the old constitution. Later in April the Lords reluctantly passed the Budget. But men, especially if they are peers of the realm, do not tamely accept any reduction of their power, and clearly, when the time came for the Lords to accept the Parliament Bill they would howl it down.

However, from the first, Asquith had had an ace of trumps up his sleeve that he could play if the King agreed to it. As a political device what Asquith suggested was not new, but never before had it been attempted on such a bold dramatic scale. The House of Lords, now overwhelmingly Tory, could be flooded by sufficient newly-created peers – five hundred, if necessary – known to be Liberal and progressive in their sympathies. But only the King could actually create peers, and Edward had been extremely reluctant to do this on such as scale, feeling that it debased the royal prerogative and that such a move, changing the old balance of the constitution, might soon threaten the Crown itself. Nothing had been settled before Edward died, and during the lull that followed – and perhaps to spare the new King from having to make difficult decisions – Asquith decided that he, Lloyd George, Lord Crewe (a Liberal peer) and Augustine Birrell should meet in conference the Opposition leaders Balfour, Lords Lansdowne and Cawdor, and Austen Chamberlain. They conferred throughout the summer but could not reach any agreement. It is significant that Lloyd George, impatient with party argument, made a very strong plea for a Coalition Government, which could defy party fanatics and then deal with the constitutional and Irish problems and combine its talents to press on with social reform. Party loyalties and habits of mind defeated his proposal. For the rest of his life, as his memoirs proved, he believed that this insistence upon party politics had had fatal consequences, not only in Ireland but also probably in Europe, where a Coalition at this time might have succeeded in preventing the drift towards war. The Conference having failed, chiefly because of the Home Rule issue, Asquith in November went down to Sandringham to explain the situation to the still bewildered King. If the Lords still vetoed the Bill, then parliament should be dissolved and there would have to be an immediate general election. But the King was much relieved to hear from Asquith that he asked for no guarantees from the King, who had not to promise that if necessary he would use his Royal Prerogative, in other words create new peers.

However, a few days later the Cabinet sent a secret note to the King telling him rather bluntly that if they had a majority in the new Parliament, then 'His Majesty will be ready to exercise his constitutional powers (which may involve the Prerogative of creating Peers)'. Guarantees were now being demanded. The King very sensibly could not see why he should be asked to make secret promises. It seemed to him – and he was right – that he was being forced into the arena of party politics, secrecy or no secrecy. All he wanted to do was to act constitutionally. If, after the election, a new Liberal Government, still deadlocked in the Lords, asked him openly to be ready to create new peers, then he could not refuse his consent – but why *now*, why in *secret*? And indeed the King had by far the more reasonable case. But Asquith and Lord Crewe saw him at Buckingham Palace, declared that the only alternative to their having this secret understanding was the immediate resignation of the Cabinet, so the King most reluctantly agreed. The General Election, the second in 1910, was rushed through in December.

It seems to me there is more than a glint or two of irony in this 1910 political crisis. To begin with, it was the simple bewildered King who was sensible and quite right, until he finally gave in, and the formidable experienced politicians who behaved unreasonably and badly. Again, after the tremendous fuss throughout the year about the Royal Prerogative, it would never in fact be used. Again, when the Liberals in their December election went rushing all over the country as champions of the People against the Lords, the result was an anticlimax. The new parliament looked almost exactly like the old one, the Liberals still depending on the support of Irish and Labour members. Finally, the People, whose cause was being championed against the Lords, were not interested, and almost all their attention was going elsewhere, as we shall see.

A Coronation postcard of 1911

George V was crowned, with all the usual ceremony and pageantry, on June 22, 1911. As I can easily recall, this was an exceptionally hot summer; it was said that in August the temperature in London rose to degrees fahrenheit. Westminster's stifling weather may partly account for unusual events in Parliament towards the end of July. Already the Parliament Bill, severely amended, had been sent back by the Lords. It was at this time that the Tory extremists, both in the Lords and Commons, earned by their fanatical obduracy a term in constant use ever since – they were 'the diehards'. But until the end of July the passage to and fro of the Bill had created no great excitement in Westminster, and even less – we could even say none at all – in the country basking or baking in the sun. But then, on July 21, Asquith, probably impatient and exhausted, made a bad move. He sent a public letter to Balfour, saying in effect he would now if necessary advise the King 'to exercise his Prerogative', and that the King had already agreed to accept and act on this advice. In short, the secret guarantees were now let out of the bag. The Tories felt they had been tricked and that

Asquith had abused his right as adviser of the Crown. Tempers flared like that sun of 1911. When Asquith rose in the House on July 24 the Tories refused him even a hearing, and for once a British Prime Minister was howled down. Margot Asquith, in her *Autobiography*, presents the astonishing scene:

The Speaker's Gallery was closely packed, and excited ladies were standing up on their chairs. My husband got a deafening reception as he walked up the floor of the House; but I saw in a moment that the Opposition was furious and between the counter-cheers I could hear an occasional shout of 'Traitor!'

When the hubbub had subsided he rose to move the rejection of the Lords' amendments; at this Lord Hugh Cecil and Mr. F. E. Smith [*later, Lord Birkenhead*] led an organised and continuous uproar which kept him on his feet for over thirty minutes.

'Divide! Divide! 'Vide! 'Vide!!!' was shouted by the Opposition in an

Margot Asquith attending a wedding at St Margaret's, Westminster in 1911

orgy of ruffianism every time he opened his mouth. The Speaker tried in vain to make them listen, but the house was out of hand and the uproar continued.

Looking at the frenzied faces from above, I realised slowly that Henry was being howled down. Edward Grey [*the famous Foreign Minister of this Government*] got up from his place four off from where my husband was standing, and sat down again close beside him. His face was set.

I scrawled a hasty line from our stifling gallery and sent it down to him. 'They will listen to you – so for God's sake defend him from the cats and the cads!'

Arthur Balfour followed, and when Grey rose to speak the stillness was formidable.

Always the most distinguished figure in the House, he stood for a moment white and silent, and looked at the enemy:

'If arguments are not to be listened to from the Prime Minister there is not one of us who will attempt to take his place,' he said, and sat down in an echo of cheers.

Mr. F. E. Smith rose to reply, but the Liberals would not listen to him and the Speaker adjourned the House on the ground of grave disorder . . .

Faced with the threat of being invaded by a host of new peers, all but 'the diehards' in the Lords changed their minds. On August 11 the Parliament Bill passed the Lords by a slender majority of 131 to 114. But the Parliament Act, as it now became, did not really face and then settle the problem of a Second Chamber. If a Second Chamber should be retained – and many radicals and Labour men did not see why it should be – there was no reason why it should be filled with hereditary peers. Clearly there ought to be some other and more rational way of finding suitable members for it. Some progress had been made, but the fundamental questions had been shelved and not answered. The trouble was that Asquith's government, in spite of the fact that it had a formidable and brilliant Cabinet, had too much to do without tackling the root problem of a Second Chamber, and it knew there had been no wide demand in the country for a complete revision. In view of what was to happen later, we should note here the high temper and fanatical resolution of the Tory 'diehards'. Typical of them was the attack, in one of their newspapers, *The Globe*, on those peers who had voted to pass the Parliament Bill: 'We hope no honest men will take any of them by the hand again, that their friends will disown, their clubs expel them, and that in politics and social life they will be made to feel the bitter shame they have brought upon us all'. The language could hardly be more intemperate if these peers had been selling their daughters into slavery. And it does at least offer some support – and there is more, much more, to follow – for my claim earlier that soon the differences would be deeper, the quarrels sharper and conducted with a new bitterness. I also added that there was a growing if largely unconscious desire for public drama, for hot news from heated presses.

3. Public Melodrama

So now, with public drama in mind, I offer a brief interlude, delaying any account of industrial conflict, newly bitter strikes and lockouts, and of the tragic progress of the women's suffrage movement, to bring a solitary murder on the scene. The people of 1910 might be indifferent to the worsening relations between the Liberals and the Lords, but they were eager to accept the tiniest detail in the story of the pursuit and arrest of 'Dr' Crippen. It was hot news indeed; something was happening for the first time in world history. I am no connoisseur of murder, but I fancy that in its grisly annals Crippen and his actual crime would not be given a prominent place; it is what happened afterwards that is important. But we ought to have a few facts before joining the hunt for him.

Crippen was an American, born and educated in Michigan and a graduate of its university. He settled down in North London, where he earned a living as a part-time dentist and as an agent for a patent-medicine company. His wife came from a Polish family called Mackamotzki but sang in third-rate music halls as 'Belle Elmore'. Though she was not without friends, as we shall see, she appears to have been an unpleasant woman and a dominating and extravagant wife. Crippen himself was smallish, short-sighted, a harmless fellow trying to do his best. Most people who knew them both felt sorry for him.

On the night of January 31, 1910, following a party, Crippen gave his wife a dose of hyoscin hydrobromide, from which she died. Panic-stricken and wildly foolish, not behaving at all like a cold-blooded premeditative murderer, the wretched little man carved up his wife's body, burned the bones, and buried the flesh in the cellar. He gave out that his wife had gone to America. He also brought to his house, as secretary, an innocent and affectionate young woman, twenty-odd years younger than he was, called Ethel Le Neve. This encouraged some gossip, and at the same time various friends of 'Belle Elmore' began to be suspicious, having had no news of her from America. Then it appeared, according to Crippen, that she had died there. Suspicion deepened – though no shadow of it touched the genuinely innocent and now loving Miss Le Neve – and, some months after the murder, an Inspector Dew of Scotland Yard called to ask a few questions. Some days later, detectives arrived to begin digging in the cellar, and they found there sufficient evidence to convince them a murder had been committed. But they were working in a deserted house. Hawley Harvey Crippen and Ethel Le Neve had vanished. There was now not only a warrant for their arrest but also a reward for any information that would enable the police to find them. Out came the big headlines: Where were Crippen and Le Neve? Nobody knew.

Dr Crippen

Captain Kendall, master of the Canadian Pacific liner *Montrose*, sailing from Antwerp to Quebec, began to observe two of his passengers,

(left) Crippen's wife who appeared on the music halls as Belle Elmore

(right) Ethel Le Neve dressed as a boy

a Mr Robinson and his son. He had noticed them surreptitiously holding and squeezing hands. During a talk with Mr Robinson, he saw that the man must have made some recent changes in his appearance, shaving off a moustache and discarding the spectacles that had left a mark on his nose. In Antwerp Captain Kendall had bought a copy of the *Continental Daily Mail*, and now he looked at the photographs and descriptions of the missing pair. He arranged for the Robinsons to be seated at his table in the dining saloon. Making a quick search of the Robinsons' cabin when he knew they had gone along to lunch, he discovered that Robinson junior had been using a piece of a woman's bodice as a face-flannel. Seeing more and more of these Robinsons during the next two days, with suspicion hardening into certainty, he ventured to send a wireless message to Liverpool: *Have strong suspicions that Crippen London cellar murderer and accomplice are among saloon passengers . . . Accomplice dressed as boy ; voice manner and build undoubtedly a girl*. Many years later, broadcasting for the BBC in one of Mr Leslie Baily's admirable *Scrapbook* programmes (to which I am indebted), Captain Kendall said, 'I remember Mr Robinson sitting in a deck-chair looking at the wireless aerials and listening to the crackling of our crude spark-transmitter, and remarking to me what a wonderful invention it was'. The wretched little man was in fact admiring the hangman's rope. The same Inspector Dew who had first questioned him was now in the White Star liner, *Laurentic*, a much faster vessel than the *Montrose*. Wireless messages were exchanged, to the effect that the inspector would board the *Montrose* in the River St Lawrence, disguised as a pilot. The actual arrest might be tricky because Captain Kendall knew that Robinson-Crippen was carrying a revolver.

This is how Captain Kendall described the arrest:

> The last night was dreary and anxious, the sound of our foghorn every few minutes adding to the monotony. The hours dragged on as I paced the bridge; now and then I could see Mr. Robinson strolling about the deck. I had invited him to get up early to see the 'pilots' come aboard at Father Point in the River St Lawrence. When they did so they came straight to my cabin. I sent for Mr. Robinson. When he entered I stood with the detective facing the door, holding my revolver inside my coat pocket. As he came in, I said, 'Let me introduce you'.
>
> Mr. Robinson put out his hand, the detective grabbed it, at the same time removing his pilot's cap, and said, 'Good morning, Dr Crippen. Do you know me? I'm Inspector Dew, from Scotland Yard.'
>
> Crippen quivered. Surprise struck him dumb. Then he said, 'Thank God it's over. The suspense has been too great. I couldn't stand it any longer.'

Crippen was tried at the Old Bailey, declared guilty, and was hanged at Pentonville on November 23, thereafter securing a place in Tussaud's 'Chamber of Horrors'. Ethel Le Neve, ably defended by F. E. Smith,

Crippen, with a scarf around his face, is led from the liner *Montrose* by Inspector Dew

A photograph taken by Captain Kendall aboard *Montrose* showing Ethel Le Neve dressed as a boy, and Crippen

was acquitted. (Captain Kendall himself was sure she was entirely innocent, believing from the first that Mrs Crippen had gone to America.) I have no natural empathy with men who dissect their wives' bodies and bury their remains in the cellar, but when I remember poor little Mr Robinson in his deckchair, admiring the new marvel of wireless, I cannot help wishing that Crippen had been able to slip away, to start a new life somewhere with his devoted Ethel. He was fifty, only five feet four inches in height, myopic, anything but handsome, yet Ethel, twenty-seven and five feet five, was ready to run away with him, even though it meant wearing boys' clothes. He must have had something that was not so much meat for the hangman.

The people, who have a sure instinct in these matters, knew they had seats in a gallery five hundred miles long for a new, exciting, entirely original drama: *Trapped by Wireless*! There were Crippen and his mistress, arriving with a smile at the captain's table, holding hands on the boat deck, entirely unaware of the fact that Inspector Dew – and there is irony even in his name – was on his way to arrest them. While they were looking at the menu, several million readers were seeing their names again in the largest type. To attempt an escape by sea was , of course, poor Crippen's last foolish mistake; they would have been far safer in Birmingham or Glasgow or any continental city; but nobody can move away from suspicion in a ship. Moreover, he had forgotten, if he ever knew, what Marconi had done for the world, which was now rapidly shrinking. So we see two hunted creatures, say a fox and a hare, with millions of hounds baying and slavering after them. I can remember the excitement at the time but cannot recall my attitude towards it; probably it was negative because a lively teenage lad has strong interests of his own and is not waiting for the press to wake him up. But if, as I believe, there was a growing taste for public drama, these last Edwardian years were now ready to supply it. We men are given what we want – but sooner or later we have to pay the bill.

Only a few weeks after Crippen was hanged there was more public drama. London seemed to have more than its share of criminal aliens, armed and ruthless. There had already been the Tottenham affair. Two foreigners, after robbing a clerk coming from a bank, had jumped on a tram and put a pistol to the head of the driver to keep the tram moving, had fired at the people running after them, killing a policeman and a boy, and had wounded fourteen people after leaving the tram. Both men died before they could be tried. That was dramatic enough, but on January 3, 1911, something like a battle was fought in London's East End at Stepney.

A week or two before, some criminal aliens – described by the police as 'anarchists' – had shot their way out of a house in Houndsditch, killing three unarmed policemen. Following a 'tip-off', the police raided another house and found there a dead man, weapons and ammunition, some oil paints and a picture signed 'Peter'. An underworld character, wanted by the police, was known in his own circle as 'Peter the Painter'. Shortly afterwards the police learnt that Peter and two members of his gang could be found in a room on the second-floor front of 100, Sidney Street, Stepney. Early in the morning fifty police, armed now, surrounded the house and contrived to bring out the other occupants. They exchanged shots with the three men in the second-floor front, and a detective sergeant was severely wounded.

Winston Churchill, who had recently been appointed Home Secretary, was told on the telephone what was happening. By the middle of the morning, no fewer than 750 police, together with a detachment of the Scots Guards bringing a machine gun, had joined the battle. Wearing a silk hat and a fur coat, Churchill himself arrived, ready to conduct operations as if he were Marlborough facing the army of Louis XIV. Two field-guns were sent for, and there was talk of Royal Engineers coming to mine the house. But just before the field-guns arrived at a gallop it was obvious that the house was on fire. Three men were supposed to have been in that room, but only two charred corpses could be found in the ruins, and neither of them could be identified as 'Peter the Painter'. It was generally believed that he had been there and then had somehow disappeared. When mythology takes over from fact, nobody should object to a little magic.

Winston Churchill, centre, conducting operations at the Sidney Street Siege in 1911

There was some criticism of Churchill with his Scots Guards and field-guns – though it is only fair to add that he had already proved to be a progressive and humane Home Secretary. Largely influenced by Galsworthy's play *Justice*, he had started some prison reform. But the importance of the Sidney Street affair lies in a quite different direction. It heightened the general feeling that there were too many armed foreigners about, that indeed there were too many dubious aliens now in Britain. Every week or two, it seemed, they made an unpleasant appearance in the newspapers. The authorities were being too lenient with these people. If they were not ordinary criminals, they were probably spies. Why didn't the Home Office and its magistrates send them packing? Public opinion was so strong that the Government had to introduce a bill in favour of new expulsion orders. So by 1911 there was xenophobia in the air, and it might be described as a disease more easily caught than checked. A hatred of foreigners or even a general vague suspicion of them does not suggest a people feeling secure and at ease. These later Edwardian years had left Victorian England, with all its proud confidence in itself, a long way behind.

However, at risk of seeming totally inconsequent, before moving on to the really 'serious' issues of the period, let me recall 1910–11 with gratitude for some totally different forms of public entertainment. These years gave us Elgar's violin concerto and 2nd Symphony, Mahler's *Das Lied von der Erde*, Ravel's *Daphnis and Chloe*, Rimsky-Korsakov's *Coq d'Or*, Strauss's *Der Rosenkavalier*, Stravinsky's *Firebird*, and Vaughan Williams's *Sea Symphony* – surely a fine rich haul of musical delight.

4. Bosses and Workers

Even if we ignore the general atmosphere of the time, increasingly militant, we can find several good reasons why relations between employers and employed rapidly deteriorated in 1911, why conflicts between 'bosses' and 'workers' came to be obstinately and bitterly fought. On one side, there was a new and far more aggressive spirit in the larger trade unions. Many of their more energetic and articulate leaders, recognised as such even when they were not nominally in control of their unions, were more or less syndicalists now, though they may not have accepted the whole of the original French doctrine. They saw themselves sooner or later abolishing capitalism. They had no patience with Liberal or even Fabian compromise and gradual reform. They regarded a strike for higher wages not as the older and milder trade union leaders did, a rather desperate move in the game of industrial bargaining, but as an early skirmish in what would be a long and grim campaign. No doubt it is easy at this remove to exaggerate syndicalist influence, yet I think it was these men who formed the hard core, who not only kept the strikes going but also insisted upon strengthening trade unionism by building small weak unions into large powerful blocks. In November, 1910, the Industrial Syndicalist Education League held a conference, at which two hundred delegates agreed that the whole trade union movement should be streamlined to give it more power and punch. Leaders like Tom Mann and A. J. Cook were busy writing pamphlets all to this effect. The men must strike now whenever the situation demanded action. The host of small unions, too often led by sleepy compromisers who had long accepted the capitalist system, must disappear. Whole industries must be represented, on the workers' side, by new and formidably large organisations, capable at any time of bringing such industries to a standstill.

Many employers and managers were prepared to offer a very stiff resistance to any new demands from their work people. So far as they were Tories – and most of them were – they disliked everything that was happening. There was, for example, the Liberal Government's feud with the Lords. There was all this talk about a Minimum Wage. There were Lloyd George's Unemployment Benefit and Health Insurance schemes. (Out of the ninepence per week that this insurance would cost, the employer would pay twopence and the employee twopence. The employer had to affix stamps on an employee's card. As employees included domestic servants, there were screams of rage and horror from Tory ladies about 'stamp licking' and I can remember they held large protest meetings, backed by the Tory press.) It is ironical that while Lloyd George was regarded by these people as a red revolutionary, in the eyes of Labour extremists he was seen as a cunning lackey of the capitalists, an adroit confidence-trick man, fooling the more innocent workers. This was a time running to extremes. The 'diehard' employers and managers felt that if they gave way to any demand for a shilling or two more in the weekly wage packet they would be encouraging revolution itself, the very ground opening under their feet. It was bad enough having the Liberals carrying their dangerous resolutions in the House – and by agreeing to pay members of it £400 a year, tempting any seedy 'agitator' to try for a seat in Parliament – but if militant trade unionism were not checked then industry, and finally the country, would be ruined. In adopting this attitude they were strongly, and not always scrupulously, supported by at least nine-tenths of the daily press. So again we can say that the fight was on.

There was a third element in this struggle. It was not concerned with syndicalism and capitalism, with Liberal or Tory points of view. It belonged to the workers themselves and their wives and families. Prices were rising but not wages. Too many men were being asked by their wives how they could expect a family to be decently fed, clothed, housed and warmed on, say, twenty-five shillings a week. Never mind politics – what about the grocer's and butcher's bills? So the women, after badgering and taunting their men, mostly stood behind them when they agreed to go on strike. I think we have to see behind these new industrial conflicts, now both sharper and more obdurate, many thousands of angry women, tired of telling their children they couldn't have something they ought to have.

Unofficial or 'wildcat' strikes, in which workmen take action without instructions from their union, are still common enough, but lockouts, when men are barred from working until some agreement has been reached, are now very rare, except on a very small scale. The lockout always suggests a tough belligerent management, believing itself to be in a strong position. In the autumn of 1910 shipyard managers locked out all members of the Boilermakers Society. The Master Cotton Spinners, a federation of employers, locked out over 100,000 work-people because of one local dispute. In both these cases a compromise was soon reached. But now it was the men's turn. There had been continual trouble and some unofficial strikes in the South Wales mining industry, and by January, 1911, the Miners' Federation of Great Britain prepared to take action in favour of a minimum wage. But before the miners could come out the union of sailors and firemen called for a strike and soon every port in the country was involved. When the shipowners brought in blacklegs (that is, non-union men whose labour would break the strike), carters and other men employed in or around the docks came out to join the sailors and firemen, who could then successfully demand better wages. This fired the dockers, who had recently become members of a new, large amalgamated union, the Transport Workers' Federation, which some of the best-known militant union men and syndicalists, men like Tom Mann and Ben Tillett, had been able to create. The Federation soon showed what it could do.

Out came the stevedores and carters in Manchester. This was followed by an even bigger strike, including railway men, in Liverpool, bringing everything to a standstill. Some of the men's demands had to be accepted, but as soon as one dispute ended another flared up. After the huge mass of workers at the Port of London had presented an ultimatum to the Employers' Association and had been given no satisfaction, the docks were deserted; the government had to send in 25,000 troops, to keep essential supplies moving. Dock workers, railway men, miners, they were now all furiously discontented, and if their union officials seemed too timid, they swept them aside. The Liberal Government, caught between angry workers and equally angry employers and managements, ran around trying to patch up truces, hurriedly improvising conciliation boards and special Commissions. Moreover, this was now the hot and temper-trying summer of 1911. There were more and more scenes of violence; so much serious street-fighting in places like Manchester and Liverpool that extra police from

(opposite) A French advertisement for Humber cycles of about 1906

La Première Marque
du Monde
Thor
The BEESTON
HUMBER
H. PETIT & Cie – Concessionnaires pour la France – 23. Avue des Champs-Elysées – PARIS

Contains
everything necessary
for producing a fine gloss
and NOTHING should
be added

ROBIN
THE New
Starch

MADE BY
Reckitt & Sons Ltd
HULL
& LONDON.
Manufacturers of the
Celebrated Paris Blue.

London and even the military from neighbouring garrisons were called in. At Liverpool two men were shot dead and two hundred injured. At Llanelly, South Wales, where there was bitter railway trouble, two men were shot, four others killed, when a petrol tank exploded. Then in the middle of August three railway unions, two of skilled men, the other of unskilled, combined to declare a general railway strike. It lasted only two or three days, and though it did compel the promise of an immediate Special Commission it was really a failure. These railway unions were not yet sufficiently strong and well organised. But the lesson had been learnt. Membership of the unions went up rapidly, and from the amalgamation of these three there rose, towering and formidable, the National Union of Railwaymen.

From now on we can say that behind the various disputes about piece rates, minimum wages, hours, conditions, there was a continual struggle between the men who were trying to amalgamate and strengthen the unions to make any major quarrel a national issue, and managements that did their best, though they might be members of an employers' federation themselves, not to widen each issue but to keep it on a local basis. There was really a secret war between the syndicalist idea and 'diehard' capitalism (with the Liberal Government running around in neutral territory.) In the later weeks of 1911 there had been various aggressive unofficial strikes among the South Wales miners and then early in 1912 the Miners' Federation officially demanded a national minimum wage and announced its intention to call a strike if necessary. Alarmed, the Government proposed a scheme for district negotiations to give colliery workers 'a reasonable minimum wage'. Various coal-owners both in South Wales and Scotland would have none of it. This brought about the largest strike the country had known so far, about a million men coming out. The Board of Trade was compelled to compromise with them. Not long afterwards there was an unusually bitter dispute at the London docks. It has a place in Cole and Postgate's lengthy social history, *The Common People*, as follows –

> The newly formed Port of London Authority had as chairman the grocer Hudson Kearley, who had been ennobled as Lord Davenport, who deeply resented not finding among the dockers the submissiveness that he expected from his unfortunate shop-assistants. But his own venom, though Labour propagandists fixed upon it, was merely characteristic of his type and indeed of a vast number of company directors. Far more than their financial loss, they resented the ending of their autocracy; it was indiscipline, the self-assertion of those born to be subordinate, that provoked their most implacable resentment. A chance dispute gave the dock authorities their opportunity in the summer of 1912; ignoring the proposals of the Government as well as the Transport Workers' Federation, Lord Davenport announced their intention of refusing to take part in any joint body or recognize the Federation. The struggle was bitter; it was on this occasion that Ben Tillet on Tower Hill led the workers in the

Two advertisement cards datable about 1905

(opposite, above) Harold Gilman's house at Letchworth Garden City, Hertfordshire, 1912, by Spencer Gore

(opposite, below) Letchworth, the Road, 1912, by Spencer Gore

(below) Letchworth Station (showing early commuters), 1911, by Spencer Gore

famous prayer: 'God strike Lord Davenport dead.' The resentment of the old-fashioned Union leaders against the Syndicalists now came into the open; J. H. Thomas, a powerful railwaymen's leader, for the first time intervened against fellow-unionists during a strike, by publicly attacking and 'deprecating' the methods of the Federation. The Federation, over-estimating its power and forgetting it was a Federation and not a Union, called a national provincial strike in support of London. It was not obeyed, and in August the strike ended in defeat.

But in the end these transport workers would find themselves members of the Transport and General Workers' Union, the largest and most powerful in the country.

If I now stretch my chronology a little, it is because in 1913 there occurred certain events of historical importance. They began in Dublin, where wages and working conditions were even worse than they were in England. James Larkin, a fierce orator and natural leader, had created an Irish Transport Workers' Union. He found a redoutable ally in James Connolly, who had spent some time in America with the exceedingly militant I. W. W. (The Industrial Workers of the World, a revolutionary organisation strongest on the Pacific seaboards, never having any influence in Britain.) Together they began making 'direct action' moves, bringing men out on strike without preliminary warnings,

A London open-top bus of about 1910

challenging the employers at every turn. By the summer of 1913 the employers had had enough; they made war on the Transport Workers' Union by dismissing its members; Larkin called a general strike; the employers decided on a general lockout. Hoping for sympathetic strikes and an immediate 'blacking' (a refusal to handle) of goods for Ireland, Larkin came over to appeal to English trade union leaders, who were too cautious to take action on any large scale. Their more militant members, however, were entirely in favour of supporting Larkin, and when, in the autumn, he was sentenced in Dublin to seven months' imprisonment for 'using seditious language', there was a storm of protest, both in Parliament and throughout the country. Not only the trade unions but also the Co-operative Societies, which had shops all over the country by this time, sent ships loaded with food for the Irish strikers and their families. It is at this point that I, aged nineteen, make a brief and exceedingly modest appearance on this huge bewildering scene. A close friend, older than I was and a boldly-progressive and enterprising fellow, asked me to join him in assisting and entertaining a group of Irish players who were touring the country to raise money for Jim Larkin. And so I did, but I must confess I can no longer conjure up a single one of their faces.

If syndicalism was making many new converts I for one never met them nor heard of them. But I would agree that during these months, 'the working class generally was more class conscious than at any time since the collapse of the Chartist Movement'. British trade unions had stretched out a long arm to the Irish strikers: working-class sympathy could cross the sea. But there was clearly still a need for a bigger and more powerful organisation; so in January, 1914, it was announced that the three largest and most effective unions – the miners, transport workers, the railwaymen – had reached agreements, actually rather fine-drawn, in what was called 'The Triple Alliance'. Such a combination had only to call a strike – though in fact it never did – and it would tie up the whole country. There was a feeling in the air, just as there was vague war talk in the air, that highly organised workers' movements could act decisively in international affairs. After all, Germany had an enormous socialist party. Moreover, the Basle Resolution of the Second International, in 1910, had made itself quite clear:

> If war threatens to break out, it is the duty of the working classes and their parliamentary representatives in the countries involved, supported by the co-ordinating activity of the International Socialist Bureau, to exert every effort in order to prevent the outbreak of war by the means they consider most effective which naturally vary according to the sharpening of the class struggle and the sharpening of the general political situation ....
>
> In case war should break out anyway, it is their duty to intervene in favour of its speedy termination and with all their powers to utilize the economic and political crisis created by the war to arouse the people and thereby to hasten the downfall of capitalist class rule . . .

But however well-meaning such language might be, it is a long way from being as short and sharp as a mobilisation order and cannot compete with a trumpet call. Moreover, all but the most fanatical class-struggle men had been having so many other things to read about and argue about: for instance, the extraordinary behaviour of those women who were demanding the vote.

5. Suffragettes

The pre-Edwardian history of the general feminist movement, with which women's suffrage was intimately connected, can be found in the earliest chapters of Mr Roger Fulford's *Votes for Women*, itself a first-class account of these later suffragette years. (I make haste to acknowledge my debt to it and to Mr Fulford.) I ought to add here that the members of the original National Union of Women's Suffrage Societies were known as *suffragists*; they held meetings and issued propaganda and kept well within the law. It was the members of the Women's Social and Political Union who became increasingly militant and defiant, broke the law, damaged public property, and it is they who were called *suffragettes*. (I shall refer to this organisation as the WSPU.) Many of the more important members had been social workers; they were desperately aware of feminine 'sweated labour' and the appalling conditions in which women and girls worked; and they believed that only female suffrage would bring about the urgently necessary sweeping reforms. But as the campaign continued and came to be more and more frantically defiant, there was a growing tendency to concentrate on the vote and see it as an end in itself. While a number of distinguished public men, mostly radicals or socialists, were in complete sympathy with the suffragettes, masculine opinion in general increasingly hardened against them. There was soon a lot of ugly caricaturing, jeering, name-calling, as if unconscious depths of masculine sadism were being disturbed. Even an avowed feminist like Wells could declare afterwards that too many of the suffragettes were simply 'man-haters'. This type could be found in their ranks but rarely among their leaders, who were or had been happily married or if single were not sexually resentful. And women like Mrs Despard or Mrs Pankhurst would have been regarded as being strikingly handsome in any company.

One familiar argument against women entering politics was that they were so naturally individualistic that they would find it impossible to

A scene from *Press Cuttings*, a play written by Bernard Shaw for the London Society of Women's Suffrage, banned by the Lord Chamberlain but privately produced at the Royal Court in 1909

Mrs Pankhurst

(right) A suffragette meeting including *(left to right)*: Mrs Drummond, Christabel Pankhurst, two unknown supporters, Mrs Pankhurst and Mrs Despard

(below) A suffragette photographed selling *Votes for Women* posters

cooperate with one another and organise themselves properly. (It is my experience with women on committees that they are more practical and sensible and less time-wasting and touchy than the men.) The WSPU as it moved into action soon made this argument look silly. The suffragettes were superbly organised and disciplined, like a guerilla force constantly taking its enemies by surprise. This, together with their extraordinary courage, impossible to overpraise, was their strength. Their weakness, to my mind – and I write as a sympathiser – was their political naivety. They could not or would not understand how the wheels went round in Westminster. After so many candidates had expressed their sympathy, the Liberal victory in 1906 had raised their hopes and when nothing happened they came to believe, in their disappointment, that the Liberal Government was deliberately deceiving them, out of contempt for their cause. After all, it had only to pass a measure, granting them even a limited suffrage, and all would be well. But they over-simplified the issue. The Government felt that it had enough on its hands without introducing a measure that might divide even the Cabinet itself. Moreover, there was something else, a deep doubt lurking in the background. (It had haunted Liberal politicians for many years.) Female suffrage would bring in votes from the grateful suffragettes and their progressive friends, even though many of the latter would vote Labour and not Liberal. But women in general were notoriously conservative in their sympathies, so their votes would be a huge gift to the Tories. (As events, much later, proved.) But most Tory politicians were strongly anti-feminist and wanted to keep women out of politics. So did most working men. The Suffragettes, like the suffragists, were largely recruited from the educated middle class.

Disappointed and increasingly angry, the WSPU energetically pursued two policies that it was often able to combine. By making demonstrations where they were not allowed, then defying the police, its members invited arrest, and then when magistrates told them they they must either pay a fine or go to prison, they chose to go to prison. (Not always in the First Division, which was easier and was usual for political prisoners, but sometimes in the Second Division, where they had to wear prison clothes and suffer various indignities. There were many public protests against this.) These tactics brought them what they wanted, plenty of publicity, some of it sympathetic, much of it antagonistic. The second and more dubious policy was to harass the Government's chief ministers, picketing their houses and constantly interrupting their most important public meetings. It would have been cleverer, I feel, to have ruined the Opposition meetings: this would have brought them as much publicity and would not have made the Liberal leaders harden their hearts. Though occasionally offering smooth words, Asquith at this time never really wanted women to have the vote; whereas Lloyd George and Winston Churchill, who came under attack most often, began by being sympathetic but inevitably resented these dangerous tactics. In his book on Lloyd George, his eldest son writes:

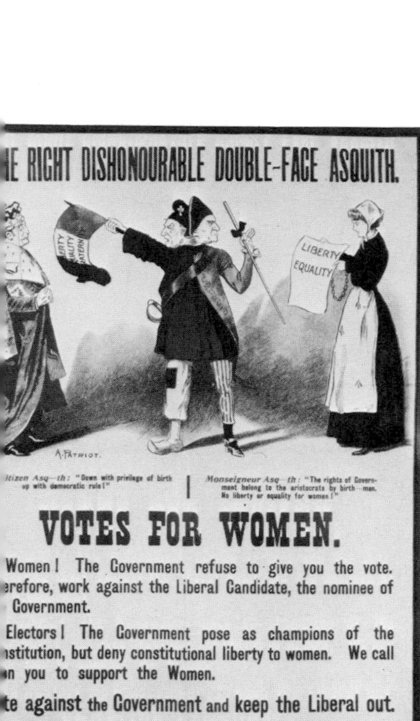

A suffragette poster designed to discredit Asquith

> . . . the militant Suffragettes expressed their hysteria by planting a bomb in our home, which wrecked four rooms. Fortunately, no one was in at the time, and maybe the women who planted it had planned it that way, blowing up almost half the furniture merely as a warning. Mrs Pankhurst took responsibility for this crass piece of criminality. She was tried at the Old Bailey, convicted and sentenced to three years' penal servitude. She immediately went on hunger strike. 'What an extraordinary mixture of idealism and lunacy!' father said, when he heard of the sentence. 'Hasn't she the sense to see that the very worst way of campaigning for the franchise is to try to intimidate or blackmail a man into giving her what he would gladly give her otherwise?' He felt sorry for her.
>
> One of the women threw a steel spike through the window of father's cab. It missed his eye by a fraction and pierced his cheek. 'Now, I simply can't do anything for them at present,' he fumed in exasperation. 'Why on earth don't they try a normal piece of feminine blandishment?' He grinned through his wounded face, and I'm sure he was picturing a recruitment of accomplished Mata Haris to undermine his resistance. I could have told them this would have been a far more potent technique of campaigning . . .

The first part of the suffragettes' campaign, chiefly directed against cabinet ministers and the House of Commons itself, reached a climax in 1909 and then almost came to an end. In one evening alone, when they laid siege to the House of Commons and hurled stones through scores of windows, over a hundred women were arrested. Such battles with the police were watched by great crowds, which rarely took sides but looked on as at a show. More impressive to some more sensitive spec-

Suffragette

(opposite, above left) Mrs Despard

(opposite, above centre) Mary E. Gawthorpe

(opposite, above right) Sylvia Pankhurst

(opposite, below left) Lady Constance Lytton

(opposite, below right) Christabel Pankhurst

(below) Gladice Keevil

tators were the large groups of the non-militant suffragists, who were peacefully picketing Parliament, while it was still sitting late at night: women of all ages and classes who waited patiently hour after hour after hour, often drenched with rain. The militants won most sympathy when the prison authorities tried to break their hunger strikes (refusing to accept food) by forcibly feeding them. Nurses and wardresses held the women down while prison doctors forced tubes into their mouths – if necessary through the nostrils – compelling them to accept various nourishing liquids. The practice was not new; it had been used for years in lunatic asylums; but now its victims were not raging maniacs but intelligent and hypersensitive women, often already weakened by their fasting. It was more disgusting than dangerous, but it raised such an outcry that during the next campaign the authorities had to adopt different tactics, as we shall see.

There was a lull in 1910 chiefly because the new Liberal Government brought in a Conciliation Bill, which on its second reading divided the House in an unexpected fashion. It was not surprising that F. E. Smith made a brilliant and unscrupulous speech against it. But even Hilaire Belloc, then a Liberal member, disposed of the argument that women should have the vote because they were intelligent enough to write books: 'I confess it turned me cold. There is perhaps nothing an educated man or woman can do which requires less intelligence than the writing of books'. On the other hand, Lord Hugh Cecil mocked Smith's argument based on the superior physique of the male: when he went to vote, he said, 'I am not conscious of performing a function either difficult or sensational or particularly masculine . . . It is a serenely tranquil, an austerely refined, and from beginning to end a thoroughly lady-like operation'. Then, to the surprise and growing fury of the suffragettes, both Lloyd George and Churchill denounced the Bill; and Asquith, in a closing speech, told the women in effect that their militant methods sentenced their cause to death

The Bill was actually passed by a majority, but a larger majority agreed that it should be referred to a Committee of the whole House, which really meant it should be sent into oblivion. Once again, after a promising start, the women's demand had been shuffled away. On a certain 'Black Friday' in November, 1910, the women demonstrating in or near Parliament Square were not quietly arrested but very roughly handled by the police, who treated educated middle-aged women and frail elderly ladies as if they were so many drunken viragoes. There were a lot of louts in the jeering crowd who had their fun too. The long-range effect of this 'Black Friday' was very considerable, though the women still had hopes of the new Liberal Government, returned in December. During the coronation rejoicings in the summer of 1911 they successfully organised a vast and peaceable procession of sympathisers. But the militants decided that they needed more publicity, and that only the most startling tactics would give them this publicity, overlooking the fact, as some more recent movements have done since, that newspaper headlines may do far more harm than good to any cause. These fanatically devoted women, bringing tremendous courage out of despair, were ready to embrace suffering. Perhaps through suffering they could reach the mass of the people. And these people would soon be aware of them, for they would no longer be content to interrupt meetings, harass cabinet ministers, try to force their way into the House of Commons: they would now declare war on the male-dominated community itself. Refused the vote that could give them some share in shaping the laws, they would now behave like outlaws. It was not a sensible decision; there was hysteria in it as well as devotion and courage; but it was one very much in the spirit of these last Edwardian years, hurrying and febrile and yet strangely fatalistic.

The new campaign began in March, 1912, when a well-organised group of suffragettes brought out hidden hammers and smashed shop windows in Piccadilly Circus, in Regent and Oxford Streets. Mrs Pankhurst and two friends threw stones, rather wildly, in Downing Street. There was also some organised stone-throwing in Kensington. Over two hundred women, including the composer Ethel Smyth, were arrested and sent to prison, where they proceeded to create as much disturbance as they could. Mrs Pankhurst, the acknowledged leader of the militants, publicly declared, while still out of prison, that property should now be attacked, adding, while actually in the dock, that she was convinced public opinion was with them. Her daughter, Christabel, fled to Paris but contrived to act as commander of the campaign. The other daughter Sylvia, the most politically-minded of the family, settled in the East End and built up a following there. A Franchise Bill, very complicated because it dealt with men still disenfranchised as well as with women, was being debated in the House; but it got lost in a maze of procedures, and the militant women, feeling they had been duped again, rose in their fury. (Two of the most valuable members of the movement, the husband-and-wife Pethick-Lawrences, now significantly withdrew from further active participation in it.) Not only in London but in various parts of the provinces flaming rags were dropped in letter boxes; racehorse grandstands and houses (usually empty) were set on fire; bombs were planted (the Lloyd George quotation belongs to this period); visiting politicians were attacked with horse whips; golf greens were ruined with acid; one of the Kew Gardens houses was destroyed; and even royalty was not spared for there were threatening demonstrations both at Balmoral and Buckingham Palace. One enterprising young woman fired a cannon captured in the Crimean War. Two small railway stations went up in flames. A bomb was found even under the Bishop's throne in St Paul's. Things were thrown in magistrates' courts, and the women's prisons were a bedlam. Though careful to avoid loss of life, the militants were now waging war.

It was not, in spite of much opinion to the contrary, a sex war, Many

(opposite) A poster showing a suffragette being forcibly fed, issued as an election poster by the militant suffragettes

TORTURING WOMEN IN PRISON
Votes for Women
PUBLISHED BY THE NATIONAL WOMEN'S SOCIAL AND POLITICAL UNION 4 CLEMENTS INN STRAND W.C. & PRINTED BY DAVID ALLEN & SONS L? 180 FLEET ST E.C.
VOTE AGAINST THE GOVERNMENT

intelligent men, both inside and outside the House of Commons, fully sympathised with the suffragettes. On the other hand, many of their own sex raged furiously against them. So Lady Bathurst, whose father owned the rigidly Tory *Morning Post*, could announce in the press: 'When a suffragette has been convicted, first have her well birched (by women), then shave off her hair, and finally deport her to New Zealand or Australia.' Perhaps even worse than this was an extraordinary long letter – it took up three columns of *The Times* – from a well-known London physician, Sir Almoth Wright. He dismissed militancy as a king of sex-lunacy all too common among middle-aged women, and went on at length to infuriate any intelligent woman by describing her as a passive appendage to man – 'there are no good women, but only women who have lived under the influence of good men' was one of his typical insights.

Meanwhile, Sir Almoth's superior beings had to devise some new method of coping with the persistent hunger strikes of the women prisoners. Forcible feeding, still going on, was condemned by moderate opinion, not represented by the Lady Bathursts, throughout the country. Churchill had now been transferred to the Admiralty, and Reginald McKenna had left it for the Home Office. McKenna, as Home Secretary, dodged forcible feeding by his Prisoners (Temporary Discharge for Ill-Health) Act, soon known everywhere as the 'Cat and Mouse Act'. Instead of being forcibly fed, the women on hunger strikes were let out of prison, but were not really free because they could be brought back at any time. But of course they were not always to be found. They went 'on the run'. They would be boarded and lodged for a few days, all in secrecy, by a chain of sympathisers who passed them on; it was rather like the famous 'underground railroad' that existed before the American Civil War to enable slaves to escape from the South to the North. I can distinctly recall that various people I knew – the same sort of people who helped Jim Larkin's Irish players – were hiding then passing on to fellow sympathisers some suffragettes wanted by the police. They were able to make use of fairly remote moorland cottages they owned or rented; but as I could offer neither accommodation nor transport I took no direct part myself, so I never really knew exactly how this hiding-and-passing-on worked. There must have been quite an elaborate organisation behind it, but then, as as I said earlier, while the extreme militants may have been responsible for some wild antics, they proved that women knew how to plan and were capable of giving and receiving efficient orders.

However, I suspect that Emily Wilding Davison had always been something of 'a loner'. She belonged to a Northumberland family and had achieved a first-class honours degree at Oxford. She was a burning enthusiast in more senses than one, for she was among the first of the letter-box arsonists, and she had been in and out of prisons several times. She was at liberty on June 4, 1913, Derby Day, and made her

The Brown Veil (Mrs Harrington Mann), 1905, by Sir William Nicholson

VOTES FOR WOMEN
COME
TO THE
HOUSE OF
COMMONS
ON OCT 13TH
AT 7.30 PM

(opposite, above) Christabel Pankhurst speaking in Trafalgar Square

(opposite, below left) A suffragette contribution to a Coronation Procession of 1911

(opposite, below right) Mrs Pankhurst being arrested by Inspector Rolf outside Buckingham Palace on May 21, 1914

(right) A procession which formed part of the Suffragette Summer Festival, 1913

(below) Mrs Pethick-Lawrence speaking in Trafalgar Square in 1908

way to the racecourse at Epsom, with the suffragette colours sewn inside her coat, dodged the police along the rails and threw herself in front of the galloping horses. By a pure coincidence it was the King's horse and jockey she brought down, slightly injuring the jockey but sustaining terrible injuries to herself. A few days later, after an operation, she died. On Saturday, June 14, her body was taken from Victoria Station to King's Cross (the station for Northumberland), and the whole of the suffrage movement staged an immense funeral procession, with thousands of women marching in groups, each dressed differently to display the suffragette colours, followed by an impressive show of women doctors and graduates. Banners with heroic inscriptions were carried, leaflets were distributed. The chief mourner should have been Mrs Pankhurst, but just as she was about to enter her carriage, a frail figure in deepest black, she was arrested under the 'Cat and Mouse Act', so immediately behind the hearse there could be seen her empty carriage. There was no counter-demonstration from the great crowd that watched the procession; this was no time for jeering and booing; but it is doubtful if many spectators were converted to the cause. Emily Davison had been known to declare that a life ought to be sacrificed for it. Her death brought at the time a graver tone into the newspaper references to the

Emily Davison having thrown herself under the King's Derby horse *Anmer* on June 4, 1913

suffragettes, but there was no fundamental change. As we shall see, defiant militancy, inspiring outrageous acts, continued throughout the next twelve months, almost to the declaration of war; but the lonely melancholy peak of determined martyrdom had been left behind. It belonged to 1913, the last whole Edwardian year. When 1914 turned its terrible corner, the whole women's suffrage movement, whether militant or constitutional, was forgotten. Afterwards, in a world that was new and yet filled with ruins, the vote that had been so bitterly fought for, that sent Emily Davison hurrying to her death, was granted without a struggle.

6. The 'Titanic'

It was not some newly rebellious women, it was the ancient hubristic folly of men, that gave 1912 its most appalling disaster. This was the loss of the *Titanic*, the largest and most luxurious liner in the world, which sank on her maiden voyage in the early morning of April 15 and drowned – or killed by shock or exhaustion in the icy water – about 1500 persons. (It is part of the strange story that nothing like an exact figure was ever established.) Even apart from official enquiries and law cases, many attempts have been made to describe in detail this disaster, to find the truth among so much rumour and legend, to fit together at least some large sections of the giant jigsaw; and I invite curious readers to consult the two most recent books on this subject, *A Night to Remember*, by Walter Lord, and *The Maiden Voyage*, by Geoffrey Marcus. Why, it might be asked, should two writers in our day, so long after the event, involve themselves in laborious research to tell the story all over again? The answer is that it is a curiously fascinating story. However, all I can do here is to set down the more important facts, making my own comment on them as we go along. Both facts and comment are necessary here because the *Titanic* tragedy will help us to understand these last Edwardian years.

The White Star Line was in constant sharp competition with the Cunard Line, which from 1907 to 1910 was ahead because its *Mauretania* and *Lusitania* were both the fastest and largest (31,000 tons) on the Atlantic run. The White Star directors, whose chairman was Bruce Ismay, a shrewd autocratic type, decided on a bold new programme of shipbuilding, financed by an American combine under Pierpont Morgan. Three liners larger and far more luxurious than the Cunarders were to be built. The first of these was the *Olympic*, which was an immediate success. Indeed, her only fault was that she had not sufficient first-class accommodation to satisfy the demand of wealthy American tourists, for whom she was chiefly intended. The second of these

"All the News That's Fit to Print."

The New York Times.

THE WEATHER.

NEW YORK, TUESDAY, APRIL 16, 1912—TWENTY-FOUR PAGES, ONE CENT

TITANIC SINKS FOUR HOURS AFTER HITTING ICEBERG; 866 RESCUED BY CARPATHIA, PROBABLY 1250 PERISH; ISMAY SAFE, MRS. ASTOR MAYBE, NOTED NAMES MISSING

Col. Astor and Bride, Isidor Straus and Wife, and Maj. Butt Aboard.

"RULE OF SEA" FOLLOWED

Women and Children Put Over in Lifeboats and Are Supposed to be Safe on Carpathia.

PICKED UP AFTER 8 HOURS

Vincent Astor Calls at White Star Office for News of His Father and Leaves Weeping.

FRANKLIN HOPEFUL ALL DAY

Manager of the Line Insisted Titanic Was Unsinkable Even After She Had Gone Down.

HEAD OF THE LINE ABOARD

The Lost Titanic Being Towed Out of Belfast Harbor.

Biggest Liner Plunges to the Bottom at 2:20 A. M.

RESCUERS THERE TOO LATE

Except to Pick Up the Few Hundreds Who Took to the Lifeboats.

WOMEN AND CHILDREN FIRST

Cunarder Carpathia Rushing to New York with the Survivors.

SEA SEARCH FOR OTHERS

The California Stands By on Chance of Picking Up Other Boats or Rafts.

OLYMPIC SENDS THE NEWS

Only Ship to Flash Wireless Messages to Shore After the Disaster

LATER REPORT SAVES 866.

The front page of the New York Times, April 16, 1912

'mammoth steamers' was launched at Belfast, Harland & Wolff being the builders, in May 1911. At 46,328 tons she was rather larger than the *Olympic*, had more first-class accommodation, including elaborate suites for the millionaires, and was designed, decorated, furnished, to be far more luxurious – indeed, she was like a floating gigantic *hotel-de-luxe*, a wonder of the world. Such a marvel needed an impressive name. Having pleased the gods with *Olympic*, the White Star had apparently decided to defy them and all auguries – with *Titanic*.

This ill-fated ship was built, finished, sent out to sea, in a bad atmosphere. No fingers were being crossed, no wood being touched – or 'knocked on' as Americans prefer to say. All was mutual congratulation, was brag and boastfulness, with an admiring and almost sycophantic press. What about the poor Germans now, still trying to catch up? How the 'unsinkable' legend began – to cast a fatal spell – I do not know. It is as if the sheer size of the *Titanic* hypnotised everybody. She was not in fact exceptionally strongly built and well-protected. She did not have the 'double skin' that the more recent Cunarders had, and probably an 'inner skin' would have saved her. It is true she had sixteen watertight compartments and could have kept afloat on the unlikely chance of two of them being holed, but not all of them went high enough and they were not strictly watertight, as events proved. A serious risk had been taken here, to provide extra passenger accommodation. But because she was such 'a beautiful, wonderful ship', she had to be unsinkable too. So one of her crew could say to a worried woman passenger, 'Lady, God himself couldn't sink this ship'. Such mounting *hubris* ought to have given some people the creeps.

It was a bad atmosphere too because the American super-rich of the time were considerably involved both as financial backers and prospective passengers. The *Titanic* carried second-class passengers, and down below a large number of the usual emigrants in the third-class, who, to give the White Star Line its due, were better accommodated and fed than they had been in other liners. But what made the *Titanic* such a marvel was what it could offer wealthy first-class travellers – the luxurious private suites, the swimming pool, the squash rackets court, the gymnasium, the Turkish Bath, the children's playroom, the Café Parisien. The ship stopped being a ship; it was another and better Ritz; it was a resort-de-luxe that moved magically from Southampton to New York. How absurd then to count those funny little boats along the upper deck! And of course Captain E. J. Smith, a sweet old bearded character, and famous too, was quite right not to bother about any boat-drill nonsense! Poor Smith, who went down with his ship, was a fine seaman of long experience; but now he began to live in this atmosphere in which the American super-rich existed all the time. They had so much money and knew so well what could be done with it that they

Titanic survivors photographed in a lifeboat

ceased to believe anything even unpleasant could happen to them – sheer disaster was unthinkable. So at noon on April 10, 1912, off they went and after a near-collision getting out of Southampton Dock (one passenger, considering this ill-omened, left the ship at Cherbourg) all was lovely smooth sailing, with everybody very gay. There were dinner parties in the first-class saloon or in private suites, supper parties in the Café Parisien, and much talk of records being broken and bets among the men on the ship's run. The White Star tycoon himself, the handsome if rather haughty Bruce Ismay, was one of the passengers, and could be seen with millionaires like John Jacob Astor and Ben Guggenheim or addressing a few remarks to a deferential Captain Smith. It was all really rather thrilling.

On April 11 the *Titanic* called at Queenstown for extra passengers and mail and then began her Atlantic crossing, carrying 1316 passengers and 891 crew. On the 14th the temperature dropped all day and there were wireless messages from other ships reporting ice ahead. The icebergs seemed to be drifting further south than was usual. The giant ship did not reduce her speed but went blinding on, all out at about 24 knots. At 11.40 p.m. there was a grinding sound from far below and she shuddered a little, but people on the upper decks felt no alarm. The ship had in fact struck an underwater projection of an iceberg that had ripped a 300-foot gash in her side and had opened one watertight compartment after another. The mocked and vengeful sea came pouring in, but the pumps were working hard, the remaining watertight compartments were not yet flooded, and the ship was so big, she was still comfortably afloat. Perhaps being 'unsinkable' she would never sink. But she soon began to list, and gradually her head went down and the water reached deck after deck. At 2.20 a.m. the *Titanic* vanished for ever. We have eye-witness accounts, from men watching in the lifeboats, of her final terrifying moments. As her head or bow went down, her stern rose higher and higher; she suddenly showed no more lights; the great boilers burst with a terrible roar; for a few moments she was a colossal dark mass standing on end; then down and down she went. The lifeboats had kept well away, to avoid the suction of the sinking. But the night was clear, the sea dead calm, and those in the boats could catch glimpses of the hundreds who were struggling among the wreckage, and, what was worse, they could hear across the water the shrieks and screams and agonised cries. The scene was so appalling that many survivors found it unbearable even in memory and were so severely affected by it that it ruined their health. Not 'a night to remember' for these people, whose dreams could so easily turn into nightmares, but certainly one that a great many other people, in fact whole communities, would do well not to forget.

But now, obviously, a question demands to be answered. What happened between 11.40, when the *Titanic* struck the iceberg, and 2.20 a.m. when she finally sank? What became of those two good hours

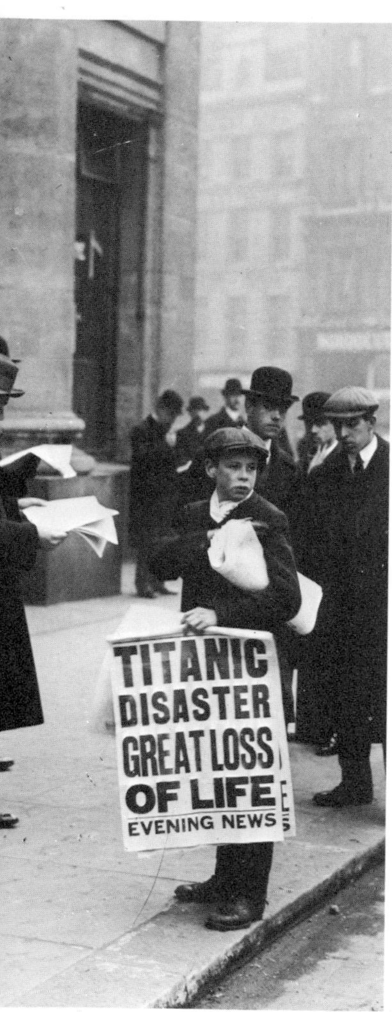

Paper boy, April 1912

when all the lifeboats could have been properly filled, with women and children plus a seaman or two for each boat, and rafts might have been improvised to take a fair number of those left behind? There was no panic, which after all, happens quickly. Instead, there was a slow-motion muddle, a kind of dreamy chaos. It was as if a fatal paralysis of the will had overcome both passengers and crew. (Could it be a sign of the times, ending in August 1914?) Or as if too many of them were still sunk too deep in the legend of the unsinkable *Titanic*. The first boat was lowered at 12.45 a.m.; the last, a collapsible, as late as 2.05 a.m.; and some of the boats even then went away half-empty. We must remember there had been no boat drill, and this was a huge ship as new and bewildering to the crew as it was to the passengers. Even so, there was a curious air of lethargy, indecision, downright fatalism, that night: it is the strangest part of a very strange story. The few persons who were energetic and decisive stood out like a young Napoleon billetted in a convalescent home: so a certain Mrs Brown, an American, was quite famous afterwards. Out of the hundreds of anecdotes, some true, some of them wild nonsense, spawned by the wreck, I will choose only one undoubtedly true, to bring a blush to any anti-semitic cheek. Mr and Mrs Isador Straus were a rich elderly Jewish couple – he was head of Macy's, the big New York store – and Mrs Straus would not leave her husband, and Mr Straus would not take a place in a boat before other women, and they went down with the ship together. Incidentally, while it is true that the band went on playing almost to the last, it was not playing *Nearer my God to Thee*.

Meanwhile, in the midst of this strangely calm confusion, Captain Smith and his officers must have been hoping for help to be on its way. They were sending out SOS wireless messages from 12.15 a.m. onwards, and firing distress rockets between 12.45 and 1.40. These rockets were actually seen by the *Californian*, a British ship that was lying idle because of the ice, only about ten miles away. She never moved. Her single wireless operator had turned in for the night, and so had her skipper, Captain Lord, who would not allow himself to believe the rockets his men had seen were coming from the *Titanic*, probably hiding even from himself his disinclination to take his ship through the ice. There is no doubt that if the *Californian* had got under way promptly she could have saved most of the people in the *Titanic*. The odds were heavily against any experienced ship's captain behaving in this fashion: it was as if the tragedy had to happen. That it was not even worse, with all the people in the boats dying of exposure to the bitter cold, was entirely due to the courageous decision of Captain Rostron, master of the *Carpathia*, one of the smaller Cunarders on her way from New York to the Mediterranean. Rostron had turned in too, but, on being given the fearful news, he bounced out of his cabin, all energy and fire. The *Titanic* was 58 miles away; at 14 knots, the Carpathia's usual speed, it would take at least four hours to reach her; so Rostron told his engineers to sacrifice everything for speed, and was finally driving north, towards the ice, at 17 knots. At the same time the whole crew were organised for a rescue operation. The *Titanic* had gone when they arrived, but there were the lifeboats scattered over a wide area, with icebergs to be seen everywhere. It took time to locate them all and bring the survivors aboard. By 8.50 a.m. Rostron, having reached the decision at once sensible and courageous, signalled a return at full speed to New York. By an odd chance, not quite eight years later, I used to listen to a first-hand account of this night of wild drama. I was up at Cambridge then, at Trinity Hall, and one of my friends there, older than I was (and after 4½ years in the army I in turn was older than most), was a musician who had come up belatedly to take his Mus. Bac. We spent many an evening smoking our pipes and working away at Haydn Symphonies arranged as piano duets. He had joined the *Carpathia* as a kind of assistant-assistant-purser, and so he had been there that night and remembered only too well how women survivors, dazed at first and then frantic, went half-blindly searching the ship for missing children and husbands.

Now that hard news is bounced off satellites into our homes immediately, we have to make an imaginative effort to understand what it was like in 1912 to face a colossal disaster like the loss of the *Titanic*. Rumour succeeded rumour, and vast crowds gathered, waiting for hours and hours, to catch the latest of them. Was the famous unsinkable ship sunk then? When it was known that she had indeed gone to the bottom and that at least 1500 lives had been lost, there was on both sides of the Atlantic a huge storm of protest. Much of it in America was directed against Bruce Ismay, who as boss of the White Star Line might be held largely responsible for the disaster, and, what was worse, had taken a place in a lifeboat and was landed at New York by the *Carpathia*. (The truth about Ismay, I suspect, was that he was one of those rather arrogant stiffly-held men who collapse under a sudden strain and hardly know what they are doing. He was under sedation in the *Carpathia*.) The Americans demanded and got an Official Inquiry at once; the Official British Inquiry came later, in May.

These two Inquiries are worth brief consideration because they well illustrate the difference between American and British methods then – and perhaps even now. The American was hasty, rather brash, and comical, because Senator Smith, who conducted the Inquiry, obviously knew nothing about ships and the sea. But it did arrive at some sharp conclusions – the lack of boat drill and 'helpful discipline', the reckless speed of the *Titanic* after she had received so many warnings, the fatal laxity of the British Board of Trade – and it shook a long finger at London, Southampton, Belfast. If the American Inquiry was all brash-brash, the British Inquiry was all hush-hush. It was long, calm, suave, heavy with expensive legal talent, and allowed no obstacle to come between it and a final discovery of nothing in particular. There

The *Carpathia*

was none of that vulgar American blaming here; an unfortunate accident had occurred; but with this smooth conclusion most seamen, including Joseph Conrad, violently disagreed. It was not any rebuke from the British Inquiry that cost Ismay, still under a cloud, his chairmanship of the White Star Line. He lived until 1937, and out of curiosity I looked to see what the *Dictionary of National Biography* had to tell us about him. 'Man of striking personality . . . those who knew him slightly found his personality overpowering . . . outward veneer of a shy and highly sensitive nature . . . a depth of affection and understanding which is given to but a few . . . became a first class shot and an expert fisherman . . .' and so on and so forth; but from the first to last not one single mention of the *Titanic*. That is the British way, but not, I fear, for all of us.

The importance of the wireless messages in the *Titanic* disaster was a great boost for Signor Marconi and the companies using his patents. Asquith's government had reached a secret agreement with these companies, which would be responsible for a chain of radio stations throughout the Empire. Then early in 1913 there were scandalous rumours that various ministers, notably Rufus Isaacs (Attorney-General), Herbert Samuel (Postmaster-General) and then later even the Chancellor of the Exchequer himself, Lloyd George, had taken advantage of this agreement to speculate in Marconi shares. But only in the American company, it was said, not the *British*, which would have been all wrong. But still the rumours multiplied. Then the Government appointed a Select Committee, which might be described as the first cousin of that Official Inquiry we noticed above. A minority report mentioned 'grave impropriety' but the majority decided to forgive the culprits. Lloyd George and Rufus Isaacs expressed their regret in the

House, and all was well, except that doubting journalists like G. K. Chesterton and his brother Cecil and their friend Hilaire Belloc still jeered and scoffed at such hush-hush conclusions.

Though my space is dwindling, I have dealt at this length with the *Titanic* for one very good reason. It is not because the Board of Trade, compelled at last to exert itself, demanded that the shipping lines should provide an adequate number of well-founded lifeboats, should make sure that crews knew how to handle them and that passengers should attend boat drill, and insisted upon various other safety precautions being taken. This indeed happened as one result of the disaster, but something else, more important, happened too. The peculiar *hubris* that had created the fatal *Titanic* legend vanished from the scene. There was to be no more defiant bragging for a long, long time. Transatlantic liners might come to look more and more like luxury hotels, but it was borne in mind that they were ships and would still have to face the ancient challenge and cruel power of the sea. But a rapidly developing technology, because it has to make things work successfully to achieve anything at all, is always in danger of *hubris*, of seeing itself as being irresistible in its might, for ever defeating this, conquering that – once the sea and now air and space. There are some places that might be healthier if they displayed large notices: Remember the *Titanic*!

7. Russian Ballet

I want to quote a short passage from a letter written by Rupert Brooke, in the high summer of 1911, to his new girl-friend 'Ka' (Katherine Cox). It can be found, along with innumerable other letters, in Christopher Hassall's full and very valuable biography of Brooke. This book, which I have been re-reading closely, seems to me to give us the spirit, feeling, flavour of these later Edwardian years as few others do – and I take this opportunity to recommend it – though I realise it may have a particular fascination for me. This is because I was alive then, very much alive, but far removed from Brooke and his various circles of friends: young Cambridge intellectuals, fellow poets, painters, splendid girls, all of them for ever meeting in or near London or packing themselves into remote country cottages. Brooke is too often remembered as the beautiful soldier-poet buried on Skyros or resented as the ultra-patriotic 1914-style sonneteer. He is more rewarding, even as a poet, before 1914. Though not a type, very much an individual, often central in his various groups because of his looks, charm, eagerness, he returns to my mind – though I never set eyes on him – as a kind of key figure of late Edwardian youth. He was the only member of the Fabian Society trying to catch the music of Pan. Gregarious and restless, he was yet determined to do great things, perhaps well outside poetry. (Close friends like Virginia Woolf said that if he had survived the war he might have turned into a man of action, choosing politics perhaps.) But his poems in the few years before the war mark his progress and partly reveal the spirit of the age. He was a brilliantly engaging young man, with an enormous zest for life, who so often felt bewildered, sometimes genuinely unhappy, that he could not help accepting the war as a release from doubt and disgust. On an intellectual and poetic level, much of 1911–12–13 can be found distilled in Rupert Brooke.

The letter I quote was written from his mother's house in Rugby, the morning after a very crowded day:

> Yesterday I got up at 4.30 – bathed above Oxford: worked in the Bodleian, went to the Grafton Galleries, saw *Schéhérazade* (*sic*), called on Geoffrey, talked to James, and caught the midnight train down here. At 2.30 I walked up, strung with bags, this mile and a half. It was incredibly hot. I crept into bed at 5.30: after a cold bath, and claret and soda. Living is sheer ecstasy. How one packs things!

Rupert Brooke, 1913

I am now ignoring the topical allusions, the Grafton Galleries and the Russian Ballet, when I suggest that a letter like this, belonging to 1911, could not have been written in 1901 or 1921. It is so very much of its own time. It exists entirely in an atmosphere that was not there in 1901 and had gone for ever in 1921. The years were just beginning to hurry somewhere – so, *one packs things*. I hope I am not being fanciful or claiming too much if I add that at eighteen, living in very different surroundings and with no such grand programmes, I breathed that air, responded to that same atmosphere. But with *living is sheer ecstasy* included? I am afraid not. To begin with, we never wrote or talked like that in Bradford. What is more important, for after all I was not completely shaped and coloured by the West Riding, I have never at any time found living to be sheer ecstasy. I have had unforgettable moments of ecstasy, but they came out of the blue, never going along with living, only paying it a very rare visit. Perhaps Brooke, writing to the girl he was in love with, was overdoing it.

Diaghilev's one-act ballet *Shéhérazade*, was only one item in Brooke's long day's programme. How much did that visit to Covent Garden contribute to the day's excitement and *living is sheer ecstasy*. I can ask the question but cannot answer it. A year or so later, lecturing on the Contemporary Theatre to the 'Heretics' at Cambridge, Brooke was not enthusiastic about the Russian Ballet and condemned Bakst's 'extremely tawdry and inharmonious scenery and dresses'. But by that time fashionable London *adored* the Russian Ballet and Bakst's designs, and young men addressing a group of Cambridge intellectuals like to cut across and not float on the tide of fashion.

Beecham had brought over from Paris the astonishing Diaghilev and

Costume design for *Shéhérazade*, 1910, by Léon Bakst

his Russian dancers to decorate the coronation season of 1911. They burst on London like a bomb filled with silks and coloured lights. Diaghilev must take most of the credit for their success. An impressive Russian with an aristocratic style, fur-coated, monocled, trimly moustached, unabashedly homosexual, combining a powerful will and ruthlessness with enormous personal charm, not afraid of roaring with laughter or suddenly bursting into tears, Diaghilev was the super-impresario, a model for all future impresarios, even those who came to work in films. They are the types who can coolly occupy the largest suites in the best hotels, ordering champagne or caviare or both at all hours, when they know they are temporarily bankrupt. (Sacha Guitry once said that impresarios are men who speak all languages with a foreign accent.) But Diaghilev had a remarkable flair for what was new and exciting in music, design, choreography, astonishing spectacular theatre. He opened doors through which the defiant twentieth century came hurtling. What is commonplace today was once a brave decision by Serge Diaghilev, taken against all odds. Ballet as we know it now – and everybody knows it now – owes everything to Diaghilev. Not only did he create highly original ballets, now familiar everywhere, but he insisted upon cutting and streamlining ballet so that what might have been spread over four acts was reduced to one. Those of us who have sat through *Swan Lake* in Moscow or Leningrad, not able to appreciate the finer points of dancing and wondering how much more we can endure, bless the memory of Diaghilev, who abridged it to one act.

His company first appeared in Paris in 1909, when it was an immediate success. London had to wait until 1911. However, two of its bewitching prima ballerinas accepted music hall engagements in London, so that Tamara Karsavina found herself, to her bewilderment at first, at the Coliseum in 1909, taking her turn with comedians and acrobats; and the following year Pavlova appeared at the Palace Theatre, first at £160 a week but soon at £1200. It would not be long before Karsavina would be seen, with the incredible Nijinsky, as the dreamy romantic girl in *Le Spectre de la Rose*. Karsavina was an enchanting person both on and off the stage, and indeed even as an author in her reminiscent *Theatre Street*. Finally, as Mrs Bruce – for she married one of us, a great tribute – she settled in London. I remember sitting next to her, at a dinner party in the 1930's, when a woman across the table, knowing her only as Mrs Bruce and merely making conversation, leant forward and said, 'Are you fond of dancing?' To the great, the incomparable Karsavina!

As for Anna Pavlova, we know she was appearing at the Palace in April, 1911, because there is an entry in Arnold Bennett's diary, dated then, about her: 'London Palace Theatre. Pavlova dancing the dying swan. Feather falls off her dress. Two silent Englishmen. One says "Moulting". That is all they say.' William Armstrong, for years the director of the Liverpool Playhouse, told me he was once watching Pavlova dancing her dying swan in Edinburgh, and just as the exquisite but pitiful creature was beginning to flutter in its death throes, he overheard a woman behind him cry, 'She's the living image o' Mrs Wishart!' Pavlova left Diaghilev's company too soon, and then had to go on and on with that dying swan. I have a very clear recollection of her performance; it was in some provincial music hall; but exactly where – or when – I simply cannot recall. I saw some of the Diaghilev ballets, including *Shéhérazade* and *The Sleeping Princess*, the most elaborate and expensive of all his productions (it ruined him – temporarily), at the Alhambra in 1921. There was then no Nijinsky, whom I never saw, and all the people I knew who had attended the pre-war seasons said that something had gone in addition to the prodigious leaps of Nijinsky, forgetting that so much had gone, even in themselves, by 1919. But no doubt freshness, *élan*, a glorious element of surprise, were missing. Repeated performances, then revivals bringing costumes and scenery out of store, little by little steal the magic out of productions. And if, for example, I found

Nijinsky in *L'Après-midi d'un Faune*, 1912

(left) Léon Bakst, photographed by E. O. Hoppé, 1913

(right) Serge Diaghilev, by Elizabeth Polunin

(below) Chaliapin as *Ivan the Terrible*, Drury Lane, 1914

Shéhérazade fairly staggering after it had been around for some years, what must have been its effect when it first blazed on London.

In 1913 the Russians captured the rank and fashion of London as if 50,000 Cossacks had swarmed into Mayfair. Diaghilev produced opera as well as ballet: *Boris Godunov* and *Khovantchina*, both by Moussorgsky, and Rimsky-Korsakov's *Ivan the Terrible*. The giant Chaliapin sang *Boris*; all the fine ladies at once lost their hearts to him, with the beautiful young Lady Diana Manners well in the lead. (Bradford used to shake its head over the gossip columns reporting her wild doings, though in fact they were innocent enough, just tearing high spirits.) One of the three new ballets that Diaghilev presented was Stravinsky's *Le Sacre du Printemps*, which had started a riot on its first performance in Paris. In London, instead of riot police, there was the music critic of the *Daily Telegraph*, who came on stage before the curtain rose to explain Stravinsky's music, leaving the audience to applaud without catcalls the strange wild sounds, the primitive rites transformed into dancing. The hothouse social atmosphere of this time is wonderfully suggested in *The Rainbow Comes and Goes* by Lady Diana Cooper (once that same Diana Manners); and she writes:

> Never since, I think, have we in England had our eyes so dazzled with new light. The comets whizzed across the unfamiliar sky, the stars danced. The time-revered old Italian opera in its buskins and farthingales, its tights and its cap-doffing, had wearied an audience older than me. Boxes at Covent Garden were hired for the season, but not for music. The darkness hid many sleepers. Wagner nights were more musically alert, because only enthusiasts could stand them. Now came a blast to awaken the dead, a blaze of blinding gold, the Kremlin bells clanged and clashed, and Boris was there, a humble giant on his way to be crowned . . .

Very well then: Diaghilev and his bold designers and composers, his dancers and singers, fascinated and then captured Lady Diana and her

(right) Karsavina and Nijinsky in *Shéhérazade*, 1910

(far right) Pavlova in her dance *The Rose*, 1911

(below left) Fokine in *Le Carnaval*, 1914, by Emmanuele Ordoño de Rosalès

(below right) Karsavina and Adolf Bolm in *L'Oiseau de Feu*, 1912

relatives and friends, all late Edwardian high life. But not a sound, not a glimpse of all this, came to us in Bradford – or to a hundred other places where the money was earned. So what – then? Why go on and on about Diaghilev and Bakst and Stravinsky and the rest of them, busy waking up and startling the rich and fashionable?

In order to answer that, I do not have to think about the women of fashion who, between 1911 and 1913, haunted by Bakst's designs, insisted upon a Russian-cum-Oriental style in their clothes and moved around apparently wearing turbans. A far better answer can be found in a brief aside by Mr Richard Buckle, in his notes on the Diaghilev Exhibition he organised in 1954: 'There are today lampshades in Scottish boarding-houses which owe their existence to *Shéhérazade*.' The first triumphant impact of Diaghilev's creations might belong to the years before the Great War, but their influence endured and widened throughout the 1920's and 1930's and even later. Indeed, it might be argued that the spirit of Diaghilev was more alive and far-reaching after his death, in 1929, than before. The designs he favoured reached Scottish boarding-houses. The scores he commissioned from Stravinsky or Ravel captured concert halls and then could be heard on thousands of recordings. If there had been no Diaghilev I doubt if the English would now be a ballet-dancing and ballet-loving nation. The Royal Ballet which now fills so many great theatres, both at home and abroad, has been largely the creation of Ninette de Valois, who was herself once a member of Diaghilev's company. But that was not all. Something happened on a deeper level. We might say that even apart from the Great War the Edwardian era with which we began, and in which most people were still living, had a time-bomb planted in it. The Russian Ballet and the audiences that wildly applauded it could be said to be existing in the 1920's years before the calendars recorded them. The harshly rebellious phase of the twentieth century blasted its way from Paris to London, then from some of the rich young to some of the poor young, mostly art students and music students. The demure but ever-present sexuality of the musical comedies and Viennese operettas was blown wide open. Young men and girls who never set eyes on the orgiastic scene of sex and death in *Shéhérazade* began to lead very different lives from their parents and grandparents. War did most of course – as it always does – but before it came crashing down, Diaghilev and his Russians and his Frenchmen had brought Dionysus out of his long sleep.

(opposite) Costume design for Nijinsky's *L'Après-midi d'un Faune*, 1912, by Léon Bakst

(overleaf) Set design for scene 1 *Pavillon d'Armide*, 1909, by Alexandre Benois

8. Science and Gowland Hopkins

In the chronology of science during these last Edwardian years some names and terms appear that are familiar enough now. Einstein is there

"L'APRÈS MIDI D'UN FAUNE"
(NIJINSKY)
BAKST

BAKST
1911

again; Rutherford is busy with the transmutation of elements; Brandenberger invents cellophane, Brearly stainless steel; research in radiation brings up Geiger; Niels Bohr is exploring the atom; and Soddy decides on isotope. But in the chronology I am using, otherwise admirably put together by Dr Williams, one name is missing, not just in these years but altogether missing. And for reasons, public and private, that will later appear, I feel I must remedy this. So in 1912, in the *Journal of Physiology*, there appeared an article – or 'paper', to use the scientists' own term – that began as follows:

> The experiments described in this paper confirm the work of others in showing that animals cannot grow when fed upon so-called 'synthetic' dietaries consisting of mixtures of pure proteins, fats, carbo-hydrates and salts. But they show further that a substance or substances present in normal foodstuffs (e.g. milk) can, when added to the dietary in astonishingly small amount, secure the utilisation for growth of the protein and energy contained in such artificial mixtures.
>
> The particular experiments, of which an account is now to be given, were undertaken to put upon a more quantitative basis results which I obtained as far back as 1906–1907. Since that time, a fuller realisation of the fact that (leaving on one side the influence of the inorganic constituents of dietaries) protein supply and energy supply do not alone secure normal nutrition, has arisen from the extremely interesting recent work upon the etiology of such diseases as beriberi and scurvy . . .

Dullish and heavy-going, no doubt, and clearly the work of a modest man. He was not alone in this new science of biochemistry; many scientists abroad were at work in this mysterious region; and he himself was very much the leader of a Cambridge team, who had a great affection for him. He was one of those splendid scientists who have imagination and intuition, encouraging a leap into the dark, but at the same time have the strength of purpose, the will and the patience, the sheer guts, to go on and on and on experimenting and checking results. Out of that dullish stuff I have quoted came the vitamins that have returned millions and millions of men, women and children to health and some chance of happiness. Still a modest unassuming man, his leadership was so widely acknowledged that he became Sir Frederick Gowland Hopkins, a President of the Royal Society, an O.M., a Nobel prize-winner. This is my public reason for introducing him here. My private reason is that although I never knew him I am married to his younger daughter, and I see a handsome feminine representation of his fine strong features every morning across the breakfast table. And if I no longer take vitamins it is because I grow fat on a diet containing A and B and C – the lot, I trust.

Costume design for the projected ballet *La Peri*, 1911, by Léon Bakst

9. Hullo Rag-time!

On the night before Christmas Eve 1912 a revue called *Hullo Rag-time!* opened at the London Hippodrome. It had a brassy-voiced American star, Ethel Levey, to belt out the big numbers. Pretty Shirley Kellogg, beating a drum, led the ragtime chorus girls along the joy plank that ran at right angles to the stage, giving the audience a fine view of their legs. (At this time, please note, the only girls' legs we had a fine view of were there on the stage, where the girls had to have good legs. We imagined in our innocence that this shapeliness was common to the whole sex, only to be disillusioned when skirts were shortened after the war.) *Hullo Rag-time!* was an immediate hit and ran for 451 performances. It appealed at once to very different sections of the public. Rupert Brooke, for instance, saw it ten times, and was always insisting upon his friends seeing it with him. If you saw it you certainly also heard it, for if it caught the eye it took the ear by storm. You could escape the full force of its ragtime numbers only by leaving the building. And even then these jagged brazen tunes followed you everywhere.

All that this revue did, however, was to bring ragtime in full blast into the West End, capturing people like Rupert Brooke and his friends as well as the usual fashionable patrons of light entertainment. The term *ragtime* had been around for some years. There were a few singers

(opposite left) A Bakst design produced by Paquin, 1912, by Léon Bakst

(opposite centre) A fashion advertisement, 1913

(opposite right) A fashion plate dated 1913

(right) The cover of the programme of *Hullo Rag-Time!*

of ragtime in the music halls two or three years before *Hullo Rag-time!* exploded at the Hippodrome. I seem to remember elaborately syncopated songs before I heard any of Irving Berlin's. But his were the most popular and they had to be put over in a certain American style. Earlier in 1912, Albert de Courville, the producer of *Hullo Rag-time!*, had gone to Coney Island, and had imported into the Hippodrome, as a single act, what he called the American Ragtime Octet. The secret of these triumphant American invaders was their colossal zest, their uninhibited enthusiasm, a world away from the genteel style of English musical comedy. It was as if the folk art of some remote hot country burst upon our audiences. Songs like those of Irving Berlin had only a vague negroid flavour, unlike the 'blues' that came later; the words were almost nonsensical – and rarely had any erotic feeling – but did suggest a wild unfocussed enthusiasm, which came to life at once with the saxophones and drums, the rasping trombones and high gleeful trumpets. The whole thing came from an America, a Walt Whitmanish democratic America, that had nothing to do with European culture; it came, though not without a hint of the Deep South, from a Coney Island of hot summers and shirtsleeves, beer and sweat. But though ragtime arrived almost like a message from the American working class, it was

never really accepted by the English working class – I never remember hearing soldiers in the Great War singing ragtime songs – and it was the younger members of the upper and middle classes who were immediately captivated by it. Perhaps they knew that the Edwardian era was now being blasted and bulldozed.

What the first encounter with ragtime meant to at least one young provincial, I have already described in my reminiscent *Margin Released*; and if I quote what I said there it is because any attempt to say it differently might falsify my impressions:

> When we went to Leeds it was generally because we wanted more cosmopolitan entertainment. One evening there, hot and astonished in the Empire, we discovered ragtime, brought to us by three young Americans: Hedges Brothers and Jacobsen, they called themselves. It was as if we had been still living in the nineteenth century and then suddenly found the twentieth glaring and screaming at us. We were yanked into our own age, fascinating, jungle-haunted, monstrous. We were used to being sung at in music halls in a robust and zestful fashion, but the syncopated frenzy of these three young Americans was something quite different; shining with sweat, they almost hung over the footlights, defying us to resist the rhythm, gradually hyptonising us, chanting and drumming us into another kind of life in which anything might happen. All right, what we were hearing for the first time was *Alexander's Ragtime Band*, *Waiting for the Robert E. Lee* and the rest, not forgetting, though its title has gone, that intoxicating refrain which went 'Fiddle up, yiddle up (BOM) on your violin'. All right, okay, so what? Well, I believe that in our time the more-than-popular song, irresistible to ordinary people everywhere, is prophetic. Out of the depths it suddenly reveals, great and terrible events will come: politicians and social historians do not keep their ears open in the right places. (They should listen now, however nauseating they find them, to the pop songs of the teenagers, so full of self-pity, so wandering and rootless and far removed from all public and national life, clinging so desperately to a sexual relationship, all expressing disinherited youth growing up with the Bomb.) Out of these twenty noisy minutes in a music hall, so long ago, came fragmentary but prophetic outlines of the situation in which we find ourselves now, the menace to old Europe, the domination of America, the emergence of Africa, the end of confidence and any feeling of security, the nervous excitement, the frenzy, the underlying despair of our century. Of course I was not consciously aware of all this on that evening, only knew that here was something new, strange, curiously disturbing. But let us keep our ears and minds open. Hedges Brothers and Jacobsen, under another name, with different words, music, tones and gestures, may be starting again next week, sketching an outline of the year 2000.

(opposite) An artist's impression of Shirley Kellogg leading the chorus along the joy plank in *Hullo Ragtime!* at the London Hippodrome in 1912

However, there was one sharp difference at that time between the provinces, at least those parts I knew, and the West End of London. Unlike the smart people there, we had not gone half out of our minds

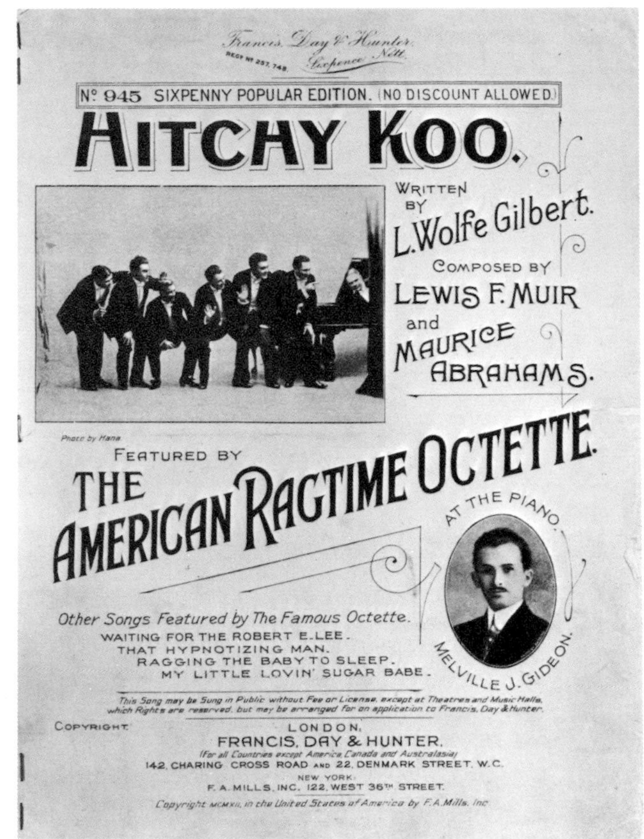

(above) The cover of the music-sheet of the song *Hitchy Koo*, composed in 1912, and performed by the American Ragtime Octet

(right) The cover of the music-sheet of *Alexander's Rag-time Band*, composed by Irving Berlin in 1911

over the new dances, the Turkey Trot, the Bunny Hug, and the rest. We did dance, though always with some reluctance on my part (my dancing time was the 1930's and especially in New York), at places like the Central Swimming Baths, but we kept going with the Military Two-step, the Valeta (a pretty dance, then unknown above the lower middle-class level) and the complicated and very Victorian Lancers. But none of your turkey-trotting and bunny-hugging! Again, unlike the smart London set, we were not staying up late and buying champagne in order to dance, nor – and this might be cheaper but it seemed sillier – were we going to hotels *at teatime* to do our dancing. The arrival of the tango – and *Hullo Rag-time!* was followed at the Hippodrome by *Hullo Tango!* –

The Turkey Trot.
This series of photographs illustrates the dance 'minus its objectionable features'

heightened the craze and deepened the disapproval. It was denounced along a wide front as an immodest dance of low South American origin, a kind of going-to-the-dogs in a very elaborate fashion. What next? – when hotels were offering tango teas and ladies who ought to have known better were actually giving tango parties. The men, not all of them young, were trying to look like the riffraff of Rio. Girls of decent parentage and upbringing were swaying and slinking into perdition. There were thunders from pulpits, letters quivering with indignation in the press. What was the country coming to? Well, one thing the country might be coming to was an appalling civil war in Ireland, and many of these very same people, so full of righteous indignation over a harmless dance, were telling one another all over again that Ulster would fight and Ulster would be right – as we shall discover, though not yet, not until another story has been told.

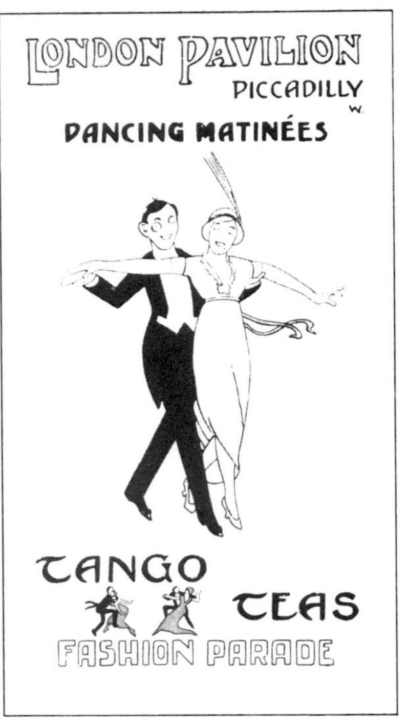

Tango teas at the London Pavilion, 1913

10. Antarctic Story

In February, 1913, Scott's ship, the *Terra Nova*, came out of the long silence to reach New Zealand, bringing terrible news. Scott and his four companions, Wilson, Oates, Bowers and Evans, had got to the South Pole on January 18, 1912, only to find that Amundsen's Norwegian expedition had been there over a month before them. Then, on the way back, ill-luck pursuing them with blizzards and lower and lower temperatures, all five had died. Why and how they died can be discovered in Scott's diary:

> *Friday, March* 16 *or Saturday* 17. – Lost track of dates, but think the last correct. Tragedy all along the line. At lunch, the day before yesterday, poor Titus Oates said he couldn't go on; he proposed we should leave him in his sleeping-bag. That we could not do, and we induced him to come on, on the afternoon march. In spite of its awful nature for him he struggled on and we made a few miles. At night he was worse and we knew the end had come.

Should this be found I want these facts recorded. Oates' last thoughts were of his Mother, but immediately before he took pride in thinking that his regiment would be pleased with the bold way in which he met his death. We can testify to his bravery. He has borne intense suffering for weeks without complaint, and to the very last was able and willing to discuss outside subjects. He did not – would not – give up hope till the very end. He was a brave soul. This was the end. He slept through the night before last, hoping not to wake; but he woke in the morning – yesterday. It was blowing a blizzard. He said, 'I am just going outside and may be some time.' He went out into the blizzard and we have not seen him since.

I take this opportunity of saying that we have stuck to our sick companions to the last. In the case of Edgar Evans, when absolutely out of food and he lay insensible, the safety of the remainder seemed to demand his abandonment, but Providence mercifully removed him at this critical moment. He died a natural death, and we did not leave him till two hours after his death. We knew that poor Oates was walking to his death, but though we tried to dissuade him, we knew it was the act of a brave man and an English gentleman. We all hope to meet the end with a similar spirit, and assuredly the end is not far.

I can only write at lunch and then only occasionally. The cold is intense, –40° at midday. My companions are unendingly cheerful, but we are all on the verge of serious frostbites, and though we constantly talk of fetching through I don't think any one of us believes it in his heart.

We are cold on the march now, and at all times except meals. Yesterday we had to lay up for a blizzard and today we move dreadfully slowly. We are at No. 14 pony camp, only two pony marches from One Ton Depôt. We leave here our theodolite, a camera, and Oates' sleeping-bags. Diaries &c., and geological specimens carried at Wilson's special request, will be found with us or on our sledge.

Sunday, March 18. – Today, lunch, we are 21 miles from the depôt. Ill fortune presses, but better may come. We have had more wind and drift from ahead yesterday; had to stop marching; wind N.W., force 4, temp. —35°. No human being could face it, and we are worn out *nearly.*

My right foot has gone, nearly all the toes – two days ago I was proud possessor of best feet. These are the steps of my downfall. Like an ass I mixed a small spoonful of curry powder with my melted pemmican – it gave me violent indigestion. I lay awake and in pain all night; woke and felt done on the march; foot went and I didn't know it. A very small measure of neglect and have a foot which is not pleasant to contemplate. Bowers takes first place in condition, but there is not much to choose after all. The others are still confident of getting through – or pretend to be – I don't know! We have the last *half* fill of oil in our primus and a very small quantity of spirit – this alone between us and thirst. The wind is fair for the moment and that is perhaps a fact to help. The mileage would have seemed ridiculously small on our outward journey.

Monday, March 19. – Lunch. We camped with difficulty last night, and were dreadfully cold till after our supper of cold pemmican and biscuit and half a pannikin of cocoa cooked over the spirit. Then, contrary to expectations, we got warm and all slept well. Today we started in the usual dragging manner. Sledge dreadfully heavy. We are $15\frac{1}{2}$ miles from the depôt and ought to get there in three days. What progress! We have two days' food but barely a day's fuel. All our feet are getting bad – Wilson's best, my right foot worst, left all right. There is no chance to nurse one's feet till we can get hot food into us. Amputation is the least I can hope for now, but will the trouble spread? That is the serious question. The weather doesn't give us a chance – the wind from N. to N.W. and —40° temp. today.

Wednesday, March 21. – Got within 11 miles of depôt Monday night; had to lay up all yesterday in severe blizzard. Today forlorn hope, Wilson and Bowers going to depôt for fuel.

Thursday March 22 *and* 23. – Blizzard bad as ever Wilson and Bowers unable to start – tomorrow last chance – no fuel and only one or two of food left – must be near the end. Have decided it shall be natural – we shall march for the depôt with or without our effects and die in our tracks.

Thursday, March 29. – Since the 21st we have had a continuous gale from W.S.W. and S.W. We had fuel to make two cups of tea apiece and bare food for two days on the 20th. Every day we have been ready to start for our depôt 11 *miles* away, but outside the door of the tent it remains a scene of whirling drift. We shall stick it out to the end, but we are getting weaker, of course, and the end cannot be far.

It seems a pity, but I do not think I can write more.

R. SCOTT.

Last entry.
For God's sake look after our people.

There was a memorial service on February 14 at St Paul's; there were government pensions for the families of the men who had died; there was a Mansion House Fund to commemorate them and to establish a polar research institute at Cambridge. It is worth noting here that while Amundsen's expedition did little or no serious scientific work, Scott's much larger expedition did a great deal and was of far greater value to later explorers. Nevertheless, the fact remains that by using skis, 52 dogs (returning with twelve of them and plenty of food still in hand for the five men), and a better route, Amundsen reached the South Pole quickly and with comparative ease, whereas Scott's motor sledges broke down, his ponies were a failure, his dog teams were inadequate, and the worst part of his journey, to the Pole and back, had to be done on foot, pulling a sledge that did not carry sufficient supplies if he was held up by blizzards. This is not an attack on the gallant Scott, even if it does suggest his judgment was not as good as Amundsen's: no man ever had more appalling bad luck. The point I wish to make is that his failure far outshone Amundsen's success. If he had reached the South Pole before Amundsen did and returned to England fit and smiling, he would have been soon forgotten by most of the English. It was not simply that five unusual men had died, though that meant something in 1913, before the casualty lists darkened the papers every morning and whole nations

Captain Scott working on his diary

existed with death at their elbow. What catches and holds the imagination of the English is not successful achievement in the ordinary sense. What they cherish, even though most of them would immediately deny it, is any action, though it may be accounted a failure, that appears when it is recorded to be epic, that takes on a poetic quality, that haunts the mind like a myth. The long silence, the sudden tragic news, the idea of Scott and his companions doomed in that remote howling wilderness of snow and ice, all of it fire the imagination, and not only then, in 1913, but ever since. But though 1913 halted a while, to mourn the dead, perhaps to lift mere news into the nation's mythology, the year had to move along, glittering on its way.

11. Fancy-dress Ball

1913 was to be the last whole year the old world knew before it vanished in the Great War. Obviously nobody was consciously aware of this, even though the Balkans had been already setting themselves alight, though the great powers were uneasy, though there was always vague war talk. But many people might have been influenced by mysterious promptings and premonitions, in the dark recesses of the mind, from the unconscious, which may have a different time scale from that of consciousness. Such people – and especially the young – may have felt that *now* they must make the most of everything, even if they could not explain why. Certainly the old world was splitting and already showed great steaming cracks in it, like some doomed volcanic region. Nationalism, which in my view is honest regionalism tainted and manipulated by ambitious politicians, was stirring in many different places and might soon come to the boil. The gap between outrageous youth and shocked age was widening. The young men were wilder, and even nicely brought-up girls were eluding chaperones to have a fling. People with more money than sense grasped every opportunity to show they had more money than sense. So, for example, in more than one capital, the 1913 season celebrated itself by elaborate and hugely extravagant fancy-dress balls, at which many a guest risked bankruptcy trying to look like somebody else for at least one night. Virginia Cowles (Mrs Aidan Crawley) is no Edwardian and indeed at this time was a baby in Boston, but she must have had all this in mind when she called her study of the year: *1913: The Defiant Swan Song*. In this she takes her readers – and I recommend the tour – to all the chief capital cities: London, Berlin, St Petersburg, Vienna, Rome, Paris and New York; and though we do not always see swans or hear any singing, she does suggest the peculiar tone, quality, atmosphere, of this perfervid year, half-desperate, half-daft.

It may be argued that the powerful, the rich and the fashionable do not represent anybody but themselves. I cannot accept this. It is true they do not represent the mass of decent quiet people who hardly know they exist, people who are not really living in their own era at all, until disaster and war drag them into it. But there are others, urban rather than rural, which means there are plenty of them, who are very much in their own era, who leap along with the times as the newspapers do. Such people are very well represented by the powerful, the rich and the fashionable, who do what these people would like to do, who are these people *with the lid off*. Certainly what is done, especially in an extravagant time, may be condemned by these people and their favourite newspapers, but this disapproval often conceals a lot of envy. It is only when we really have not the least desire to attend a fancy-dress party in Venice that we can smile or shrug it away.

In 1913 no fewer than three Imperial Majesties were making their final year-long peacetime appearances on the world's stage. Praising

(opposite) Ethel Levey in *Hullo Tango!* London Hippodrome, 1913. The costumes were designed by Léon Bakst

Fielding's *Tom Jones*, Gibbon said it would outlive the imperial eagle of Austria. It was now about to outlive the imperial eagles of the Hapsburgs, the Romanovs, and the Hohenzollerns, the empires of Austria, Russia and Germany being doomed to melt away in the furnace of war. The restless and neurotic Kaiser Wilhelm II did not want war, was indeed genuinely afraid of it, though in between making private moves to preserve peace he could not help making tactless public statements likely to undo all that he had done in private. He was greatly annoyed by the militarist antics of his son, the Crown Prince, who appeared to be half out of his mind when wearing the improbable uniform of the Death's Head Hussars. The young Edward, Britain's Prince of Wales, paid the Kaiser a fairly successful visit, though Berlin must have seemed narrow and provincial after London. This aspect of his capital worried the Kaiser, who did what he could (there must be evening dress at the opera) to add glitter and glamour. But *his* aristocrats, the Prussian 'Junkers', either kept to their estates or served hard in the army, and refused to hobnob with rich industrialists in order to cut a dash in Berlin. However, the marriage of his one daughter, Princess Victoria Louise, to the Duke of Brunswick, was a grand affair. King George V and Queen Mary attended it, and the Kaiser enjoyed their company far more than he had ever done that of his impressive twinkling uncle, Edward VII, who had always made him feel uncomfortable. Oddly enough, Princess Victoria Louise, only twenty-one, had fretted so much during her engagement that she had lost weight, continually being driven to tears by a premonition that war was coming. Moreover, throughout the year, the Kaiser's realm and subjects were constantly being disturbed by melodramatic or bizarre incidents, too numerous to describe here, involving not only strange disappearances (like that of Diesel, the inventor of the engine) and suicide and murder among the aristocracy, but also, as at Zabern in Alsace, even making the Army itself look ridiculous.

To Vienna the Serbs, who had won some battles against the Turks and were being encouraged by Russia, looked dangerous, so much so that part of the Austrian army had been mobilised. It did not improve the situation when Captain Redl, a well-born member of the General Staff, was proved to be a spy in the pay of Russia. The old Emperor Franz Josef, now in his eighties and having reigned for sixty-five years, who lived no better than a railway clerk retired on a tiny pension, could hardly be said to exist at all in the world of 1913. Violent death having struck his family over and over again, he contrived to be a tragic character who was also extremely dull, spreading tedium all round him. Neither he nor his aristocrats cared anything for the arts; it was the Jews they despised who gave Vienna its aesthetic life. The Emperor's nephew, the Archduke Franz Ferdinand, paid a state visit to George V, and together they blazed away happily together, so that it rained dead ducks in Windsor Great Park. The Archduke was not without ideas that

Lord Ribblesdale, 1902, by John Singer Sargent

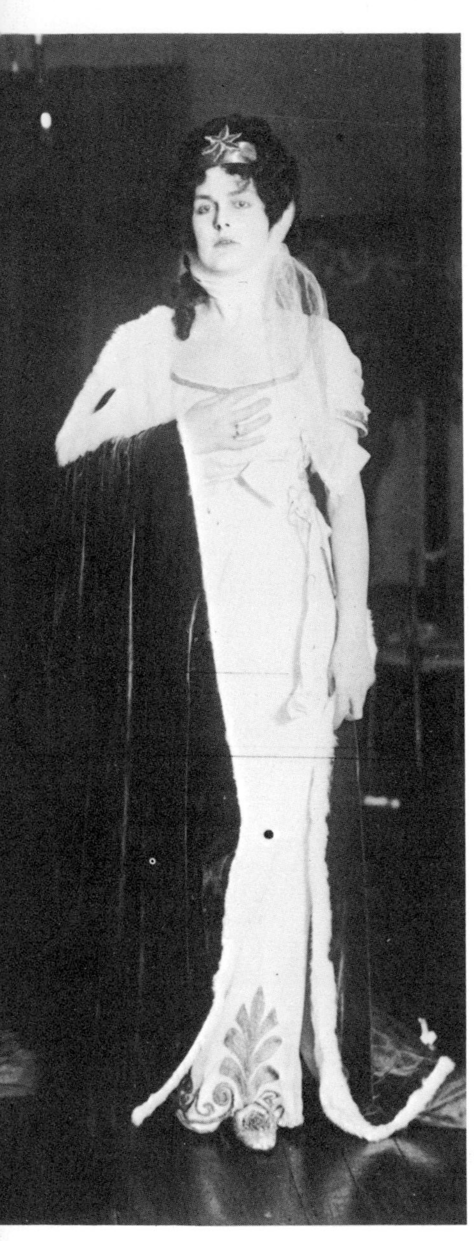

Miss Dubose Taylor as Queen Louise on the occasion of the Picture Ball at the Albert Hall, early in 1914

might help to save the ricketty Hapsburg Empire – and it might have been better if some federal form of it had been preserved – but before the end of 1913 he had already planned to visit Bosnia in June 1914, making an appointment with assassination, which in turn would light the match setting Europe on fire.

In St Petersburg the Empress never showed herself to the public; there were no dances in the Winter Palace; she was said to be now entirely under the influence of the dirty monk, Rasputin, because she believed he had saved the life of little Alexei, her only son. (The boy had haemophilia, and though Rasputin's hypnotic power could not cure that, it could at least make the Empress feel better.) Dominated by his wife, the mild Nicholas did nothing to heighten the power and glory of the House of Romanov, though 1913 was its three-hundredth anniversary. The wealthy families entertained one another with fancy dress parties, *tableaux vivants*, amateur acting; the younger noblemen went out of the city to drink champagne with the famous gypsy troupes of singers and dancers, sometimes staying for days; and far away, in Cracow, a man called Lenin was busy organising and addressing conferences. Further away still, in Rome, handsome titled men were fairly hard at work for once, in the dollar-importing business, marrying the daughters and widows of American millionaires. Attractive male partners in the tango tea rooms were two a penny. The notorious Marchesa Casati, who almost ran a zoo, arrived at one party with a macaw on her shoulder and an ape on her arm, followed by an attendant with a leopard or puma. Not to be outdone, the Princess Radziwill rode through the ballroom of the Hotel Excelsior with a leopard on one side of her, a lion on the other. At the British Embassy a thousand guests were invited to a fancy-dress ball, and Prince Liechtenstein of the Austrian Embassy brought a bevy of beautiful Roman ladies to stage some daring scenes from the *Arabian Nights*. The Swiss guards at the Vatican, who might be said to be attending a permanent fancy-dress party, went on strike. There was not a dull moment, except perhaps for the millions of peasants trying to scratch up some kind of living.

In Paris the rather absurd but charming Marcel Proust, who was seen in all the *salons* at one time, produced out of his retirement a peculiar sort of novel about somebody called Swann. But the Countess Greffuhle, taken by Proust later as the chief model for his Duchess of Guermantes, was still a leader of the high society from which the novelist had fled. In 1913, however, the Faubourg St Germain was being invaded by the new rich and the American heiresses. Tired of St Petersburg, Russian grand dukes were enjoying gypsy music in Montmartre; the cabarets, traps for tourists, were moving in. New fast into grand pianos. The poets and painters were moving out of Montmartre, the cabarets, traps for tourists, were moving in. New fast motorcars were roaring and honking in the Bois de Boulogne, ruining the noon parade of horses and carriages. There was increasingly sharp

(right) The Countess of Warwick dressed as the Queen of Assyria

(below) Isadora Duncan about 1900

competition between the famous fashion houses, Poiret, Paquin, Worth, Lanvin, and others, and the flimsy garments worn by their models were more and more daring, quite shocking in fact. Poiret gave tremendous parties, and Isadora Duncan, now the rage of Paris, danced for him. It was in April this year that the car in which her two children and their governess were riding into the Seine, and all three were drowned. It was that kind of year: unlikely accidents, duels, various types of *crime passionel*, being all too common. There was a widening division, there was more and more tension, between the war-mongering 'patriots' of the Right, seeking closer relations with Russia, and the pacifist writers and the groups on the Left, which had as their chief orator the picturesque and impassioned Jean Jaurès, to be murdered in July 1914.

One argument in favour of monarchy is that if you no longer have the real thing, combining mystique and professional training, your high society is liable to have absurd imitations imposed upon it. In 1913 New York, though it contained plenty of scoffing democrats, was still accepting a mock-monarchy-and-aristocracy, based on huge fortunes and the time of their acquisition. Triumphant deals in railways or real estate in the 1880's might put a man and his wife, especially his wife, in line for the throne and certainly among the aristocrats. But a killing in tin plate about 1910, let us say, would not guarantee an entry into the best society of Newport, the seaside resort of the queens and their courtiers. Mrs Astor, dying in 1908, was succeeded by Mrs Cornelius Vanderbilt – and the Vanderbilts were more narrowly and rigidly aristocratic than almost anybody in Europe – though her reign was not free from occasional disloyal moves by Mrs Oliver Belmont or Mrs Stuyvesant Fish. The more solemn New York press, closing its columns to low jeering fellows, acted as an unfailing Court Circular. When J. P. Morgan died in Italy this year, the innumerable columns might have been mourning the loss of Lincoln, all the Medicis, Aristotle and Napoleon.

It was still the era, though perhaps a shade less wild, of conspicuous waste and daft extravagance, as if too many of the dollars were beginning to smell a little. New millionairesses were under dreadful pressure to do the right thing and then be accepted, and had to work nearly as hard as the waiters who suddenly came out on strike in 1913 or the girls in the garment trade who dreamt of a minimum wage of nine dollars a week. Mrs Mable Dodge solved her problem by living sumptuously down in Greenwich Village, among the poets and painters and rebels, and even organised a Socialist Costume Ball. It was she who was largely responsible for the huge show in the 69th Street Armory, where a group of unfashionable and more realistic American painters could hang their work. But out of the 1600 pictures and pieces of sculpture, it was the importations from Paris – work by Picasso, Matisse, Brancusi, Picabia, Marcel Duchamp – that raised a storm of protest. In particular, Duchamp's *Nude Descending a Staircase* achieved a kind of mixed ill-fame and fame that it neither earned nor deserved. Like so many things, that year.

Back then to London and its brilliant 1913 season. Lady Diana Cooper, in *The Rainbow Comes and Goes*, remembering her youth, sends the season flashing on its way again, beginning with 'eligibles':

> A foreign eligible didn't carry the same stigma. Count Clary for instance was very eligible. He taught me the Viennese waltz and we would spin ourselves to a standstill to the strains of Cassano's band. Count Wilczeck was eligible, so was Count Hoesch, another Dream Waltzer. But the most eligible of all was Prince Felix Youssupoff. He was later to kill Rasputin, but at the time he was an innocent at Oxford and deeply in love with my

Nude Descending a Staircase, No. II, 1912, by Marcel Duchamp

The 69th Street Armory Show, 1913, arranged largely by Mrs Mabel Dodge

sister Marjorie. A mystic, and of transcendent beauty, he sang to his guitar the Russian gypsy songs, now so hackneyed, then new to us. At the many fancy balls he wore his eighteenth-century Russian dress of gold and pearls and sables and aigrettes, with embroidered boots and jewelled scimitar. He rode in the procession with me at the revived Eglinton Tournament. This historic second-time failure took place at Earl's Court. The tickets were fabulously expensive – twenty pounds, I think – so very few were sold. The challengers were the Duke of Marlborough, Lord Ashby St Ledgers, Lord Craven, Lord Tweedmouth and others. Lady Curzon was the Queen of Beauty and I was a lady of her Court. Letty was part of a musical ride mounted on ordinary-looking horses loaned by the Household Cavalry. The Queen of Beauty's steed was little better. These well-breds were not dramatic enough for me, nor were the ugly Elizabethan costumes, so I designed myself a black velvet Holbein dress (quite out of period) and hired Richard II's stage horse, Roan Barbary, with mane and tail that swept the ground. It was as broad as a circus galumpher, but never mind. Felix wore his Russian robes and mounted himself on a mettlesome snow-white Arab, foaming and flecking and pawing. Of course they were cross with us for cheating, and another score was marked up against me. I see why – now. Publicity was building me my pedestal. I never encouraged it knowingly. I think I was not aware of it. If I was, I simply didn't care.

I prayed for Marjorie to marry Felix. I bought her a *Hugo's Russian Grammar,* but her heart was set and its desire at hand. In a few months she was engaged to Charles Anglesey and sailed away from me in a fine yacht, and I knew that, as with Letty, we could never be the same to each other again.

No time to mope – she was happy and I had friends and more friends and many that I love wholeheartedly. There were Raymond and Katharine Asquith, and Viola, now married to my adored Alan Parsons, Felicity and Iris Tree, Phyllis Boyd, just coming into my life, and then all the young men who were making and moulding me and would so soon be lost. The favourites were Edward Horner, Patrick Shaw-Stewart, George Vernon, Denis Anson, the Grenfells, Sidney and Michael Herbert, Tommy Bouch, and Duff Cooper . . . .

They were so clever, so handsome, so gay, these young men of the 1913 season; and I believe still that theirs was a very special generation and that after more than half a century we have not yet recovered from the loss of it: *They carry back bright to the coiner the mintage of man.* It was in 1896 that Housman first published *A Shropshire Lad.* Half the little book was twenty years ahead of its time: it belonged to 1916.

12. Ulster and Home Rule

The Moon in the Yellow River is not an oriental piece; it is a play about Ireland by an Irishman, Denis Johnston. At the end of the second act, a German engineer, working in Ireland, trying to settle something, complains bitterly that this is not a country but a debating society, that everybody talks and talks and talks but nothing ever happens. He has no sooner said that than one of the Irishmen there – *without any demonstration*, the stage direction runs – shoots another one dead. That little scene takes us very close to Ireland. The amount of talk, often as cross-purposes, becomes farcical, then suddenly there is violence, there is tragedy. The Home-Rule-and-Ulster story of 1913–14 reproduces this pattern while immensely enlarging it; the talk, with large elements of comedy in it, mounts and swells gigantically; while tragedy waits in the wings for its cue, for there might be a bloody civil war together with mutiny in the British Army. And this was not simply a crisis for the United Kingdom. Germany was observing events closely, and indeed, as we shall see, took a hand in them. It has been argued that the German General Staff might not have followed the Schlieffen plan if Britain had not seemed to be facing a civil war. This plan involved a sweep through Belgium, as part of the invasion of France, a move that contemptuously dismissed the neutrality of Belgium, which Britain had guaranteed. But a Britain split in two by the Irish quarrel, with an army threatening mutiny, might forget its obligations to Belgium. So the argument runs, and though it may not be sound, it does show us the startling interdependence of things in this world (it always takes us by surprise), and that we cannot regard the Home-Rule-and-Ulster crisis as one huge comedy. It is indeed more than that, even to this day.

The Liberal Party had been talking about Home Rule, in one form or another, for over thirty years.Now at last Asquith would have to do something about it, because, as we saw earlier, he depended upon John Redmond and his Irish Nationalist members for his majority in the House. The Liberal social reforms and the party's challenge of the Lords would have been impossible without the support of the Irish. Now that Asquith and his ministers had enjoyed the meal, they would have to pay the bill. This would not be easy; any mention of Ireland and Home Rule would immediately stiffen and then enrage the opposition.

Earlier when discussing politics I called the Unionists (their own name for themselves) simply Tories, but now, when the Irish question is all-important, I shall reverse the procedure and call the Tories Unionists. They were the politicians who believed – and there were a few Liberals who shared this belief – that the union of Great Britain and Ireland, dating from 1801 and creating the United Kingdom, should be preserved at all costs. They did not call themselves Unionists for nothing; they would display their disgust and anger at once at the very rumour of a Home Rule Bill. They would declare, as they soon did with great vehemence, that so grave a step, splitting the United Kingdom, could not be taken unless it was clearly shown that a large majority in the country wanted it. There was no evidence of such a demand; the English displayed little interest in Home Rule. So the Unionists argued that only a General Election, fought on the Home Rule issue, could test the feeling of the country.

Asquith knew that an election might bundle the Liberals out of office, just at the time they had so much at stake. Redmond and his Irish Nationalists did not want an election; a Unionist victory would mean there would be no hope of Home Rule for years. This left Asquith to face the Unionist taunts in the House, telling him that his Home Rule Bill was merely parliamentary jobbery, that he was ready to wreck the United Kingdom without the shadow of a people's mandate: he was greeted with cries of *Traitor*! more than once. From first to last in this Irish affair Asquith was in a weak position, though he was always ready to defend himself and the Government with his usual superb parliamentary skill. But he did not whole-heartedly *want* Home Rule, never brought to it any real concentration of will. He was utterly unlike the fanatics on the other side. He had to keep shifting his ground. Though he lost no personal respect, there was a growing feeling, not altogether confined to his Unionist opponents, that while Asquith was a weighty advocate, a solid party leader, he was not a statesman committed to causes and so prepared to take swift decisive action. And this may partly explain what happened to him later, when he lost his leadership in the war.

His chief Unionist opponent – though he was not the Leader of the Opposition – was entirely without such weakness, being indeed a fanatic. This was Sir Edward Carson, who had made a great name at the bar, where in cross-examination he terrified hostile witnesses. (In private life he could be charming and had many friends.) A fanatically dedicated man, with a tall impressive figure, a formidable face, the fluent but impassioned speech of a born advocate, Carson was a priceless gift to any side in complete agreement with him. Though born in Dublin and educated at its Trinity College, he had chosen his side from the first: he was the implacable and ruthless enemy of Irish self-government. Home Rule to him meant that the Protestants of Northern Ireland, the Orangemen (so-called because they had helped William of Orange to rid the country of the Papist James II), would come under priest-ridden rule of the Southern Irish, and this was unthinkable. Ulster the home of the Orangemen, the most prosperous part of Ireland (it had Belfast and the great shipyards), would never allow Asquith and John Redmond or anybody else at Westminster to tear it out of the United Kingdom.

The men of Ulster – that is, the Protestant majority, for there were beleaguered Catholics in the province – were as fanatical as Carson. They were mostly a Scots-Irish mixture, formidably aggressive. Though the Battle of the Boyne, in which the Orangemen defeated the Papists, had taken place as long ago as 1690, Protestant Ulster was still celebrating it, as if James II might still be around. They waved the Union Jack as if it had just been created for them. (The largest ever made was unfurled at a great Ulster demonstration against Home Rule.) As British military records testified, they were at all levels first-class fighting men. They hardly needed fiery speeches from Carson, though they heard plenty of them. There was something in the air of Northern Ireland that encouraged belligerent oratory. The official Leader of the Opposition was Bonar Law, and even he, a cautious Scots-Canadian, could not resist making inflamatory statements as soon as he spoke in Ulster. With Home Rule looming up, the Ulster men in scores of thousands signed, sometimes in blood, a Solemn Covenant. Its text began:

(top) Sir Edward Carson

(below) Major-General Henry Wilson (detail), 1922, by Oswald Birley

> Being convinced in our consciences that Home Rule would be disastrous to the material well-being of Ulster as well as the whole of Ireland, subversive of our civil and religious freedom, destructive of our citizenship, and perilous to the unity of the Empire, we, whose names are underwritten –

SOUTH LONDONDERRY
WE WILL NOT HAVE
HOME RULE

Ulster Anti-Home-Rule demonstration in Hyde Park, September 1914 *(left to right)*: H. J. Barrie, M.P., Sir Edward Carson and Mr F. E. Smith

And then they pledged themselves to defend their citizenship in the United Kingdom and 'to defeat the present conspiracy to set up a Home Rule Parliament in Ireland'. The Ulster women were as fanatical as their men, signed their own covenant, and made it available in various centres in Great Britain. There were now monster demonstrations, torchlight processions, do-or-die oratory everywhere, drilling and marching with dummy rifles, and, in spite of the heady atmosphere, some very efficient staff work. By the end of 1912 Ulster was far better organised to resist Home Rule than the Liberal Government was to make it legal and then act upon it. Carson and his dashing fellow advocate, F. E. Smith, a kind of brandied Carson, were already publicly defying the Government to take any action against them.

Early in 1913 the Home Rule Bill, having survived many stormy sessions in the Commons, went forward to the House of Lords, where it was immediately denounced and thrown out. Ulster was now working on a scheme for a provisional government, and was rapidly recruiting religious, legal, military men of experience, authority, distinction. An old Indian Army fire-eater, recommended by Lord Roberts, came out of retirement to take command in Belfast of what was potentially the largest army he had ever commanded, at least 60,000 men and soon to be over 100,000. They still lacked real rifles and ammunition, but there was such a thing as gun-running, and the British Army had some stores of arms in Ulster. Before the end of the summer the Lords had rejected the Bill for the last time; the constitution recently amended by the Liberals did not allow them any further rejection; King George had only to give his consent and the Bill would be transformed into an Act of Parliament: Home Rule would be imbedded in the law of the realm, and all the rebellious Ulstermen, together with all their Unionist supporters, would be potential lawbreakers. Poor King George, who had already been called upon to face more crises than his father had ever known, found himself protesting in a cleft stick. Whatever he did, he pointed out, he would offend half the population; he could not help feeling that the Government was drifting and taking him with it. Was it not possible to arrive at some 'settlement by consent?' So up at Balmoral that September, when he might have been enjoying himself in the open air, he had to keep inviting Liberal ministers and Unionist leaders to join him in a series of intimate and urgent talks. Every piece of information coming from Belfast heightened the crisis.

The Ulster Provisional Government had taken definite shape. There was to be a £1,000,000 special fund to indemnify the Ulster Volunteer Force. If there were strong speeches in the North of Ireland by Carson and his friends, there were equally strong speeches in the South by John Redmond and the Nationalists, who declared that Home Rule was for all Ireland with no exclusion of Ulster. The King pointed out that he was the titular head of the Army, that its officers and men had opinions of their own and could not be expected to engage in a civil war against their own judgement: there must be more consultations, conferences, compromises. And so there were, except that the compromises did not mature. Here I find it impossible to disagree with Mr A. P. Ryan, whose *Mutiny at the Curragh* is a detailed but lively account of these doings, when he says –

> Thus the King's first patient attempt to keep the peace had, at the close of 1913, failed. But his determination to succeed was undaunted and his influence was to be felt again in the coming months. It was fortunate for the country that it had in George V a monarch who was the reverse of a Hamlet. The more the time was out of joint, the stronger did his common sense assert itself behind the scenes. It was to be needed, for as the Asquith-Bonar Law negotiations failed, the professional soldiers began to be drawn in by the civil authorities . . .

As the comedy-near-tragedy takes shape, we ought to take a look at the chief members of the cast. As leading man, Asquith was out of luck.

If Carson and F. E. Smith made truculent speeches, so did Winston Churchill, whether his Government needed them or not. He was still at the Admiralty and often sounded as if his battleships could swing 12-inch guns towards Ulster at a few hours' notice. On the other hand, Augustine Birrell, the minister responsible for Ireland, talked and behaved as if nothing of any importance was happening. Birrell was a delightful man, an occasional essayist and critic who can still be read with pleasure, and one of the best after-dinner speakers I have ever heard, but in this crisis he was rather like a man-at-the-helm busy trying to recall the best passages in Boswell's *Johnson*.

General Paget was in command of the army in Ireland. He had distinguished himself in the Ashanti War in the 1870's, was a brave but never a thoughtful man, and ought to have been retired to his garden – he was an excellent gardener – long before these troubles began. The Director of Military Operations was Major-General Henry Wilson, as fanatical an Ulsterman as Carson himself, and a tireless and unscrupulous intriguer, then and later throughout the Great War. A fervent Unionist himself, Wilson was always ready to keep the Unionist leaders well informed about the Army and the attitude of its officers towards any possible conflict with Ulster. With such support, Asquith's position, always weak, was weaker still. If there was to be Home Rule at all, something would have to give, and clearly it would not be Ulster. Already, officers whose troops would have to control the Ulstermen were resigning their commissions. Asquith could only press Redmond to accept some modified version of Home Rule.

It was announced by Asquith in the House on March 9, 1914. The Ulster counties would be excluded from Home Rule, but only for six years, after which they would come under the Irish Parliament unless a majority of the electorate in the whole British Isles agreed to their

(opposite) The Blue Hat, *c.* 1913, by Walter Richard Sickert

(overleaf) Dinner on board the yacht Vanderbilt at Cowes (detail), 1909, by Jacques-Emile Blanche

further exclusion. Redmond said that his Nationalists had agreed to make this sacrifice, but that if it should be rejected, they would expect the Government to use all its resources to suppress the Ulster rebels. The Unionists noisily rejected the modified Bill at once. Carson cried: 'We do not want sentence of death with a stay of execution for six years', and went on to say that the forces of the Crown belonged to the country and not to 'any political caucus', to a Government that might be here today and gone tomorrow. So there was no way out. And the military situation was going from bad to worse. It looked as if Ulster might soon turn into a huge armed camp. Arms and ammunition were being smuggled in, and it was not long before about 25,000 modern rifles, with an ample supply of ammunition, were landed on the Ulster coast. (This gun-running adventure, which kept a tramp steamer going in and out of various ports under different flags and names, is quite a saga in itself, and a spirited sketch of it can be found in Mr Ryan's book. The arms were bought and first loaded in Hamburg, but it was a secret private deal, not part of some official German plot.) Once the Ulster Volunteers were armed in this fashion, the Unionists in London and elsewhere were quite openly triumphant; the press rushed out special editions; Lord Roberts, a Field-Marshal of the British Army, even if retired now, cried to Carson, 'Magnificent! Magnificent! Nothing could have been better done!' If the rifles were going to be used against Britain's worst enemies, he could not have been more enthusiastic. But now they were all, so to speak, in ragtime.

At the Curragh, only thirty-five miles from Dublin, the British Government maintained its own highly professional armed camp. All was confusion there; it was as if military affairs now slipped through the Looking Glass, like Alice. In the centre of the muddle, busy muddling it more and more, was old General Paget in Dublin, commanding and not commanding, suggesting peace and war in alternate sentences: the Irish Command was really Irish now. Brigadier-General Hubert Gough, a fine soldier in charge of the Cavalry Brigade, announced that while he and his officers were ready to maintain order and protect Government property in Ulster if necessary (there was a danger that the Army depots would be seized), he and the large majority of his officers would prefer to be dismissed rather than initiate active military operations against Ulster. Some officers in the infantry and engineers were taking the same attitude. There were conferences at the Curragh, more meetings with muddled Paget in Dublin, who swore that he had had direct orders from the King himself, which was wildly untrue; telegrams flashed between headquarters in Dublin and the War Office, where Seely gave orders that any senior officers disputing authority should be suspended from duty at once. Catching the flying rumours, the Unionists declared triumphantly that the Army was ready to mutiny rather than take any part in what they called 'The Plot', largely hatched by Churchill, sending his ships closer to Ulster, and by Seely with his

Robin, *c.* 1912, by Augustus John

The army and police (in an armoured car), during a strike in Liverpool in 1911

arrogant telegrams. It was a plot, they declared, to goad the Ulster Volunteers into active resistance, and it could not work because the soldiers themselves would have none of it.

While so many hitherto responsible men were losing their heads, at the madder end of this mad March, Asquith kept his, became Secretary for War himself, and made a number of cool statements. All talk of a plot was nonsense. He issued a White Paper, very guarded in its reference to the Admiralty and the War Office, to prove it. On the first Saturday in April, the Unionists, who had had much public support, organised a vast and indeed unique demonstration in Hyde Park, to protest against the use of the army and navy against Ulster, and to demand that 'the Government shall immediately submit this grave issue to the people'. But comedy was still in charge here. Fourteen platforms had been set up in a great circle. Processions representing different orders of society marched towards these platforms, bands playing and Union Jacks by the thousand. Conservative clubmen, silk-hatted and black-coated, marched in one procession, peers and members of Parliament in another, City men in another, and all the marching members of the Ladies' Imperial Club carried a Union Jack. The workers, who may or may not have been enthusiastic Unionists but knew how to enjoy an outing when they were offered one, arrived in waggonette loads. There were veteran buglers *en masse*, more bands, more Union Jacks, choral contributions from the crowd ranging from *O God, our help in ages past* to *He's a Jolly Good Fellow*, and speeches, speeches, speeches from the fourteen platforms. Churchill appears to have been the villain of the piece; any mention of his name drew angry cries from the crowd; he was called everything from a blackguard to 'a Lilliput Napoleon'; and Robert Cecil, who really ought to have known better, announced that he knew Churchill 'contemplated the slaughter of hundreds of thousands of his fellow men'. That afternoon there was some dirty fighting from the Unionist leaders, perhaps under the influence of bugling, band-playing, flag-waving.

During one of the stormy sessions in the Commons that followed this demonstration, when Churchill in particular was under attack, he made a big fighting speech. It contained some good debating points, though it ended with a conciliatory appeal to Carson; but one strongly partisan point it made seems very important to me, if only because I

The Great Ulster Rally in Hyde Park, April 4, 1914

remember making it myself in print years before I read this speech of Churchill's. I will quote his actual words:

> . . . Let me point out to the Conservative party, and those who are associated with them, that there is in this country a great democracy, millions of whom are forced to live their lives under conditions which leave them stripped of all but the barest necessities, who are repeatedly urged to be patient under their misfortunes, repeatedly urged to wait year after year, and Parliament after Parliament, until, in the due workings of the Constitution, some satisfaction is given to their clamant needs, all the time this great audience is watching and is learning from you, from those who have hitherto called themselves 'the party of law and order' how much they care for law, how much they value order when it stands in the way of anything they like!

Certainly it is only fair to the Unionists to remember that it is they who demanded a General Election, to be fought on this Home Rule, and that the Liberal Government would not agree. Yet Churchill's point drives home, not only on this but on other occasions. It is the gentlemanly party of law and order that is ready at a pinch to break the law and create disorder. Moreover, the Labour members did not hesitate at this time to make their own very sharp point. Army officers who were ready to resign rather than take their troops to curb any rebellion in Ulster, which was already drilling its own army, showed no such decision, not even any hesitation, when they were ordered to South Wales and there, if necessary, use their guns and bayonets against strikers, who after all had been merely refusing to work, had not been drilling, smuggling in arms, and flying their own flag. It was one thing to be a belligerent country gentleman in Antrim, and quite another thing to be a hungry miner or railwayman in Glamorgan.

However, in the world of fact and not of rumour, just as there was not an elaborate Government 'plot' to provoke Ulster into active military resistance, there was not any actual mutiny at the Curragh, because direct orders were never openly disobeyed. Some of its heat and bitterness left the Liberal-Unionist conflict during the summer of 1914, and in July Asquith finally agreed, after considerable pressure from King George, that a Conference should meet at Buckingham Palace – the Government, the Conservative Party, the Irish Nationalists, the Ulster Unionists, each sending two leaders. By the fourth – and last – morning, they were arguing about the boundaries of two small North Ireland counties, but they were still obdurately disagreeing. And then there was news of Austria's ultimatum to Serbia, and suddenly Home Rule was not important at all. But something else was very important, though this was far from being realised at the time. If the Ulstermen could go shopping for foreign arms, so could the National Volunteers in Dublin. After much time was lost exploring various arms black-markets on the Continent, at last about 1500 Mauser rifles and nearly 50,000 rounds of ammunition were loaded into three yachts. (One of them belonged to Erskine Childers, who, as a rebellious Sinn Feiner, was captured in 1922, sentenced to death by the new Free State Government, and shot.) Late in July, 1914, these arms were landed and then vanished among the National Volunteers. Compared with what Ulster had smuggled in, this was a trifling consignment. But unlike Ulster's arms, these were used; the crack of these Mausers could have been heard in the Easter Rising of 1916; and probably some of them were still seeing service in the frequent ambushes during the 'troubles' after the war. What might have been settled sensibly round a table in 1913 came in the end to be settled by force, violence, murder, fire and anguish. Nor was it really the end, for in this very week, while I am writing here, I have already seen more pictures than I want to see of houses blazing in Ulster, of death again in the streets.

13. Nineteen-fourteen

On New Year's Day, 1914, the *Daily Chronicle* published an interview with Lloyd George, whose Celtic intuition did not seem to be hard at work when he offered his readers a wide prospect of peace and tranquillity, all under an unclouded blue sky. But his references to the cost of naval armaments and to the danger of Liberalism betraying its trust suggested, at least to more sophisticated readers, that he was not staring at the world in a crystal ball; he was making another political move, and was continuing in public his private quarrel with Winston Churchill and the Admiralty. It is worth adding that during this month of January, 1914, many readers, far more than Joseph Conrad usually had, were enjoying his new complicated tale, *Chance*. It was a good time to begin appreciating the mysterious operations of chance, which soon appeared to be imposing its own patterns on any designs created by will and purpose. Writing about these months in his *Modern History of the English People*, Gretton makes the same point in a different way:

> Indeed, the strongest feeling just now of the average man was that the disastrous element in the outlook lay not in any insuperable and fatal deadlock anywhere, but in the growth of a strange tendency to play with fire. Politicians tempted further and further by their own extravagances of language, suffragists going always a little deeper into destructiveness, Labour and Ulster moulding forces more and more into the machinery of conflict, and all the while a most dangerous number of the more comfortable classes making up their minds that something was bound to happen – the whole situation had the mounting unreality of a nightmare, in which a man knows himself to be more sane than the creature he is for the moment being . . .

It may seem frivolous – though the charge should be delayed – to announce that in April one of the leading West End theatres, the Palace, produced its very successful revue, *The Passing Show of 1914*. (It was in this show that the handsome and husky-voiced Basil Hallam, who was killed in the war, sang 'I'm Gilbert the Filbert, the Knut with a "K"', enravishing all the debs and many of their mothers.) The title was well-chosen, though it cut deeper than the Palace Theatre intended it to do. 1914 itself was a show, and a show that was swiftly passing. Among those who felt they had to make the most of it were the suffragettes, who went wild again, in fact wilder than ever. They quite literally played with fire. They set the torch to all manner of buildings; they planted bombs in many famous churches, not even exempting Westminster Abbey itself; and, determined now to get publicity at all cost, they smashed a case of porcelain in the British Museum and began chopping at and slashing pictures. So the Velasquez 'Rokeby Venus', newly acquired by the National Gallery, was damaged, and so were Sargent's portrait of Henry James and Herkomer's Duke of Wellington at the Royal Academy. This led to a great outcry and the closing of some public galleries and museums. It was stupid vandalism, arising from the equally stupid notion that any publicity is good publicity; it made no converts among the mass of ordinary people; it alienated the very persons not entirely unsympathetic to female suffrage. It was now bold propaganda out of control and self-defeating – a weakness of propaganda both then and now.

But then we might say, without venturing into the morass of art history, that on another level those paintings had already been chopped at and slashed before the suffragettes got at them. The axes and knives had been supplied by the *avant garde* rebels who had sent their work to the two shows at the Grafton Galleries. In their own sphere, these painters and the poets and critics who praised them had destroyed the era even before it began to destroy itself. They were no more Edwardian than the bulldozer and the four-engined bomber. This *avant garde* belonged to another age before it existed. They were breathing another, colder air, already staring at a harsher world. They were battering their way out of a culture centuries old, leaving arts that could be public behind them, offering work that was intensely private like so many necromancers selling secrets. No doubt their work can be widely enjoyed now, packing public galleries, but the relation between the arts and society suffered a change that is with us yet, when indeed we are so far removed from order that we seem to be looking at chaos. Our own English *avant garde* was revealed during these months when *Blast* came roaring at us, telling and not asking us to accept 'Vorticism'. I remember buying a copy – it was printed in varying types on horrible paper – and discovering that Percy Wyndham Lewis and his friends (if this gifted but wilful and refractory character really *had* friends) had more cheerful impudence to offer than they had wit and insight. But there anyhow was

Basil Hallam, 1914

Blast, which we read and discussed while drifting on our way towards some real blasting.

I have described elsewhere, in *Margin Released,* what my own life was like during these first seven months of 1914 – how I seemed to be 'running round at a standstill', cramming the hours with experience and yet finding that in the centre of it all nothing much was happening. Though never a clear hard planner at any time, I was living through these months without the vaguest glimmer of a plan. I am not cheating by using hindsight when I say that I neither knew nor cared what I was going to do. Now I know something I did not know when I was writing *Margin Released,* simply because for this present book I have had to go through memoirs, letters, biographies, to understand the era and its people. They have left me with the feeling that my drifting and planless state of mind was far from being uncommon then, that other people, in situations very different from mine, did not know where they were going or what they wanted to do in the near future. If they were not aware of this blank, this emptiness never flashing the signal *War*, then they were haunted during these months by the idea of something going, something being lost.

There is plenty of evidence to prove that we were expecting war. I have not produced any of it here because I deny its conclusion: on anything like this level, where rational evidence is important, we were not expecting war. (I am of course excluding the men commanding the armed forces, always professionally concerned with the expectation of war.) There had been for some years so much vague war talk that we shrugged it away. The First World War must not be confused with the Second. By the middle of the 1930's, many of us knew there would *have* to be war, at least either that or, sooner or later, humiliation followed by slavery. Compared with the Second World War, the First was senseless. Historical rationality cannot reach it. We can of course point out – and it is wise to do so – that the very things that were supposed to preserve peace did in fact greatly help to end it. Thus the great powers – these include Britain on a naval basis – were prepared for war, whereas if they had all been unprepared for war there would not have been one. Again, the very system of alliances, interlocking for better protection, pulled one country after another into war: the powers were like mountaineers roped together but with the rope itself nowhere securely fastened above or below them. Even so, and at the risk of offending every historian, I believe it is useless examining and brooding over every document, telegram, mobilisation order, putting the blame first on one foreign office and then another. If the war had not arrived one way, it would have arrived some other way. What was certain was its arrival.

I have lived too long, have spent too much time both with the world and with myself, to be disturbed by any charge of irrationality. Like the *Titanic* – and I keep remembering that doomed ship and the queer

(opposite) The Tub, 1912, by Duncan Grant

(right) Two Mechanics, *c.* 1912, by Percy Wyndham Lewis

(opposite) Recruiting poster 'There's room for you', *c.* 1914

paralysis of the will that followed its fatal injury – we move, as civilizations, societies, individual human beings, among icebergs with more bulk and power below the water level than above it, ready to inflict a 300-foot gash and open the watertight compartments. I believe that some of us behaved so oddly during those 1914 months because in our unconscious, which has a different time scale from consciousness, *the war had already begun, our world had already ended.* This suggests at least some shadowy communication between the unconscious and consciousness, a queer shift in the background emotional pattern. Determined to make the most of the present time, we were like those young artists destined to enjoy only a short life and somehow constantly aware of it. But this surely is determinism, denying the free will we feel we have? We do not know enough to settle and then be rid of this age-old argument. Some things are determined, so far as individuals are concerned. and though we are not without free will, it is more limited than we usually imagine it to be. Time and scale come in here, but not into this book.

Because I began this Part Three with George V I feel we ought to return to him for the very last week of the era. The extracts that follow are from his Diary:

July 29th. Austria has declared War on Servia. Where will it end? . . . . . Winston Churchill came to see me, the Navy is all ready for War, but please God it will not come. These are very anxious days for me to live in.
July 30th. Foreign telegrams coming in all day, we are doing all we can for peace and to prevent a European War but things look very black . . . . . The debate in H. of C. on Irish question today has been postponed on account of gravity of European situation.
July 31st. The Prime Minister came to see me and we discussed the European situation which he thinks is more grave . . . . . Lord Kitchener came to see me, he returns to Egypt on Monday. He is most anxious to go to India as Viceroy when Hardinge's time is up . . . . . Very tired, bed at 11.30. Colin (Keppel) came and woke me up at 12.45 saying the Prime Minister wanted to see me. I got up and saw him in Audience Room & he showed me a draft of a telegram he wanted me to send to Nicky (Czar Nicholas) as a last resort to try to prevent War, which of course I did. Went to bed again at 1.40.
August 1st. Saw Sir Edward Grey. Germany declared War on Russia at 7.30 this evening & German Ambassador left Petersburg. Whether we shall be dragged into it God only knows, but we shall not send Expeditionary Force of the Army now. France is begging us to come to their assistance. At this moment public opinion here is dead against our joining in the War but I think it will be impossible to keep out of it as we cannot allow France to be smashed.
August 2nd. We issued orders to mobilise the Fleet last night . . . . . Worked all the evening, masses of telegrams and papers to read. At 10.30 a crowd of about 6000 people collected outside the Palace, cheering & singing, May & I went out on the balcony, they gave us a great ovation.

THERE'S ROOM FOR YOU

ENLIST TO-DAY

> *August 3rd*. Saw Winston Churchill who told me the Navy was absolutely ready for war & all the ships mobilised . . . . . Crewe came to see me to tell me what had taken place at the last Cabinet. John Burns has resigned. Morley, Beauchamp & Sir John Simon probably will do so. May & I went for a short drive in Russian carriage down the Mall to Trafalgar Square through the Park & back by Constitution Hill. Large crowds all the way who cheered tremendously . . . . . We were forced to go & show ourselves on the balcony three different times, at 8.15, 9.0 & 9.45, tremendous cheering. Public opinion since Grey made his statement in the House today, that we should not allow Germany to pass through English Channel & that we should not allow her troops to pass through Belgium, has entirely changed, & now everyone is for war & helping our friends. Orders for mobilisation of the army will be issued at once.
> *August* 4th. Warm, showers & windy. At work all day. Winston Churchill came to report at 1.0 that at the meeting of Cabinet this morning we had sent an ultimatum to Germany that if by midnight tonight she did not give satisfactory answer about her troops passing through Belgium, Goschen would ask for his passports. Held a Council at 4.0. Lord Morley & John Burns have resigned & have left the Cabinet . . . . . I held a Council at 10.45 to declare War with Germany, it is a terrible catastrophe but it is not our fault . . . . . When they heard that War had been declared the excitement (of the crowds outside the Palace) increased & it was a never to be forgotten sight when May & I with David went on to the balcony, the cheering was terrific. Please God it may soon be over & that He will protect dear Bertie's life . . . . .

The 'Bertie' in that last sentence was the Duke of York afterwards George VI, and at that time, still in his teens, he was a midshipman in the Navy. The 'David' who went on to the balcony was the Prince of Wales, later a staff officer in France, where, disobeying orders, he kept slipping away to visit the front line trenches. The Royal Family had its weaknesses, but lack of courage was certainly not one of them.

There was a lot of cheering in August 1914, not only outside Buckingham Palace but in many other places. Was it simply so much mob hysteria? Before we say it was, we must remember there had been no great crowds demonstrating and screaming for war, an unpleasant spectacle that many capital cities had seen before 1914 and some have seen since. (Cairo, for instance, just before the Six Days' War.) On the other hand, we know there was very little cheering for the Second War. Why then this sudden 1914 jubilation? Before I try to answer that, I must explain that my friends and I, soon to volunteer for active service, never did any cheering: we have no behaviour of our own to excuse, we were not hysterical mob types ourselves. But does this justly describe all the cheerers or the crowds that brought King George and Queen Mary on to the balcony? I doubt if it does. (Though for the gangs of patriots who went around wrecking pork butchers' shops because some had German names, much harsher language would be justified.) These crowds were not drawn from one class. For the time being they could forget the class

(opposite) Girl in Blue, 1910, by Philip Wilson Steer

system. They could ignore the splitting splintering of society, its show of partial militancies, of fanatics here and cynics there, because the idea of an embattled nation, of which the King was the symbol, now took possession of them. It made them feel part of a greater and richer totality, so they had to cheer. They were celebrating unity, not war.

14. Illusion and Fact

Before saying Goodbye to these Edwardian years, I want to quote the opening paragraph of Mr A. J. P. Taylor's admirable study, *From Sarajevo to Potsdam*. I bring in Mr Taylor not simply because he is a good historian but also because he grew up in the 1920's, not in the 1910's as I did, and cannot be accused of any feeling of nostalgia. So here he is:

> In 1914 Europe was a single civilised community, more so than even at the height of the Roman Empire. A man could travel across the length and breadth of the Continent without a passport until he reached the frontiers of Russia and the Ottoman empire. He could settle in a foreign country for work or leisure without legal formalities except, occasionally, some health requirements. Every currency was as good as gold, though this security rested ultimately on the skill of financiers in the City of London. There were common political forms. Though there were only two republics in Europe (France and Portugal – Switzerland was technically a confederation, not a republic), every state except Monaco possessed some form of constitution limiting the power of the monarch to a greater or lesser degree. Nearly everywhere men could be sure of reasonably fair treatment in the courts of law. No one was killed for religious reasons. No one was killed for political reasons, despite the somewhat synthetic bitterness often shown in political disputes. Private property was everywhere secure, and in nearly all countries something was done to temper the extreme rigours of poverty.

And he goes on to enlarge upon the unity of habits and customs in urban Europe, the 'common outlook in morality and philosophy, vaguely Christian and a good deal more emphatically, optimistically liberal'.

With travel and individual liberty in mind I can contrast very sharply my situation today and the one I knew so many years ago. At seventy-five I must collect visas, permits, photographs, official grants to spend a little of my own money on foreign currency; and even so there are many totalitarian states and semi-military dictatorships that I would not visit even to buy a cup of coffee in them. But as an Edwardian youth of eighteen and nineteen I was able to visit, even if only briefly, five

The Student, 1902, by Gwen John

foreign countries, without any fuss at all, with no more palaver than taking a train today from Leamington Spa to Paddington. The most hopeful sign now, when we must have more authoritarian-military governments than the world has ever known before, comes from our own young people, who cheerfully set out for Anatolia, East Africa or the Himalayas, as if they were already existing in a new freer world, somehow creating an atmosphere of their own. An ancient Edwardian youth salutes them. Though they often talk a lot of nonsense – as I did – they seem to be taking their defiant beards and intrepid girls into another era of hopeful debate, not unlike that of the Edwardian Age. Though the wheel is so much larger and has so many missing spokes, it is turning in a direction I knew long ago.

Far back in these pages I rejected the garden-party idea of the Edwardian era, all the long afternoons bathed in lost sunlight, the myth of its Golden Age. Now when I am about to leave it, I feel I must bring something gleaming out of the wreck. Some gold can be found in there, and not simply the fairy gold of childhood and youth. (Nor, of course, the pinchbeck of the gossip columns.) As I hope I have shown, the era was not really all of a piece; during its last few years it changed rapidly; 1913 was a long way from 1901. But the rich were hardly poorer; the poor no richer; the gap was still appallingly wide. The Edwardian rich I never knew, and my reading has not convinced me that I missed very much. The North-country industrial working class I knew very well indeed, and while they did too much work for too little money, mostly living in ugly mean streets, those I knew cannot be honestly presented as miserable down-trodden creatures. Their lives were narrow but somehow they contrived to bring to them a great deal of zest, humour, innocent excitement. If they had not cars, washing machines, holidays on the Costa Brava, they were not worrying how to pay for cars, washing machines, holidays on the Costa Brava. The bulk of the upper and lower middle classes were nearly as stupid in 1913 as they had been in 1901. Yet, as we have discovered, it was from a minority in each of these classes, energetic, alert-minded, defying and then escaping from prejudice, that shining talents and progressive movements emerged. They might then meet with an unfriendly reception. Edwardian England was no 'land of smiles'. It ran to extremes of opinion and feeling. A writer who was trying to reach 1950 might come under the lash of a critic who was still living in 1850. Suffragettes on hunger strike, miners' wives who existed on bread and margarine, could be angrily condemned by men and women whose livers were suffering from four heavy rich meals a day. Those 'lean tanned fellows', returning on leave from the outposts of Empire (going at once, we are told, to the promenade of the Empire music hall), could be surprised and shocked if English working men did not see themselves as lascars and coolies. Middle-aged men – and I knew some – who were frock-coated, top-hatted, very solemn, every Sunday morning, but kept pretty young mill girls as mistresses on the side, could be outraged if girls of their own class were presented as human beings inspired or tormented by sexual desires. Tablets of stone came down every day from mountains of English cant and humbug.

I do not believe I have any illusions about Edwardian England. I was there – 'a chield's amang you taking notes'. But when the last illusion has been stripped away, something solid remains; there is that gleam of real gold in the wreck. The age somehow created an atmosphere in which English genius, talent, generosity of mind, could flourish. Yes, of course, these were 'the spacious years', which have been mentioned often, too often, when the Empire seemed to remain unchallenged, when Britain appeared to be a very great power indeed. It may be that a calm sense of security gave something to the spirit of the age. Yet it is not what I have in mind. Insularity certainly played its part, the idea that we were different and on our own, breathed our own air and must consider our own particular destiny, an idea responsible for a dangerously limited attitude of mind. Yet it was far from being altogether a bad thing. The Edwardians, as we have seen, could be quarrelsome, militant, with various aggressive sections of society bitterly opposed to one another; yet they could create and maintain that atmosphere of hopeful debate which never survived the Great War. The civilised and liberal Europe, which Mr Taylor describes, flourished even more freely at this insular Western edge of it. And something alien, belonging to a new spirit – harshly derisive, intolerant, arrogant, ultimately dehumanising – already breaking through from 1910 onwards, could still be softened, intuitively transmuted, by the English temperament. (It is a point made more than once by Santayana in his *Soliloquies in England*.) Had there been no Great War, we might have saved ourselves and the world.

In that war we lost the better part of a fine generation of young men. This is not sentimentality, no uprush of self-pity: the facts bear it out. During the earlier time of voluntary enlistment our young men of greatest promise, the future leaders in everything except making money quickly, became junior officers, and it was the junior officers who were mown down. Our national life during the 1920's and 1930's had to recruit its younger leaders from a mere remnant. Moreover, we had to move into a world largely alien to the English temperament. (This is true even today when we wonder, bearing in mind our inventiveness and technical skill, why we are not more successful competing in high-pressure industry and salesmanship, forgetting that we are instinctively opposed to high-pressure industry and salesmanship, wanting something better than a huge national rat race.) As I suggested earlier, the Golden Age myth of Edwardian England, together with its flood of nostalgic feeling, is not really based on garden party lovelies in big hats and tight skirts, nor on a low cost of living so that a poet might be housed and fed for a year on a legacy of £100, nor even – because it is important

– on the fact that in those days there did not seem to be too many people everywhere. Edwardian England is a time and a land seen across the vast dark chasm of war. Over there the afternoons seem to linger in the mellow sunlight, the nights are immediately romantic. There is illusion here, of course, but it is not all a cheat: something *did* go, something *was* lost. Yet again a smaller something did not go, was not lost, but survives in those of us who grew up as Edwardians and went into the war and came out of it. There is, I think, behind our grousing and grumbling a kind of optimism, not large and wide and one huge smile, almost tiny but very compact and somehow indestructible. It encourages us to engage in all manner of doubtful ventures – as, for instance, trying to huddle Edwardian England between the covers of a book.

The British Cemetery at Bayeux

Select Bibliography

ASHBEE, Charles Robert, *Craftsmanship in Competitive Industry being a Record of the Guild of Handicrafts, and some Deductions from their Twenty-One Years' Experience,* 1908

ASQUITH, Emma Alice Margaret (Margot), *Autobiography of Margot Asquith,* 1936

BAILY, Leslie, *Scrapbook 1900–1914,* 1957

BRIGGS, Asa, *They Saw It Happen . . . 1897–1940,* 1960

COLE, G. D. H., and POSTGATE, R., *The Common People 1746–1946,* 1956 (first edition 1938)

COOPER, Diana, *The Rainbow Comes and Goes,* 1958

COWLES, Virginia, *1913: the Defiant Swan Song,* 1967

FUCHS, Carl, *Autobiography,* 1942

FULFORD, Roger, *Votes for Women, the story of a struggle,* 1957

GARDINER, A. G., *Prophets, Priests and Kings,* 1908

GRETTON, R. H., *A Modern History of the English People 1880–1922,* 1930

HASSALL, Christopher, *Rupert Brooke,* 1964

HYNES, Samuel, *The Edwardian Turn of Mind,* 1968

JULLIAN, Philippe, *Edward and the Edwardians,* 1967

LAVER, James, *Edwardian Promenade,* 1958

LLOYD GEORGE, Richard, *Lloyd George,* 1960

MACCARTHY, Desmond, *Memories,* 1940

PRIESTLEY, J. B., *Margin Released,* 1962

RYAN, A. P., *Mutiny at the Curragh,* 1956

SACKVILLE WEST, V., *The Edwardians,* 1930

TAYLOR, A. J. P., *From Sarajevo to Potsdam,* 1966

WELLS, H. G., *The New Machiavelli,* 1911

WOOLF, Virginia, *Roger Fry,* 1940

Full Captions, Locations, Photographic Credits and Acknowledgments

(reverse of frontispiece) A poster advertising the Palace Theatre, 1904.
Mander and Mitchenson Theatre Collection, London
(frontispiece) The Mantelpiece, *c.* 1907, by Walter Richard Sickert. Oil on canvas, 30 × 20 in. (76·2 × 50·8 cm.).
Art Gallery, Southampton
Page 10 The christening of Albert Edward, Prince of Wales, in St George's Chapel, Windsor, January 25, 1842, *c.* 1842–45, by Sir George Hayter. Oil on canvas, 76 × 108 in. (184 × 275 cm.).
The Royal Collection
Page 11 (right) The Royal Family at Balmoral, September 29, 1855.
Gernsheim Collection, the University of Texas, Austin
Page 11 (below) The Prince of Wales during his visit to the United States in 1860.
Mansell Collection, London
Page 11 (below) Edward, Prince of Wales during his visit to the United States in 1861.
Mansell Collection, London
Page 13 Nanny in Kensington Gardens, *c.* 1910, by Brake Baldwin. Oil on canvas, 14 × 12 in. (35·6 × 30·5 cm.).
Collection Mrs Brake Lochhead (Photo W. G. Belsher)
Pages 14 & 15 The Imperial Hunt in the Forest of St Germain, August 25, 1855, by Hippolyte Bellange. Watercolour, 18½ × 12¾ in. (47 × 32·4 cm.).
The Royal Collection, Windsor (Photo J. R. Freeman)
Page 16 The Arrival of Princess Alexandra for her marriage to the Prince of Wales: driving through the City at Temple Bar, March 7, 1863 from *An Historical Record of the Marriage of H.R.H. Albert Edward, Prince of Wales . . . an account of the Progress of the Princess from Copenhagen to London*, 1863.
Guildhall Library, London (Photo J. R. Freeman)
Page 18 The Prince of Wales descending a timber slide near Ottawa in 1860.
Mansell Collection, London
Page 19 (below) Sandringham, Norfolk.
Mansell Collection, London
Page 19 (bottom) Marlborough House, London.
Radio Times Hulton Picture Library, London
Page 20 (top) The Prince and Princess of Wales at Sandringham, autumn 1863.
Mansell Collection, London
Page 20 (above) Queen Alexandra, founder of the Rose Day, in 1912, receiving a rose from a small child.
W. Gordon Davis, London
Page 21 Caricature by Sir Max Beerbohm entitled: 'The Rare, the rather awful visits of Albert Edward, Prince of Wales, to Windsor Castle', 1921, from *Things New and Old*, by Max Beerbohm, Heinemann, 1923.
Victoria and Albert Museum, London (Photo J. R. Freeman)
Page 22 Catherine Walters, 'Skittles'.
Radio Times Hulton Picture Library, London
Page 23 Cremorne Gardens (closed 1877): 'The Chinese Platform', 1857.
Radio Times Hulton Picture Library, London
Page 24 (above left) Sarah Bernhardt as *Théodora*, 1902.
Mander and Mitchenson Theatre Collection, London
Page 24 (above right) The Prince of Wales, photographed by Bassano, *c.* 1875.
Bassano and Vandyk Studios, London
Page 26 (above) Four generations: Queen Victoria, George VI, Edward VII and Prince Edward of York, 1899.
W. Gordon Davis, London
Page 26 (below) The Prince of Wales leading in Persimmon after winning the Derby in 1896.
Radio Times Hulton Picture Library, London
Page 27 Queen Victoria's funeral procession at Windsor, February 2, 1901.
Gernsheim Collection, the University of Texas, Austin
Page 29 King Edward VII, 1907, by Sir Arthur Stockdale Cope. Oil on canvas, 50 × 36 in. (127 × 91·5 cm.).
Broadlands, Hampshire (Photo Derrick Witty)
Page 30 Coronation postcards, 1902.
Collection Mrs Norbury
Page 32 Princess Alexandra on the occasion of Queen Victoria's Golden Jubilee, photographed by Bassano, 1887.
Bassano and Vandyk Studios, London
Page 33 The Coronation of Edward VII, August 9, 1902, 1904, by Laurits Tuxen. Oil on canvas, 66½ × 54½ in. (169 × 138 cm.). The Royal Collection

Page 34 (top) President Kruger.
Mansell Collection, London
Page 34 (below) Rudyard Kipling.
Mansell Collection, London
Page 35 Lord Roberts.
Radio Times Hulton Picture Library, London
Page 35 (right) Lord Kitchener.
Radio Times Hulton Picture Library, London
Page 35 (far right) Christian de Wet.
Mansell Collection, London
Page 37 Cheering the Chief Scout (later called 'Send Us!'), 1913, by W. H. Y. Titcomb. Oil on canvas, 50 × 44 in. (127 × 111·8 cm.).
City Art Gallery, Bristol
Page 38 The Doctor, by James Pryde, exhibited 1909. Oil on canvas, $33\frac{3}{4} \times 28\frac{1}{4}$ in. (85·7 × 71·7 cm.).
Tate Gallery, London (Photo Derrick Witty)
Page 40 (above) A blockhouse in South Africa.
Gernsheim Collection, the University of Texas, Austin
Page 40 (below) An evacuated Boer dwelling.
Gernsheim Collection, the University of Texas, Austin
Page 43 Souvenir election postcard of 1906.
Mansell Collection, London
Page 44 Edward VII after his arrival at Bois de Boulogne Station, Paris, May 1, 1903, driving away with President Loubet.
Mansell Collection, London
Page 45 Edward VII in Paris, a caricature by the German, Bruno Paul, 1905.
Mansell Collection, London
Page 46 Cecil Rhodes, 1896.
Mansell Collection, London
Page 47 (right) William Randolph Hearst, a caricature by Oliver Herford.
Radio Times Hulton Picture Library, London
Page 47 (below) Theodore Roosevelt, the 26th President of the United States.
Mansell Collection, London
Page 48 Edward VII and the Kaiser during the State visit to Berlin in February 1909.
Mansell Collection, London
Page 49 (below left) A South African comment on the Tory government's decision to allow the importation of Chinese labourers into Transvaal.
Africana Museum, Johannesburg
Page 49 (below right) A poster used by the Liberals in 1906.
Radio Times Hulton Picture Library, London
Page 51 Britta the Danish ballerina as the 'Spirit of the Flag' in *Oor Flag*, a ballet at the Alhambta Theatre in 1910, painted by Spencer Gore. Oil on canvas, 30 × 25 in. (76·2 × 63·5 cm.).
Private Collection, London (Photo Derrick Witty)
Page 52 A leaded glass panel for Miss Cranston's Willow Tea Rooms, 1903, by Margaret Macdonald.
Daly's Bridal Boutique, Glasgow
(Photo *Daily Telegraph* Colour Library)
Page 54 (above) Waiting for parcels of food in Cheapside, London, 1901.
W. Gordon Davis, London
Page 54 (below) Waiting for lights out in the Salvation Army Shelter, Medland Hall, 1901.
W. Gordon Davis, London
Page 55 Fashions seen at Ascot.
Sport and General Press Agency Limited, London
Page 56 Laundry Girls, 1906, by Albert Rutherston. Oil on canvas, 36 × 46 in. (91·5 × 117 cm.).
Tate Gallery, London
Page 57 Maid darning socks, *c.* 1910, by Brake Baldwin. Oil on canvas, 24 × 20 in. (61 × 50·8 cm.).
Collection Mrs Brake Lochhead (Photo W. G. Belsher)
Page 59 In Sickert's House, 1907, by Harold Gilman. Oil on canvas, $18\frac{1}{2} \times 12\frac{3}{4}$ in. (47 × 32·4 cm.).
City Art Gallery, Leeds
Page 60 Maid cleaning silver, *c.* 1910, by Brake Baldwin. Oil on canvas, 12 × 14 in. (30·5 × 35·6 cm.).
Collection Mrs Brake Lochhead, on loan to the Ashmolean, Oxford
Page 62 Cowes Regatta, with the Royal yacht (centre), July 1909.
Radio Times Hulton Picture Library, London
Page 63 (right) Edward VII shooting at Sandringham, *c.* 1907.
Radio Times Hulton Picture Library, London
Page 63 (below) The visit of King Carlos I and Queen Amelia of Portugal to Windsor Castle on November 15 and 16, 1904.
Gernsheim Collection, the University of Texas, Austin
Page 64 The Butler, 1910, by George Percy Jacomb-Hood. Oil on canvas, $30\frac{1}{4} \times 10$ in. (76·8 × 25·4 cm.).
City Art Gallery, Bristol
Page 65 A spring morning in London, 1911.
Radio Times Hulton Picture Library, London
Page 67 Tranby Croft, September 11, 1890.
Radio Times Hulton Picture Library, London
Page 68 Beauty without make-up, 1902.
Radio Times Hulton Picture Library, London
Page 69 (left) The Corset of 1903.
William Gordon Davis, London
Page 69 (right) 'Gibson Girl' Miss Camille Clifford, 1906
Mander and Mitchenson Theatre Collection, London
Page 70 (above left) Zena and Phyllis Dare.
Mander and Mitchenson Theatre Collection, London
Page 70 (above right) Gabrielle Ray.
Rainbird Picture Library
Page 70 (below left) Marie Studholme.
Mander and Mitchenson Theatre Collection, London
Page 70 (below right) Gertie Millar as 'Mitzi' in *The Girls of Gothenburg*, Gaiety Theatre, 1907.
Mander and Mitchenson Theatre Collection, London
Page 72 Waiting for work, London.
William Gordon Davis, London
Page 73 Ploughing on the Downs, 1907, by Robert Bevan. Oil on canvas, $24\frac{1}{4} \times 32\frac{1}{4}$ in. (61·6 × 81·9 cm.).
Art Gallery and Museum, Aberdeen
Page 74 A Primrose seller, 1905.
William Gordon Davis, London
Page 75 (above) Dancing to a street organ in the slums of the East End of London during the early part of the century.
William Gordon Davis, London

Page 75 (below) Taking the air in Whitechapel, London, 1901.
William Gordon Davis, London
Page 76 (above) An artist's impression of a tailor's sweat shop in the East End of London, 1904.
Mansell Collection, London
Page 76 (below) Women at work in a cycle factory, *c.* 1901.
William Gordon Davis, London
Page 80 Guglielmo Marconi at Signal Hall, Newfoundland.
Marconi Company
Page 81 (above left) Wilbur Wright.
Radio Times Hulton Picture Library, London
Page 81 (above right) Samuel Franklin Cody.
Sport and General Press Agency Limited, London
Page 81 (below) Poster for England's first aviation races at Doncaster, 1909.
Science Museum, London (Photo Derrick Witty)
Page 85 Lytton Strachey, 1914, by Henry Lamb. Oil on canvas, $96\frac{1}{4} \times 70\frac{1}{4}$ in. (250×178 cm.).
Tate Gallery, London
Page 86 Flying at Hendon, 1913, by Tony Sarg. Gouache, $33 \times 20\frac{1}{2}$ in. ($83{\cdot}9 \times 52{\cdot}1$ cm.).
Museum of British Transport, Clapham, London (Photo Derrick Witty)
Page 88 (above left) Miss Liebmann's 1906 Darracq car outside the Albert Hall, London.
Radio Times Hulton Picture Library, London
Page 88 (above right) *La Belle Chauffeuse*, 1904, by Sir William Nicholson. Oil on canvas, $30 \times 25\frac{1}{8}$ in. ($76{\cdot}2 \times 63{\cdot}8$ cm.).
National Gallery of Victoria, Melbourne, Australia
Page 88 (below) The model for the Rolls-Royce mascot, 'The Spirit of Ecstasy', 1911, by Charles Sykes. Height 28 in. (71·2 cm.).
Rolls-Royce Limited, London
Page 89 A scene from *An Englishman's Home,* by Major Guy du Maurier, Wyndham's Theatre, 1909.
Mander and Mitchenson Theatre Collection, London
Page 90 George Bernard Shaw, 1912, by Alick P. F. Ritchie, *Vanity Fair*, 'Men of the Day', No. 1292.
Mander and Mitchenson Theatre Collection, London
Page 91 (left) G. K. Chesterton, *c.* 1907.
Radio Times Hulton Picture Library, London
Page 91 (right) H. G. Wells, *c.* 1900.
Radio Times Hulton Picture Library, London
Page 92 Henley Regatta, 1914.
Radio Times Hulton Picture Library, London
Page 93 The Salvation Army Penny Sit-up at Blackfriars, *c.* 1901.
William Gordon Davis, London
Page 94 (above) Mrs Sterry.
Radio Times Hulton Picture Library, London
Page 94 (below) A. F. Wilding.
Radio Times Hulton Picture Library, London
Page 95 (above) The Tottenham Hotspur side of 1912.
Radio Times Hulton Picture Library, London
Page 95 (below) The dramatic finish of the Marathon at the White City Stadium, London, in the Olympic Games of 1908.
Sport and General Press Agency Limited, London

Page 96 (above) The historic touring M.C.C. Cricket party of 1911/12.
Radio Times Hulton Picture Library, London
Page 96 (below) Yorkshire, the reigning county cricket champions of 1902/3.
Radio Times Hulton Picture Library, London
Page 99 Cabyard at Night, 1910, by Robert Bevan. Oil on canvas, 24×27 in. ($61 \times 68{\cdot}6$ cm.).
Museum and Art Gallery, Brighton
Pages 100–01 Paulhan flying a Henry Farman machine over the London and North Western Railway during the London to Manchester Air Race, April 1910, by I. E. Delaspre.
Science Museum, London (Photo Derrick Witty)
Page 102 (above left) 1904 Wolseley; **(above right)** 1901 Sunbeam Mabley; **(centre left)** 1912 Lanchester; **(centre right)** 1909 Rolls-Royce; **(below left)** 1913 Morris; **(below right)** 1913 Vauxhall.
Montagu Motor Museum, Beaulieu, Hampshire
Page 104 The Breakfast Table, 1911, by Harold Gilman. Oil on canvas, $27 \times 20\frac{3}{4}$ in. ($68{\cdot}6 \times 52{\cdot}7$ cm.).
Art Gallery, Southampton
Page 105 (below left) *Ennui*, *c.* 1913, by Walter Richard Sickert. Oil on canvas, 60×44 in. (152×112 cm.).
Tate Gallery, London
Page 105 (below right) Edwardian Interior, *c.* 1901–5, by Harold Gilman. Oil on canvas, $21 \times 21\frac{1}{4}$ in. ($53{\cdot}4 \times 54$ cm.).
Tate Gallery, London
Page 107 The author's childhood home in Bradford, Yorkshire.
Courtesy *Telegraph and Argus,* Bradford
Page 109 A Liberal poster of 1906.
Mansell Collection, London
Page 111 Lloyd George and Asquith, 1910.
Mansell Collection, London
Page 115 Woman seated on a bed *c.* 1909, by Spencer Gore. Oil on canvas, $19\frac{5}{8} \times 15\frac{7}{8}$ in. ($49{\cdot}8 \times 40{\cdot}3$ cm.).
Collection J. B. Priestley
Page 116 Bank Holiday, 1912, by William Strang. Oil on canvas, $60\frac{1}{8} \times 48\frac{1}{4}$ in. (153×123 cm.).
Tate Gallery, London
Page 121 Hilaire Belloc, 1909.
Radio Times Hulton Picture Library, London
Page 123 Robert Bridges.
Mansell Collection, London
Page 124 (above) W. B. Yeats, *c.* 1905.
Radio Times Hulton Picture Library, London
Page 124 (below) Walter de la Mare.
Mansell Collection, London
Page 125 Thomas Hardy, *c.* 1905
Radio Times Hulton Picture Library, London
Page 126 (right) The Cloud, 1901, by Arthur Hacker. Oil on canvas, 51×52 in. (130×132 cm.).
Art Gallery and Museum, Bradford (Photo the Royal Academy of Art, London)
Page 126 (below) The Elf, 1910, by Sir William Goscombe John. Bronze, height. 40 in. (101·6 cm.).
Royal Academy of Art, London
Page 128 (left) Joseph Conrad, *c.* 1911.
Mansell Collection, London

Page 128 (right) Arnold Bennett.
Radio Times Hulton Picture Library, London
Page 129 (above) John Galsworthy, *c.* 1910.
Radio Times Hulton Picture Library, London
Page 129 (below) W. H. Hudson, *c.* 1905.
Radio Times Hulton Picture Library, London
Page 130 The blocking design by Arthur Rackham for *Undine* by De la Motte Fouqué, published by Heinemann in 1909. 10 × 7½ in. (25·4 × 19 cm.).
Collection Bertram Rota Limited, London
Page 132 (left) Illustration for *The Tailor of Gloucester*, 'Simpkin at the Tailor's Bedside', *c.* 1902 by Beatrix Potter. Watercolour, 4⅜ × 3⅝ in. (11·1 × 9.2 cm.).
Tate Gallery, London
Page 132 (right) The Dance in Cupid's Alley, 1904, by Arthur Rackham. Watercolour, 12¾ × 23½ in. (32·4 × 59·7 cm.).
Tate Gallery, London
Page 132 (below) Peter Pan, erected in Kensington Gardens in 1911, by Sir George Frampton.
(Photo Derrick Witty)
Page 134 Miss Evie Green singing to her own voice, 1902.
Mander and Mitchenson Theatre Collection, London
Page 135 Caruso as Canio in *I Pagliacci*.
Radio Times Hulton Picture Library, London
Page 136 Henry Wood, *c.* 1905.
Mander and Mitchenson Theatre Collection, London
Page 137 The Queen's Hall, Langham Place.
Mander and Mitchenson Theatre Collection, London
Page 138 Edward Elgar, 1911, by William Strang.
Chalk, 17½ × 11¼ in. (44·4 × 28·6 cm.).
The Royal Collection, Windsor
Page 139 Thomas Beecham, 1908, by 'Emu' from *The World*.
Mander and Mitchenson Theatre Collection, London
Page 141 The Fabian Window at the Beatrice Webb House, Leith Hill, Surrey.
(Photo Derrick Witty)
Page 142 Gauguins and Connoisseurs at the Stafford Gallery, *c.* 1911, by Spencer Gore. Oil on canvas, 32 × 28 in. (81·3 × 71·2 cm.).
Private Collection (Photo Edwin Smith)
Page 144 (above) Crows over a wheat field, 1890, by Vincent van Gogh. Oil on canvas. 20 × 40¾ in. (50·8 × 103·5 cm.).
Gemeentemuseum, Amsterdam
Page 144 (below) The House of the Hanged Man at Auvers-sur-Oise, 1873, by Paul Cézanne. Oil on canvas, 21⅞ × 26⅛ in. (73·3 × 66·4 cm.).
Musée de L'Impressionisme, Paris
Page 145 Caricature of Roger Fry, 1913, by Max Beerbohm 'We needs must love the highest when we see it' from *Fifty Caricatures* by Max Beerbohm published by Heinemann in 1913.
Victoria and Albert Museum, London (Photo J. R. Freeman)
Page 146 Horace Brodzky, 1913, by Henri Gaudier-Brzeska. Bronze, height 26¾ in. (67·9 cm.).
Tate Gallery, London
Page 147 (above left) The eldest daughter of Mrs William K. Vanderbilt, 1910, by Prince Paul Troubetzkoy. Bronze, height including base 21¼ in. (54 cm.).
Museum and Art Gallery, Birmingham
Page 147 (above centre) Putting the weight, 1913, by Reginald Fairfax Wells. Bronze, height 12½ in. (31·8 cm.).
Fine Art Society Limited, London
Page 147 (above right) Orpheus and Eurydice, *c.* 1905–7, by Charles Ricketts. Bronze, height 13½ in. (34·3 cm.).
Fine Art Society Limited, London
Page 147 (below left) Nan the Dreamer, 1911, by Jacob Epstein. Bronze, height 10½ in. (26·7 cm.).
Fitzwilliam Museum, Cambridge (Reproduced by permission of the Syndics of the Fitzwilliam Museum, Cambridge)
Page 147 (below right) Bathsheba, by Sir Charles Holroyd, exhibited 1912. Bronze, height 8½ in. (21·6 cm.).
Fine Art Society Limited, London
Page 149 Homage to Manet, 1901, by Sir William Orpen. Oil on canvas, 62 × 51 in. (158 × 130 cm.).
City Art Gallery, Manchester
Page 150 A gathering of habitués in the now vanished Domino Room at the Café Royal, 1912, by Sir William Orpen. Oil on canvas.
Musée de L'Impressionisme, Paris (Photo R. Lalance, Meudon-la-Foret, France)
Page 152 (above) Marsh Court, Stockbridge, Hampshire, 1901, by Sir Edward Lutyens.
(Photo Country Life)
Page 152 (below) Home Place, Kelling, Norfolk, 1904, by E. S. Prior.
(Photo Country Life)
Page 153 (above) Hill House, Helensburgh, Dunbartonshire, 1902–3, by Charles Rennie Mackintosh.
(Photo Country Life)
Page 153 (below) Liverpool Cathedral, 1903, by Sir Giles Gilbert Scott.
(Photo Country Life)
Page 154 (above left) Dresser designed by Ernest Gimson.
Museum and Art Gallery, Leicester
Page 154 (above right) Armchair in satinwood with ebony and boxwood stringing sold by Pratts of Bradford, 1904.
City Art Gallery and Museum, Bradford
Page 154 (below left) Chair in mahogany with satinwood and ebony stringing sold by Pratts of Bradford, *c.* 1904.
City Art Gallery and Museum, Bradford
Page 154 (below right) Cabinet and stand in brown ebony inlaid with mother of pearl, with bright iron handles, 1908, by Ernest Gimson.
Museum and Art Gallery, Leicester
Page 155 Chair designed by Ernest Gimson.
Museum and Art Gallery, Leicester
Page 157 The Jester (W. Somerset Maugham), 1911, by Sir Gerald Kelly. Oil on canvas, 40 × 30 in. (101·6 × 76·2 cm.).
Tate Gallery, London (Photo Derrick Witty)
Pages 158–59 The London Hippodrome, 1902, by Everett Shinn. Oil on canvas, 26⅜ × 35¼ in. (67 × 89·5 cm.).
Art Institute, Chicago
Page 160 Five postcard throw-aways advertising Edwardian melodramas.
Mander and Mitchenson Theatre Collection, London

Page 162 (left) Martin Harvey as *Oedipus Rex*, Covent Garden, 1912.
Mander and Mitchenson Theatre Collection, London
Page 162 (right) Lily Elsie and Bertram Wallis in *The Count of Luxembourg*, Daly's Theatre, 1911.
Mander and Mitchenson Theatre Collection, London
Page 163 (above left) Annie Horniman.
Mander and Mitchenson Theatre Collection, London
Page 163 (above centre) Postcard throw-away advertising The Duke of York's Theatre.
Mander and Mitchenson Theatre Collection, London
Page 163 (above right) J. M. Barrie, 1904, by Sir William Nicholson. Oil on canvas 23 × $20\frac{3}{4}$ in. (58·5 × 52·7 cm.).
Scottish National Portrait Gallery, Edinburgh
Page 163 (below) The poster for *Man and Superman* by George Bernard Shaw, Criterion Theatre, 1911.
Mander and Mitchenson Theatre Collection, London
Page 164 (above) Harley Granville-Barker, *c.* 1907.
Radio Times Hulton Picture Library, London
Page 164 (below) Lillah McCarthy and Granville-Barker in *Man and Superman*, Royal Court Theatre, in 1905.
Mander and Mitchenson Theatre Collection, London
Page 165 (above) Norman Wilkinson's stylised *décor* for Granville-Barker's *Twelfth Night*, Savoy Theatre, 1912.
Mander and Mitchenson Theatre Collection, London
Page 165 (centre) *The Whip,* 1909, one of the many grand scale melodramas produced at Drury Lane.
Mander and Mitchenson Theatre Collection, London
Page 165 (below) Frank Benson as *Richard III* at the Shakespeare Memorial Theatre, Stratford-upon-Avon, 1906.
Mander and Mitchenson Theatre Collection, London
Page 167 Marie Tempest, 1908, by Jacques-Emile Blanche. Oil on canvas, $38\frac{1}{2}$ × 31 in. (97·8 × 78·8 cm.).
Garrick Club, London
Page 168 Seated Nude: The Black Hat, *c.* 1900, by Philip Wilson Steer. Oil on canvas, 20 × 16 in. (50·9 × 40·7 cm.).
Tate Gallery, London (Photo Derrick Witty)
Page 170 (below left) Mrs Patrick Campbell, *c.* 1901.
Radio Times Hulton Picture Library, London
Page 170 (below right) Ellen Terry, *c.* 1903.
Radio Times Hulton Picture Library, London
Page 171 (right) A Viking costume design by Gordon Craig for Ibsen's *The Vikings,* Imperial Theatre, 1903.
Victoria and Albert Museum, London (Photo Malcolm Keep)
Page 171 (far right) Portrait by Gordon Graig of (?) Ellen Terry as Mistress Page in *The Merry Wives of Windsor*.
Victoria and Albert Museum, London (Photo Malcolm Keep)
Page 171 (below) Costume design for W. B. Yeat's *The King's Threshold,* 1904, by Charles Ricketts.
Victoria and Albert Museum, London (Photo Malcolm Keep)
Page 172 Gladys Cooper, photographed by Bassano, 1910.
Bassano and Vandyk Studios, London
Page 173 (above) Lewis Waller as *Monsieur Beaucaire*, Comedy Theatre, 1902. He was the first man to have a 'fan club' Mander and Mitchenson Theatre Collection, London
Page 173 (below) Paul Cinquevalli.
Mander and Mitchenson Theatre Collection, London
Page 174 (left) Vesta Tilley.
Enthoven Collection, The Victoria and Albert Museum, London
Page 174 (right) Marie Lloyd.
Mander and Mitchenson Theatre Collection, London
Page 175 (above) Little Tich ('The Droll Dancer'), by Alick P. F. Ritchie.
Mander and Mitchenson Theatre Collection, London
Page 175 (below left) Harry Tate in his 'Golfing' sketch.
Mander and Mitchenson Theatre Collection, London
Page 175 (below right) George Robey as Mother Hubbard in Pantomime.
Mander and Mitchenson Theatre Collection, London
Page 176 (above left) A music hall gallery, *c.* 1902.
Mander and Mitchenson Theatre Collection, London
Page 176 (above right) Advertisement for the Biograph, 1905.
Mander and Mitchenson Theatre Collection, London
Page 177 Charlie Chaplin 'snapped' aboard the liner *Cairnrona* on his way to America with Fred Karno's *Mumming Birds* in 1910.
Mander and Mitchenson Theatre Collection, London
Page 180 Mrs Keppel.
Gernsheim Collection, the University of Texas, Austin
Page 181 Edward VII and Queen Alexandra, 1905.
Radio Times Hulton Picture Library, London
Page 182 (above) Edward VII at Monte Carlo, 1909.
Gernsheim Collection, the University of Texas, Austin
Page 182 (right) Edward VII walking with Colonel Holford, Equerry-in-Waiting, during his last visit to Biarritz in 1910.
Mansell Collection, London
Page 183 Black Ascot in mourning for Edward VII, 1910.
William Gordon Davis, London
Pages 186–87 Buckingham Palace as it was before the façade was altered in 1911.
Gernsheim Collection, the University of Texas, Austin
Page 188 George V and Queen Mary, *c.* 1911.
Private Collection, London
Page 189 Review of the Home Fleet by George V shortly after his succession.
Collection Mrs Norbury
Page 190 Lieutenant Shackleton who attempted to reach the South Pole in 1908.
Private Collection, London
Page 191 Captain Scott and his comrades at the South Pole on January 18, 1912.
Popperfoto, London
Page 193 A Coronation postcard of 1911.
Collection J. B. Priestley
Page 194 Margot Asquith attending a wedding at St Margaret's, Westminster in 1911.
Radio Times Hulton Picture Library, London
Page 196 Dr Crippen.
Syndication International, London
Page 198 (left) Crippen's wife, who appeared on the music halls as Belle Elmore.
Syndication International, London

Page 198 (right) Ethel Le Neve dressed as a boy. Syndication International, London
Page 199 Crippen, with a scarf around his face, is led from the liner *Montrose* by Inspector Dew.
P. A. Reuter photo
Page 200 A photograph taken by Captain Kendall aboard *Montrose* showing Ethel Le Neve dressed as a boy, and Crippen.
Courtesy Leslie Baily
Page 201 Winston Churchill, centre, conducting operations at the Sidney Street Siege in 1911.
Syndication International, London
Page 205 A French advertisement for Humber bicycles of about 1906.
Montagu Motor Museum, Beaulieu, Hampshire
Page 206 Two advertisement cards datable about 1905. Victoria and Albert Museum, London (Photo Derrick Witty)
Page 208 Letchworth Station (showing early commuters), 1911, by Spencer Gore. Oil on canvas, 25 × 30 in. (63·5 × 76·2 cm.).
Collection J. Peter W. Cochrane
Page 209 (above) Harold Gilman's house at Letchworth Garden City, Hertfordshire, 1912, by Spencer Gore. Oil on canvas, 25 × 30 in. (63·5 × 76·2 cm.).
Private Collection London (Photo Derrick Witty)
Page 209 (below) Letchworth, the Road, 1912, by Spencer Gore. Oil on Canvas, 16 × 17 in. (40·7 × 43·2 cm.).
Private Collection, London (Photo Derrick Witty)
Page 210 A London open-top bus of about 1910.
London Transport Board, London
Page 212 A scene from *Press Cuttings* a play written by Bernard Shaw for the London Society of Women's Suffrage banned by the Lord Chamberlain but privately produced at the Royal Court in 1909, from *The Sketch*, July 21, 1909.
Victoria and Albert Museum, London (Photo Malcolm Keep)
Page 213 Mrs Pankhurst.
Collection Mrs Michael Foot (Photo J. R. Freeman)
Page 214 (right) A suffragette meeting.
Collection Mrs Michael Foot (Photo J. R. Freeman)
Page 214 (below) A suffragette photographed selling *Votes for Women* posters.
London Museum, London
Page 215 A suffragette poster designed to discredit Asquith
Collection Mrs Michael Foot (Photo J. R. Freeman)
Page 216 (above left) Mrs Despard.
Radio Times Hulton Picture Library, London
Page 216 (above centre) Mary E. Gawthorpe.
London Museum, London
Page 216 (above right) Sylvia Pankhurst.
London Museum, London
Page 216 (below left) Lady Constance Lytton.
London Museum, London
Page 216 (below right) Christabel Pankhurst.
London Museum, London
Page 217 Gladice Keevil.
London Museum, London
Page 219 A poster showing a suffragette being forcibly fed. Collection Mrs Michael Foot (Photo J. R. Freeman)
Page 220 The Brown Veil (Mrs Harrington Mann), 1905, by Sir William Nicholson. Oil on canvas, $29\frac{3}{4} \times 24\frac{1}{2}$ in. (75·6 × 62·2 cm.).
Museum and Art Gallery, Birmingham
Page 222 (above) Christabel Pankhurst speaking in Trafalgar Square.
London Museum, London
Page 222 (below left) A suffragette contribution to a Coronation Procession of 1911.
London Museum, London
Page 222 (below right) Mrs Pankhurst being arrested by Inspector Rolf outside Buckingham Palace on May 21, 1914.
Central Press, London
Page 223 (right) A procession which formed part of the Suffragette Summer Festival, 1913.
Radio Times Hulton Picture Library, London
Page 223 (below) Mrs Pethick-Lawrence speaking in Trafalgar Square in 1908.
Radio Times Hulton Picture Library, London
Page 224 Emily Davison having thrown herself under the King's Derby horse *Anmer* on June 4, 1913.
Sport and General Press Agency Limited, London
Page 226 The front page of the *New York Times*, April 16, 1912.
William Gordon Davis, London
Page 227 *Titanic* survivors photographed in a lifeboat.
Radio Times Hulton Picture Library, London
Page 229 Paper boy, April 1912.
Radio Times Hulton Picture Library, London
Page 231 The *Carpathia.*
(Photo Cunard Line)
Page 233 Rupert Brooke, 1913.
Mansell Collection, London
Page 234 Costume design for *Shéhérazade*, 1910, by Léon Bakst.
Wadsworth Atheneum, Hartford, Conn.
Page 235 Nijinsky in *L'Après-midi d'un Faune*, 1912.
Victoria and Albert Museum, London (Photo Malcolm Keep)
Page 236 (left) Léon Bakst, photographed by E. O. Hoppé, 1913.
Mander and Mitchenson Theatre Collection, London
Page 236 (right) Serge Diaghilev, by Elizabeth Polunin. Oil on canvas, 28 × $21\frac{1}{2}$ in. (71·1 × 54·6 cm.).
Radio Times Hulton Picture Library, London
Page 236 (below) Chaliapin as *Ivan the Terrible,* Drury Lane, 1914.
Mander and Mitchenson Theatre Collection, London
Page 237 (right) Karsavina and Nijinsky in *Shéhérazade*, 1910.
Mander and Mitchenson Theatre Collection, London
Page 237 (far right) Pavlova in her dance *The Rose,* 1911.
Mander and Mitchenson Theatre Collection, London
Page 237 (below left) Fokine in *Le Carnaval,* 1914, by Emmanuele Ordoño de Rosalès. Plaster, height $13\frac{1}{4}$ in. 32·5 cm.).
Toneelmuseum, Amsterdam

Page 237 (below right) Karsavina and Adolf Bolm in *L'Oiseau de Feu*, 1912.
Mander and Mitchenson Theatre Collection, London
Page 239 Costume design for Nijinsky in *L'Après-midi d'un Faune,* 1912, by Léon Bakst. Watercolour.
Wadsworth Atheneum, Hartford, Conn. (Photo Shah Scharier)
Pages 240–41 Set design for scene 1 *Pavillon d'Armide,* 1909, by Alexandre Benois. Watercolour.
Private Collection, London (Photo Derrick Witty)
Page 242 Costume design for the projected ballet *La Peri,* 1911, by Léon Bakst. Watercolour.
Bibliothèque Arzenal, Paris (Photo Photographie Giraudon, Paris)
Page 244 (left) A Bakst design produced by Paquin, 1912.
Victoria and Albert Museum, London (Photo J. R. Freeman)
Page 244 (centre) A fashion advertisement, 1913.
Mander and Mitchenson Theatre Collection, London
Page 244 (right) A fashion plate dated 1913.
Victoria and Albert Museum, London (Photo J. R. Freeman)
Page 245 The cover of the programme of *Hullo Rag-Time*!
Mander and Mitchenson Theatre Collection, London
Page 246 An artist's impression of Shirley Kellogg leading the chorus along the joy plank in *Hullo Ragtime!* at the London Hippodrome in 1912.
Mander and Mitchenson Theatre Collection, London
Page 248 (above) The cover of the music-sheet of the song *Hitchy Koo,* composed in 1912, and performed by the American Ragtime Octet.
Mander and Mitchenson Theatre Collection, London
Page 248 (right) The cover of the music-sheet of *Alexander's Rag-time Band,* composed by Irving Berlin in 1911.
Mander and Mitchenson Theatre Collection, London
Page 249 The Turkey Trot from *The Sketch* of February 14, 1912.
Mander and Mitchenson Theatre Collection, London
Page 250 Tango teas at the London Pavilion, 1913.
Mander and Mitchenson Theatre Collection, London
Page 253 Captain Scott working on his diary.
Popperfoto, London
Page 255 Ethel Levey in *Hullo Tango,* London Hippodrome, 1913. The costumes were designed by Léon Bakst.
Mander and Mitchenson Theatre Collection, London
Page 256 Lord Ribblesdale, 1902, by John Singer Sargent.
Oil on canvas, $101\frac{3}{4} \times 56\frac{1}{2}$ in. (256×143 cm.).
Tate Gallery, London (Photo Derrick Witty)
Page 258 Miss Dubose Taylor as Queen Louise on the occasion of the Picture Ball at the Albert Hall, early in 1914.
Radio Times Hulton Picture Library, London
Page 259 (right) The Countess of Warwick dressed as the Queen of Assyria.
Radio Times Hulton Picture Library, London
Page 259 (below) Isadora Duncan, about 1900.
Mander and Mitchenson Theatre Collection, London
Page 261 Nude Descending a Staircase, No. II, 1912, by Marcel Duchamp.
Oil on canvas, 58×35 in. ($148 \times 88{\cdot}9$).
Museum of Art Philadelphia, Pa.
Page 262 The 69th Street Armory Show, 1913, arranged largely by Mrs Mabel Dodge.
Culver Pictures Inc., New York
Page 265 (top) Sir Edward Carson.
Private Collection, London
Page 265 (below) Major-General Henry Wilson, 1922, by Oswald Birley. Oil on canvas 48×38 in ($122 \times 96{\cdot}6$ cm.).
Marlborough College, Marlborough (Courtesy the Photographic Society)
Page 266 Ulster Anti-Home-Rule demonstration in Hyde Park, September 1914.
Radio Times Hulton Picture Library, London
Page 269 The Blue Hat, *c.* 1913, by Walter Richard Sickert. Oil on canvas, 20×16 in. ($50{\cdot}8 \times 40{\cdot}7$ cm.).
City Art Gallery, Manchester
Page 270–71 Dinner on board the yacht Vanderbilt at Cowes, 1909, by Jacques-Emile Blanche. Oil on canvas, $28 \times 39\frac{1}{2}$ in. ($71{\cdot}2 \times 100{\cdot}3$ cm.).
Leicester Galleries, London (Photo Derrick Witty)
Page 272 Robin, *c.* 1912, by Augustus John. Oil on panel, $17\frac{3}{4} \times 12$ in. ($45{\cdot}1 \times 30{\cdot}5$ cm.).
Tate Gallery, London (Photo Derrick Witty, London)
Page 274 The army and police (in an armoured car) during a strike in Liverpool in 1911.
Courtesy Leslie Baily (Photo J. R. Freeman)
Page 275 The Great Ulster Rally in Hyde Park, April 4, 1914.
Radio Times Hulton Picture Library, London
Page 279 Basil Hallam, 1914.
Mander and Mitchenson Theatre Collection, London
Page 280 The Tub, 1912, by Duncan Grant.
Watercolour and tempera, 30×22 in. ($76{\cdot}2 \times 55{\cdot}9$ cm.).
Tate Gallery, London
Page 281 Two Mechanics, *c.* 1912, by Percy Wyndham Lewis. Drawing and wash, $22 \times 13\frac{1}{4}$ in. ($55{\cdot}9 \times 33{\cdot}7$ cm.).
Tate Gallery, London
Page 283 Recruiting poster 'There's room for you', *c.* 1914.
Lord's Gallery, London
Page 285 Girl in Blue, 1910, by Philip Wilson Steer. Oil on canvas, 29×24 in ($73{\cdot}7 \times 61$ cm.).
Municipal Gallery of Modern Art, Dublin
Page 286 The Student, 1902, by Gwen John.
Oil on canvas, $22\frac{1}{8} \times 13$ in. ($56{\cdot}2 \times 33{\cdot}1$ cm.).
City Art Gallery, Manchester
Page 290 The British Cemetery at Bayeux.
British Legion Headquarters

Index

References in *italic type* indicate illustrations